DEGROWTH

Degrowth is a rejection of the illusion of growth and a call to repoliticize the public debate colonized by the idiom of economism. It is a project advocating the democratically-led shrinking of production and consumption with the aim of achieving social justice and ecological sustainability.

This overview of degrowth offers a comprehensive coverage of the main topics and major challenges of degrowth in a succinct, simple and accessible manner. In addition, it offers a set of keywords useful for intervening in current political debates and for bringing about concrete degrowth-inspired proposals at different levels [en] local, national and global.

The result is the most comprehensive coverage of the topic of degrowth in English and serves as the definitive international reference.

Giacomo D'Alisa is Research Fellow at the Autonomous University of Barcelona, Spain.

Federico Demaria is a PhD candidate at the Autonomous University of Barcelona, Spain.

Giorgos Kallis is Professor at the Autonomous University of Barcelona, Spain.

The three editors are members of Research & Degrowth, www.degrowth.org

More information at: vocabulary.degrowth.org

PRAISE FOR THE BOOK

This book is an excellent introduction to the politics of 'degrowth' in its different meanings and dimensions that are analyzed and catalogued in dozens of entries providing an indispensable point of reference for anyone interested in joining the debates surrounding this perspective. It is also an eye-opener to the evolution of the concept. For as the editors' introduction demonstrates, 'degrowth' for many signifies a variety of initiatives [en] time banks, local currencies, urban gardens, solidarity economies [en] proposing an alternative to capitalist accumulation and the reconstruction of our reproduction on more cooperative terms. This then is a volume that those committed to building non-exploitative relations will need to consult as it offers a map to the world of alternatives to capitalisms.

Silvia Federici, Emeritus Professor at
Hofstra University, New York

At a time in history when political, economic and intellectual leaders assure us that nothing fundamental can any longer be questioned, nothing could be more important than the movement – of thought, and of action – that this volume on Degrowth represents. It raises the prospect of finally ejecting the twin demons of productivism and consumerism that are responsible for so many historical failures of the left as well as the right, and begins to set about the real work of imagining and building a society fit for human beings to live in.

David Graeber, Professor of Anthropology,
London School of Economics, London

This book is one of the most thorough and insightful presentations and discussion of economic theory and practice in the field of de-growth economics, a revolutionary attempt to understand the economy as if humans and Nature matter.

Manuel Castells, Professor Emeritus of City And Regional
Planning, University of California, Berkeley

A thought-provoking, wide-ranging, spirited, and deeply original analysis; this book is a must-read on degrowth debates.

Karen Bakker Professor and Canada Research Chair Director,
Program on Water Governance, University of British Columbia, Vancouver.

Degrowth takes the false coin of economic growth via capital accumulation and confronts it head on: There is no wealth but life and to protect life on the planet and to ensure the future for all it is necessary to exit the current system of production. This is the essential message for our time.

John Bellamy Foster, Professor of Sociology
at the University of Oregon, Eugene

Breaking away from myths has always been difficult . . . But this is the spirit of the contributions of this book which ask: will it be possible to escape from the monster of growth? The answer is simple. It is is not only possible, but indispensable. But is also not sufficient. We also need to think new utopias to orient us. And these one can find in this book . . . Those utopias imply a critique of perverse reality as well as the patient construction in solidarity of new and diverse options. . . . Alternatives imagined collectively and implemented democratically . . .

Alberto Acosta, Professor of Economics, FLACSO University and
ex-President of the National Constitutional Assembly of Ecuador

We really need to develop a vocabulary for a new era, and this timely book takes us a great step forward by providing an impressive collection of concepts and ideas related to the degrowth debate. It is a very useful resource for both newcomers and seasoned participants. Everyone can find inspiration and new links between ideas by following one's own personal track through the entries – it is a pleasure.

Inge Røpke, Professor of Ecological
Economics Aalborg University, Copenhagen

This volume is indispensable for anybody interested in moving beyond mere retrofit solutions to the most important economic and ecological conundrums of our time. This book helps bury several oxymoron-constructs masquerading as solutions to the human predicament. It achieves this by landing definitive intellectual and political blows to both the desirability and possibility of unfettered economic growth as a panacea for all ills.

Deepak Malghan, Professor of Ecological Economics
at Indian Institute of Management, Bangalore

What a splendid vocabulary! A range of international authors brilliantly surveys the emerging field of an economics which bids farewell to the obsession of growth. The entries are compact yet eloquent, learned yet action-oriented. In the new style of economic thought, ideas like sharing, frugality, debt-free money, dematerialization, and digital commons play a leading role. Whoever wants to know more about an economy of permanence for the 21th century should reach for this book.

Wolfgang Sachs, Professor of Social Science
at the Wuppertal Institute, Berlin

This collection is an invaluable source of knowledge and inspiration for anyone interested academically or politically in alternative ways of thinking and acting about the environment and development. The collection is of interest to economists, political scientists, ecologists, geographers, planners, environmentalists, activists, development scholars, anthropologists, policy makers, and to anyone who wishes to think and act in ways that transcend the current environmental and economic impasse.

Maria Kaika, Professor in Human Geography,
University of Manchester, Manchester

Degrowth thinking is a strategic meeting place for many trends in contemporary environmental politics, and this encyclopaedic compendium, at once widely accessible and deeply informative, will be invaluable in advancing the work of both academics and activists committed to building eco-sufficiency and global justice.

Ariel Salleh, Professor of Social Science
at Friedrich Schiller University, Jena

Degrowth is more than just an idea: it is a dream. Born in the 1970s, this recurrent, collective dream has survived the neo-liberal hegemony and – as this book convincingly shows – has gone more political (and more feminist) through collective thinking and social practices. Like it or not, this persistence of the concept must be recognized, and credit given to its capacity of spurring new debates and new forms of social mobilization, appealing to all those who continue to see 'growth' as a false solution to social problems and a true disaster for the environment.

Stefania Barca, Environmental Historian
at University of Coimbra, Coimbra

Degrowth illuminates diverse concepts for clear thinking, provides us with new languages for political discourse, and outlines the many steps we can take to recreate our economy, our lives, and our relations to planet Earth. Call it what you want: happiness, living within limits, community, real democracy – *Degrowth* both calls and empowers us to bold action.

Richard Norgaard, Professor Emeritus of Energy
and Resources, University of California, Berkeley

In times marked by political stupor, it is refreshing to have such a light-footed guide through a universe of anti-mainstream ideas ranging from conviviality to Ubuntu, and from urban gardening to entropy.

Marina Fischer-Kowalski, Professor of Social Ecology
at Alpen Adria University, Vienna

The editors invite the reader to make their own voyage through this book. It is sage advice, for readers will wander through a wonderland of radical thoughts, intriguing observations and bold visions for a different kind of world. It's exciting and deeply subversive.

Clive Hamilton, Professor of Public Ethics at the
Centre for Applied Philosophy and Public Ethics, Melbourne

This dictionary is a vital resource for those who want to engage with the diverse networks of ideas and traditions, analytical concepts and theories known as 'Degrowth'. It is also one indispensable compass to find orientation in the complex simplicity of alternatives.

Massimo De Angelis, Professor of Political Economy and
Development at the University of East London, London

For the poor to grow up to a steady-state economy that is sufficient for a good life and sustainable for a long future, the rich must make ecological space by de-growing down to the same sufficient (not luxurious) steady-state level. Essays in this collection recognize the necessity to face this difficult convergent task of justly sharing our finite world.

Herman Daly, Professor Emeritus of Ecological
Economics, University of Maryland, Maryland

This exciting book is a pioneering exploration of the recently come-of-age field of degrowth economics and policy. It will be landmark for all those who want to transcend the growth fetish that has so many enthralled today.

James Gustave Speth, Professor of Law at
the Vermont Law School, Royalton

Degrowth is less a theory of development as it is a theory of societal change. This must-read collection of thoughtful and accessible essays provides many contrasting perspectives that will stimulate rethinking what kind of society we want and could have.

Nicholas A. Ashford, Professor of Technology
and Policy, at MIT, Massachusetts

DEGROWTH

A vocabulary for a new era

*Edited by Giacomo D'Alisa,
Federico Demaria and Giorgos Kallis*

Routledge
Taylor & Francis Group

NEW YORK AND LONDON

First published 2015
by Routledge
2 Park Square, Milton Park, Abingdon, Oxon OX14 4RN

and by Routledge
711 Third Avenue, New York, NY 10017

Routledge is an imprint of the Taylor & Francis Group, an Informa business

British Library Cataloguing in Publication Data
A catalogue record for this book is available from the British Library

Library of Congress Cataloging in Publication Data
Degrowth: a vocabulary for a new era/edited by Giacomo D'Alisa,
    Federico Demaria and Giorgos Kallis.
pages cm
Includes bibliographical references and index.
1. Economic development—Moral and ethical aspects. 2. Stagnation
(Economics) 3. Poverty. 4. Sustainable development. I. D'Alisa, Giacomo.
II. Demaria, Federico. III. Kallis, Giorgos.
HD75.D4375 2014
338.9—dc23
2014017043

ISBN: 978-1-138-00076-6 (hbk)
ISBN: 978-1-138-00077-3 (pbk)
ISBN: 978-0-203-79614-6 (ebk)

Typeset in Bembo
by Swales & Willis Ltd, Exeter, Devon, UK

The cover image and the illustration on page xxiv were created by Bàrbara Castro Urío, and appear with her permission.
© Bàrbara Castro Urío, labarbara.net 2014

CONTENTS

CONTRIBUTORS

Editors

Giacomo D'Alisa, PhD in Economics, is a young ecological economist and political ecologist. Since 2012, he has been working as Assistant Coordinator of the EU funded European Network of Political Ecology project at the Institute of Environmental Science and Technology (Autonomous University of Barcelona). In the last five years, his research focused on the waste mismanagement in Campania (Italy) and the commons. He is currently a Research Fellow at the University of Rome 'La Sapienza' working on the illegal waste trafficking in Europe. He is a member of Research & Degrowth (Spain). For him a shift towards a degrowth society implies a smooth change of the hypertrophic modern individual toward a sober person committed to the social *dépense*. giacomo_dalisa@yahoo.it

Federico Demaria is a PhD candidate at the Institute of Environmental Science and Technology, Autonomous University of Barcelona with an affiliation at the Center for Studies in Science Policy, Jawaharlal Nehru University (JNU), India. He works in ecological economics and political ecology with a focus on waste policy in India and is part of EJOLT (www.ejolt.org), a global research project bringing science and society together to catalogue and analyze ecological distribution conflicts and confront environmental injustice. Since 2006 he has been part of the degrowth movement and debate, first with the Italian Association for Degrowth and then as a co-founder of Research & Degrowth (Spain). federicodemaria@gmail.com

Giorgos Kallis is an ecological economist coordinating the Marie Curie funded European Network of Political Ecology. Before becoming a professor in Barcelona he did a postdoc at the Energy and Resources Group at the University of California at Berkeley and a PhD in environmental policy and planning at the University of the Aegean in Greece. He has a Masters in Economics from Universitat Pompeu Fabra in Barcelona, and a Masters in environmental engineering and a Bachelors in chemistry from Imperial College, London. He is a member of Research & Degrowth (Spain). giorgoskallis@gmail.com

Contributors

Blake Alcott hails from Oklahoma and Connecticut and worked until 2001 in Zürich as a cabinet-maker. He received his MPhil in environmental policy from Cambridge University in 2006 and his PhD in sustainability strategies from the University of East Anglia in 2013, and is now a retired ecological economist living in Cambridge. www.blakealcott.org blakeley@bluewin.ch

Samuel Alexander is co-director of the Simplicity Institute (www.simplicityinstit ute.org) and teaches a course called 'Consumerism and the Growth Paradigm' for the Masters of Environment at the University of Melbourne, Australia. He is also co-founder of Transition Coburg and has recently published his second book, *Entropia: Life Beyond Industrial Civilisation* (2013). s.alexander@simplicityinstitute.org

Diego Andreucci is a 'Marie Curie' predoctoral fellow of the European Network of Political Ecology (ENTITLE) project at the Institute of Environmental Science and Technology, Autonomous University of Barcelona. He researches critical geographies of environment and development, with a focus on the politics of resource extraction in Latin America. diego.andreucci@gmail.com

Isabelle Anguelovski is trained in urban studies and planning. Her research is situated at the intersection of urban inequality, environmental policy and planning and development studies. She has just published *Neighborhood as Refuge: Community Reconstruction, Place Remaking, and Environmental Justice in the City* (MIT Press, 2014). Isabelle.Anguelovski@uab.cat

Viviana Asara is a PhD candidate at the Institute of Environmental Science and Technology, Autonomous University of Barcelona and is currently undertaking research on degrowth and democracy and the political ecology of the indignados movement. She is currently a visiting student at the European University Institute (Florence). viviana.asara@gmail.com

Denis Bayon is a member of Research & Degrowth.

David Bollier is an author, activist, blogger and independent scholar who has studied the commons as a new paradigm of economics, politics and culture for the past 15 years. He pursues this work primarily as co-founder of the Commons Strategies Group. His most recent book is *Think Like a Commoner: A Short Introduction to the Life of the Commons*. www.bollier.org

Mauro Bonaiuti has taught at the universities of Bologna, Modena, Parma, and is currently teaching at the University of Turin. He has mostly worked on the relations between economy, ecosystems and society, following a complex systems approach. He is co-founder of the Italian Degrowth Association and promoter of the Italian Solidarity Economy Network. He is the author of *The Great Transition*, (2014) and the editor of *From Bioeconomics to Degrowth: Georgescu-Roegen's New Economics in Eight Essays* (2011), both published by Routledge. mauro.bonati@unito.it

Rita Calvário is a PhD candidate at the Institute for Environmental Science and Technology (ICTA) at the Autonomous University of Barcelona (UAB) and a predoctoral Marie Curie fellow of the European Network for Political Ecology (ENTITLE). She holds a BA in agronomic engineering, an MA in environmental and territorial planning (2010) and a MPhil in climate change and sustainable development policies (2012). ritamcalvario@gmail.com

Chris Carlsson, co-directs the multimedia history project Shaping San Francisco (www.shapingsf.org), and is a writer, publisher, editor and community organizer. He has written two books (*After the Deluge, Nowtopia*) and edited six books, (most recently: *Shift Happens! Critical Mass at 20*). He has given hundreds of public presentations based on Shaping San Francisco, Critical Mass, Nowtopia, and his 'Reclaiming San Francisco' history anthologies since the late 1990s, and has appeared dozens of times in radio, television and on the internet. www.chriscarlsson.com

Claudio Cattaneo did his PhD at the Institute of Environmental Science and Technology, Autonomous University of Barcelona, where he remains a Research Associate. His doctoral thesis explored the ecological economics of Barcelona squatters. His research interests focus on alternative life-styles, urban and squatting movements, do-it-yourself, human ecology and political ecological economics. Claudio combines research with practical and social work as a squatter, a bicycle mechanic and an olive farmer. claudio.cattaneo@liuc.it

Marta Conde is pursuing her PhD at the Institute of Environmental Science and Technology, Autonomous University of Barcelona. Her research looks at social reactions to the expansion of the extractive industries at the commodity frontiers. mcondep@gmail.com

Chiara Corazza graduated from Ca'Foscari University (Venice) with a thesis on Kumarappa's Economy, presented at the Venice Degrowh Conference (2012). She is a member of the Editorial Board of «DEP» (*Deportate, esuli, profughe*) www.unive.it/dep. chiaracory@hotmail.it

Sergi Cutillas is a PhD candidate at the School of Oriental and African Studies. His research focuses on the political economy of money and finance, with a special interest in the nature and dynamics of credit money. Sergi also works as researcher at the Observatory on Debt in the Globalization. He also participates in the citizen debt audit campaign in the Spanish state (PACD), partner of the CADTM network and part of the International Citizen Audit Network. sergi.cutillas@odg.cat

Marco Deriu is Assistant Professor of Sociology of Political Communication at the University of Parma (Italy). As a member of the Italian Degrowth Association and Maschile Plurale Association, he was part of the Organizing Committee of the 3rd International Conference on Degrowth (Venice, 2012). marco.deriu@unipr.it

Kristofer Dittmer is a PhD student in ecological economics at the Institute of Environmental Science and Technology, Autonomous University of Barcelona. kristofer.dittmer@gmail.com

Arturo Escobar is Professor of Anthropology at the University of North Carolina, Chapel Hill. His main interests are: political ecology, design, and the anthropology of development, social movements and science and technology. Over the past twenty years, he has worked closely with several Afro-Colombian social movements in the Colombian Pacific, particular the Process of Black Communities (PCN). His most well-known book is *Encountering Development: The Making and Unmaking of the Third* World (1995, 2nd ed. 2011). His most recent book is *Territories of Difference: Place, Movements, Life, Redes* (2008). aescobar@email.unc.edu

Silke Helfrich is an author and independent researcher, networker and activist of the commons. She is founding member of the Commons Strategies Group. She blogs at www.commonsblog.de. Silke.Helfrich@gmx.de

Joshua Farley is an ecological economist and full Professor in Community Development and Applied Economics and Public Administration. His broad research interests focus on the design of an economy capable of balancing what is biophysically possible with what is socially, psychologically and ethically desirable. He is co-author with Herman Daly of *Ecological Economics, Principles and Applications*, 2nd ed. Island Press (2010). joshua.farley@uvm.edu

Fabrice Flipo is a social and political philosopher, he teaches at Telecom & Management SudParis and is a member of the *Laboratoire de Changement Social et Politique* at Paris 7 Diderot University. fabrice.flipo@telecom-em.eu

Mayo Fuster Morell is a postdoctoral researcher at the Institute of Government and Public Policy, Autonomous University of Barcelona and fellow at the Berkman Center for Internet and Society, Harvard University. In 2010, she concluded her PhD thesis at the European University Institute on the governance of digital commons. She is the principal investigator of IGOPnet for the European project P2Pvalue and of the Spanish National Research programme Information, culture and knowledge: New citizens' practices, new public policies. mayo.fuster@eui.eu

Erik Gómez-Baggethun, PhD in ecology and the environment, is an environmental scientist working in the fields of ecological economics and political ecology. He is a member of Research & Degrowth and a senior researcher at the Norwegian

Institute for Nature Research and at the Institute of Environmental Science and Technology, Autonomous University of Barcelona. The focus of his research is on ecosystem services and long term resilience. erik.gomez@nina.no

Eduardo Gudynas is a leading scholar on buen vivir. Gudynas is the executive secretary of the Latin American Centre for Social Ecology in Uruguay and author of over ten books and many academic articles. His expertise is on sustainable development and alternatives to development. www.gudynas.com

Tim Jackson is Professor of Sustainable Development at the University of Surrey and Director of RESOLVE. He also directs the follow-on project: the Sustainable Lifestyles Research Group (SLRG). He authored the controversial report, later published by Earthscan as *Prosperity without Growth – Economics for a Finite Planet*. Tim's current projects include – in collaboration with Professor Peter Victor (York University, Toronto) – the development of the green economy macro-model and accounts (GEMMA). t.jackson@surrey.ac.uk

Nadia Johanisova is an assistant professor at the Faculty of Social Studies, Masaryk University (Brno, Czech Republic). She works in the fields of ecological economics and degrowth. She has published a comparative study of Czech and British social enterprises (*Living in the Cracks*, 2005). Her current interests lie in 'alternative economic practices' (including social enterprises, co-operatives, local food projects, community currency schemes, etc.) in the Global North and South and their role in current and future degrowth economies. nadia.johaniso@fss.muni.cz

Christian Kerschner holds a PhD in ecological economics from the Institute of Environmental Science and Technology, Autonomous University of Barcelona. His main area of interest are resource scarcities and general issues of economic scale. Christian authored an influential article consolidating the steady-state economy with the newly emerging field of economic de-growth and provided insights into the backgrounds of the Steady State Economy. christian.kerschner@gmail.com

Serge Latouche is a French Professor Emeritus in Economy at the University of Paris-Sud. He is a specialist in North-South economic and cultural relations, and in social sciences epistemology. He has developed a critical theory towards economic orthodoxy and he is one of the leading thinkers and most renowned partisans of the degrowth theory. He is the author of many books, among others *Farewell to Growth* (2009).

David Llistar is author of the book *Anticooperación. Interferencias globales Norte-Sur* (2009). He is a co-founder of the *Observatorio de la Deuda en la Globalización* (ODG). He is a physicist and has given classes on political ecology at different universities. His main research interest regards the impacts of the Spanish economy upon countries in the South. david.llistar@odg.cat

Sylvia Lorek, head of the Sustainable Europe Research Institute, Germany, holds a Ph.D. in consumer economics and diploma in household economics and nutrition. She is engaged in CSO activities towards sustainable consumption at national, European and global levels. sylvia.lorek@t-online.de

Joan Martinez-Alier is Professor Emeritus at the Autonomous University of Barcelona (Spain) and FLACSO, Quito, Ecuador. He is the author of *Ecological Economics: Energy, Environment and Society* (1987) and *The Environmentalism of the Poor: A Study of Ecological Conflicts and Valuation* (2002). joanmartinezalier@gmail.com

Terrence McDonough is Professor of Economics at the National University of Ireland, Galway. His primary interest is in Marxist approaches to stages in capitalist history. He is the co-editor of *Contemporary Capitalism and its Crises: Social Structure of Accumulation Theory for the 21st Century* (2010). terrence.mcdonough@nuigalway.ie

Mary Mellor is Professor Emeritus in the Department of Social Science at Northumbria University, UK. She is the author of *The Future of Money: From Financial Crisis to Public Resource* (2010). She has also published widely on ecofeminist political economy, including a book entitled *Feminism and Ecology* (1997). She is currently working on a book on public money. m.mellor@northumbria.ac.uk

Barbara Muraca is a postdoctoral researcher at the Institute for Sociology at the Friedrich-Schiller-Universität Jena, with the German Research Foundation-Advanced Research Group 'Post-Growth-Societies'. Barbara works in the research field of ethics, environmental philosophy and social philosophy. barbara.muraca@uni-jena.de

Dan O'Neill is a lecturer in ecological economics at the University of Leeds, and Chief Economist at the Center for the Advancement of the Steady State Economy. He is co-author (with Rob Dietz) of *Enough Is Enough: Building a Sustainable Economy in a World of Finite Resources*. d.oneill@leeds.ac.uk

Iago Otero, PhD in Environmental Science, is a postdoctoral researcher at IRI THESys (Humboldt Universität zu Berlin) and works with the project groups 'Changing rural-urban linkages across the world' and 'Transformations and uncertainties of land-water systems'. He wrote his PhD thesis on the rural-to-urban social-ecological transformation of Mediterranean mountain areas. iago.otero.armengol@hu-berlin.de

Philippa Parry is a graduate of the University of Birmingham (UK) and a Masters graduate of Forum for the Future (London) in Leadership for Sustainable Development. Her experience in The Ecology Building Society seeded an interest in co-operative structures, leading to the setting up of a co-operatively-run organic cafe in Barcelona. philippa01@gmail.com

Susan Paulson explores interactions among gender, class, ethnicity and environment in diverse contexts in Latin America. Collaboration in research and theory building on rural territory dynamics led to her 2013 book *Masculinidades en movimiento, transformación territorial* and the 2005 volume *Political Ecology Across Spaces, Scales, and Social Groups*. She teaches sustainability at the University of Florida. spaulson@latam.ufl.edu

Antonella Picchio is a feminist economist with a research interest on social reproduction and un-paid work. Her best-known book is *Social Reproduction: the Political Economy of the Labour Market* (1992). Picchio has also edited *Unpaid Work and the Economy: A Gender Analysis of the Standards of Living* (2003). She has been a militant in the feminist movement since the 1970s. picchio@unimo.it

Mogobe B. Ramose is Head of the Department of Philosophy at the University of South Africa, Pretoria. ramosmb@unisa.ac.za

Xavier Renou is a former nuclear disarmament campaigner at Greenpeace France. He initiated the activists' network called *"Les désobéissants"* ("those who disobey"), which trains people into civil disobedience tactics in a large number of countries and provides help to those who struggle against injustice whatever its nature, be it environmental, social or international. An activist and a trainer himself, he is also the author of a dozen books and the editor of a series of handbooks, *Desobeir* (at Le Passager clandestin, Paris). xrenou2@gmail.com

Onofrio Romano is professor of Sociology of Culture at the University of Bari (Dept. Political Sciences), Italy. His writings focus on post-modern cultures and the Mediterranean societies. Among his recent books is *The Sociology of Knowledge in a Time of Crises* (2014). onofrio.romano@uniba.it

François Schneider is a degrowth researcher, practitioner and activist. Since 2001, he is active in the development of the degrowth concept and debate in France, Spain and Europe. francois@degrowth.net

Juliet Schor is Professor of Sociology at Boston College and author of *Plenitude: the New Economics of True Wealth*. Previous books include *The Overworked American* and *The Overspent American*. Schor is also the principal organizer of the Summer Institute in New Economics, and a past recipient of the Herman Daly Award from the US Society for Ecological Economics. juliet.schor@bc.edu

Filka Sekulova is a researcher at Institute of Environmental Science and Technology, Autonomous University of Barcelona, in transition studies and well-being. Having a background in psychology and environmental economics, she wrote her PhD on the economics of happiness and climate change. She has been writing on degrowth, happiness and ecological economics. filka@degrowth.net

Alevgül H. Şorman is a researcher in the Integrated Assessment group at the Institute of Environmental Science and Technology, Autonomous University of Barcelona. She focuses on the multi-scale integrated analysis of energy systems and societal metabolism. alevgul@gmail.com

Ruben Suriñach Padilla works at the Centre of Research and Information on Consumption (CRIC) as a project manager and consultant on sustainable consumption and new economies. Through *Opcions* magazine, he has developed investigative research projects about cooperativism, social and community innovation and sustainable lifestyles. He is an economist and has a Masters degree in environmental studies, specialising in ecological economics. rubens@pangea.org

Erik Swyngedouw is Professor of Geography at the University of Manchester in its School of Environment, Education and Development. Swyngedouw has published several books and research papers in the fields of political economy, political ecology and urban theory and culture. He focuses on politically explicit yet theoretically and empirically grounded research that contributes to the practice of constructing a more genuinely humanizing geography. erik.swyngedouw@manchester.ac.uk

Gemma Tarafa holds a PhD in molecular biology at the Universitat de Barcelona, then she obtained a postdoctorate degree at the Yale University. She was a researcher at the Catalan Institute of Oncology and is currently a public health researcher at the Universitat Pompeu Fabra (UPF) in the Health Inequalities Research Group (GREDS). She has been a researcher at the Observatory on Debt in Globalisation (ODG) since its creation in 2000 and a member of the PACD (Plataforma Auditoría Ciudadana de la Deuda). gemma.tarafa@odg.cat

Sergio Ulgiati is Professor of Life Cycle Assessment and Environmental Certification at the Parthenope University of Napoli, Italy. His research interests are in the fields of environmental accounting and emergy synthesis, life cycle assessment and energy analysis. sergio.ulgiati@uniparthenope.it

B. J. Unti is a PhD candidate in the Department of Economics at the University of Missouri-Kansas City and currently teaches at Bellevue College in Washington state. bjufz5@mail.umkc.edu

Peter A. Victor is Professor in Environmental Studies at York University, Canada. His teaching and research focus on ecological economics. He is now involved in an ongoing collaboration with Professor Tim Jackson (UK) to develop ecological macroeconomics, in particular the construction of a simulation model of national economies designed to explore alternatives to economic growth. petervictor@ sympatico.ca

Solomon Victus is a social analyst. He holds a PhD in religion and philosophy from Madurai Kamaraj University and a Master of Theology (M.Th) in social analysis from Serampore University. He has been senior theologian in Tamilnadu Theological Seminary, Madurai. He is the author of seven books and hundreds of articles in journals of national importance. solomonvictus@gmail.com

Mariana Walter is a researcher at the Institute of Environmental Science and Technology, Autonomous University of Barcelona and at the International Institute of Social Studies, Erasmus University Rotterdam. She holds a PhD in environmental studies. Her thesis addresses the political ecology of mining conflicts in Latin America. She has taken part in research projects in Argentina (UNGS) and Europe (ALARM, CEECEC), and currently works in the European-funded ENGOV Project, aiming to develop a framework for sustainable and equitable natural resource use. marianawalter2002@gmail.com

PREFACE

When the ordinary language in use is inadequate to articulate what begs to be articulated, then it is time for a new vocabulary.

We live in an era of stagnation, rapid impoverishment of a vast part of the population, growing inequalities, and socio-ecological disasters - from Katrina, Haiti and Philippines, to Fukushima, the spill in the Gulf of Mexico, or the burial of toxic waste in Campania, to climate change and the continuous disaster of preventable deaths by lack of access to land, water, and food.

There is a failure, even by radical thinkers, to come up with new responses that are not articulated around the twin imperatives of growth and development. If the desire for growth causes economic, social, and environmental crises, as the authors in this volume argue it does, then growth cannot be the solution.

Fortunately, alternatives are springing up on the ground. They range from new forms of living, producing, and consuming in common to new institutions that can secure the livelihoods of all without growth. However, more comprehensive counter-hegemonic narratives are necessary for articulating and connecting these new alternatives. We hope this book offers keywords for constructing such narratives.

Degrowth has multiple interpretations. Different people arrive at it from different angles. Some, because they see that there are limits to growth. Others, because they believe we are entering a period of economic stagnation and we should find ways to maintain prosperity without growth. Yet others because they believe that a truly egalitarian society can only be one that liberates itself from capitalism and its insatiable pursuit of expansion, one that learns to collectively limit itself and work without the calculus of self-interested utility. And yet others, simply because "degrowth" sounds pretty much like the way they choose to live.

Contributions in this book come from different schools of thought, different disciplines, and different spheres of life: ecological (bio- and steady-state) economists, anti-utilitarianists, (neo)Marxians, political ecologists, cooperativists, nowtopians, and various activists and practitioners. Each of our contributors sees degrowth slightly differently. Not all of them necessarily share what is said in other entries. Yet degrowth is what brings them together and connects them.

Degrowth defies a single definition. Like freedom or justice, degrowth expresses an aspiration which cannot be pinned down to a simple sentence. Degrowth is a frame, where different lines of thought, imaginaries, or courses of action come together. We see this versatility as a strength. This is why we decided to represent degrowth in a (loose) form of a dictionary. The vocabulary of degrowth is a network of ideas and conversations, strongly rooted in the radical and critical traditions, but open-ended and amenable to multiple connections.

The book starts with an essay written by the three of us. It is longer than the other entries in the book, not because we were more lenient with the word limit for ourselves, but because it attempts to present "degrowth" linking this core keyword of this book all the other keywords of this book. In this introductory chapter, we present the history of the term degrowth and the various propositions and ideas that express it.

The remainder of the book is divided into four parts. The first part examines intellectual roots that nourish degrowth, i.e. the epistemologies of degrowth. The entries summarize in a few words entire schools of thought, explaining their relevance for degrowth. The second part presents the concepts that are at the core of degrowth's critique to the *pensée unique* of growth. Each entry in this part represents a different entry-point into degrowth. Together, these entries form the theory of degrowth. The third part moves to action and focuses on concrete institutional proposals and on living examples of how degrowth looks on the ground. The entries span from state policies to activist projects and try to cover the whole range of the post-capitalist imaginary of degrowth. Finally, the fourth and shortest part of the book, looks at "alliances"; it presents schools of thought, actors, and concepts, which share a lot with the degrowth project but which have only had loose connections with degrowth up to now. It is there where the most fertile geographical links and future extensions of degrowth are to be found and strengthened.

The reader may approach the book in the standard linear way, reading it entry by entry. But, according to us, this will probably be the most boring way to engage with it. An alternative would be to start from what seems as the most intriguing entry and then wander through the cross-references (marked in bold) to other entries. A meticulous reader might want to read one by one all entries mentioned in a single entry, then move to the next unread entry and do the same, until he or she has read the whole book. Readers are encouraged to make their own voyage through the book and reach their own sense of what degrowth means to them.

At the end of this book, in an essay called "From austerity to depense," we state what degrowth has come to mean to us in the process of preparing this book and reading the contributions. This is our own politically committed and selective take on the book.

The authors contributing to this volume were instructed to write as simply as possible, but not simpler than that. The entries are written for a general public, not for the specialist. They do not demand previous knowledge of the debates or the terminology. Still, they are framed and composed with the desirable rigor and expertise of academic book chapters. At the end of each entry there is a references list for those who want to delve deeper into each topic.

The book is a collective output, but with our own spin on the selection and arrangement of entries and contributors. As with any intellectual product, our contributions for this book are not only our own, but the output of accumulated work from the people we have read and the people we have discussed with. It embodies and is embedded in the social and familial work of reproduction. It is a result of commoning.

In the Monday reading group of Research & Degrowth in Barcelona we formulated most of the ideas we express in this book. Many of the members of this collective, some of them researchers also at the Institute of Environmental Science and Technology (ICTA) at the Autonomous University of Barcelona, are also contributors to this book. But let us acknowledge them also one by one: Filka, Viviana, Claudio, Marta, Kristofer, Erik, Christian, Iago, Christos, Daniela, Diego, Rita, Lucha, Aggelos, Marco, and the various occasional participants of the reading group, too many to mention here. Our special thanks to Joan Martinez-Alier, who created at ICTA a wonderful haven of radical thought without which we would never have come together to work in common, and to François Schneider, who brought to Barcelona his passion for degrowth and shared it with all of us. Let us also thank all these people without whom this volume would have not been completed. Jacques Grinevald who passed to us generously his knowledge of the history of degrowth; our translators from French and Spanish, Bob Thompson and Cormac De Brun; our editors at Routledge Robert Langham, Andy Humphries, Lisa Thomson, Laura Johnson, and Natalie Tomlinson; and Valerie McGuire (aided by Jason Badgley), who not only translated entries from Italian, but painstakingly read and edited all entries of the book, improving the English of non-native speakers, and allowing this to be a truly international volume. We also thank Bàrbara Castro Urío (labarbara.net), our graphic designer, who created the cover and the illustrations of this book, because aesthetics matters too. We acknowledge the financial support of the Spanish government through the project CSO2011-28990 BEGISUD (Beyond GDP growth: Investigating the socio-economic conditions for a Socially Sustainable Degrowth) and of the European Union through the Marie Curie Action Initial Training Networks - FP7 – PEOPLE - 2011; contract No 289374 — ENTITLE (European Network for Political Ecology).

This book has several chapters and authors. We are not the only ones who worked on it, but we did work a lot on it. We would like to dedicate our contributions to those we most care for. Giacomo D'Alisa to his present and future: his wife Stefania and his children Claudia Pilar and Nicolas Mayo. Federico Demaria to his partner Veronica, his parents Maria and Mario, and his brother Daniele. Giorgos Kallis to his wife Amalia, his parents Vassili and Maria, and his sister Iris. And last but not least, to all our close friends and companions.

Giacomo D'Alisa, Federico Demaria, Giorgos Kallis
Barcelona, April 2014
vocabulary.degrowth.org

FOREWORD

The issue of economic degrowth and the prospect of a more sustainable and just society entered the domain of scientific research in 2008 when we, the authors of this foreword, co-organized the first international conference on the subject in Paris. Success was immediate and a promising future opened up. The Paris conference was followed by conferences in Barcelona, Montreal, Venice, and Leipzig (among a large array of local events). An international network is developing in 30 countries, research agendas and multi-dimensional political proposals are being debated, and several scientific journals have been publishing the work of the burgeoning degrowth research community. Of course, when we convened the Paris conference we were well aware that we were not the first to criticize the "growth society." The Club of Rome in the 1970s had already questioned the possibility of continuous material growth, the basis of productivist societies (capitalist or socialist). This question has only become more insistent since then, due to six drivers: the continuing degradation of the natural environment; resource depletion and the challenge it poses to economic growth; exhaustion of the growth potential due to the unsustainable contradictions that capitalism remains locked into; renewed interest in seeking a path of civilization not based on utilitarian exchange with ever-growing increasing returns; a growing counter-productivity of institutions, namely their tendency to act as barriers with respect to users, rather than as tools; and finally the "crisis of meaning" and the attempt by many to disconnect from mass consumption and give new meaning to their lives (through frugality, Do-It-Yourself, eco-communes, etc.).

These six forces will not weaken in the near future. To take the environmental dimension, for example, even the International Energy Agency now recognizes that we reached the peak of conventional oil in 2011.[1] The coming oil shortage explains the rush for unconventional energy sources, such as shale gas, economically attractive despite the environmental and social destruction they bring. The Millennium

Ecosystem Assessment (2005) clearly established that ecosystems are increasingly exploited, in many cases beyond their limits. The National Bureau of Economic Research, where the "*crème de la crème*" of American economists sit, many of them awardees of Nobel prizes, published an article in August 2012 that asked whether the long period of continued US economic growth was coming to an end. Similarly, in Europe, where the average rate of economic growth has been declining for four decades, a "crisis of meaning" has become evident, manifested in the growing public distrust of science and technology. Many conferences reflect on this "crisis of meaning," as do documents such as the recent "Convivialist Manifesto" – where several important personalities dared to utter for the first time the word "degrowth." There is willingness from diverse political and economic actors to abandon their usual positions and radically question the present situation. Finally, there is a looming institutional crisis. More and more people reject "democratic" processes. This rejection is manifested not least in a growing electoral abstention and the electoral rise of extreme right nationalists almost everywhere in Europe.

This multi-fold crisis relates to the unsustainability of the post-war consumption-based economic model as well as the exclusion from it of individuals, whole countries, or even continents. If we continue to uphold an unsustainable level of consumption in privileged areas of the globe – and even worse, continue to imagine that this level will grow in the future – we must also acknowledge that this "growth" can only come by means of "closure," of leaving out those for whom "there is not enough." Hence we witness the proliferation of gated communities, national borders closed for the poor of the world (and opened for the rich), and the internal closure of social groups with the development of essentialist or racist discourses. These closures sustain, for the selected few, the present unsustainable ways of life that Western societies have grown accustomed to.

In the West, the idea of economic degrowth and of the construction of a society of sharing, frugality and conviviality continue to strengthen. Yet the vast majority still live in denial. This denial is reinforced by economists – the apostles of industrial modernity – by whom the question of degrowth remains largely ignored, if it is not a taboo. Witness the sharp reaction at the mention of the word "degrowth" in front of economists. In economics, the degrowth perspective is scarcely present, even among those economists who oppose capitalism or liberalism. Heterodox economics may distance themselves from the extremely narrow vision defended by the liberal orthodoxy, but they often do not offer original thinking as far as the question of the overall direction of an economy is concerned. In fact many "heterodox" economists (but not all) simply defend theoretical positions and public policies that have been held for decades, such as stimulus to push demand, or tax reforms.

Like other scientists, economists adopt a strategy of willful blindness, reducing the object of their research to ensure the manageability and feasibility of their investigation. This is not necessarily wrong. What is wrong is the fixation on certain absolute rules, such as the growth objective, and the production of recommendations that, if they were to be applied, would direct societies down the same narrow path. With this global policy in place, we experience a societal lock-in, continuously reproduced, which constrains genuine reflection on truly original futures, commensurate with the challenges faced by our societies. These challenges are great if one considers that an industrial society with an excessive productive capacity is also a society with very strong social inequalities (exploitation of labor power, expulsion of peasants from their subsistence lands, material misery of the unemployed). Degrowth has nothing to do with a simple greening of existing techniques, nor with a "democratization," to make them accessible to all (assuming they are wanted), or merely with the collective self-management of capitalist techniques. Degrowth signals a radical critique of society: it challenges techniques, rather than just calling for their control. Some technologies are to be rejected (nuclear, GMOs, nanotechnologies) because they are not amenable to limits, others are acceptable up to certain limits, which should be deliberated by the whole of society. Degrowth is not an idea made to seduce. It is a revolutionary idea.

Today, degrowth faces two risks. The first is that it could lose its meaning and become a new version of how to consume and produce differently, omitting for example the inconvenient idea that degrowth is, also, about consuming and producing less, *much less,* at least in the wealthy regions of the world. The second risk is that degrowth could be put aside and its radical content watered down if subsumed within vaguer notions such as "post-growth," which, like sustainable development before it, leaves tactically open the possibility of "win-win" solutions. We are equally sceptical of the notion of the "steady-state," which focusses on the biophysical dimension and evades hard political and social questions.

In this context, the vocabulary that this book offers is important in two ways. On the one hand, it conveys the diversity of approaches and ideas co-existing within the term "degrowth." On the other, it manifests the great breadth of concerns and proposals that degrowth thinkers and actors have put forward by being involved in many areas (arts, science, activism) and working to develop imaginaries and concrete practices that are alternative to productivism, both local and global, in different places on the planet, within or outside the major knowledge producing institutions. We stress here the importance of combining different political strategies (opposition, building alternatives, but even some reformism) in order to bring true social change in a degrowth direction.

Like or hate the term degrowth, you can't deny that it opens up all sorts of debates that were previously closed. The emotions it stirs mean it can never become an issue of secondary importance. The valuable contribution of this volume, the first of its kind in English, is that it clarifies some of the most important and difficult to comprehend concepts mobilized in the debates about degrowth. Anti-utilitarianism, capitalism, environmentalism, conviviality, Illich's critique of big institutions, new forms of wealth or happiness, buen-vivir, and concrete aspects of voluntary simplicity, co-operatives, civil disobedience. The entries in this book are numerous and connected to one another, enabling the reader to become gradually more familiar with the key ideas associated with degrowth.

Of course such work cannot be exhaustive: degrowth is more of an exploratory avenue than a completed and sealed doctrine. This is what makes it a living and dynamic set of ideas. Let us hope that it remains this way for a long time to come and that new reflections arise to enrich, criticize, and transform the thoughts presented here.

Fabrice Flipo and François Schneider
Founders and members of Research & Degrowth

Note

1   AIE, World Energy OutInteook, 2010.

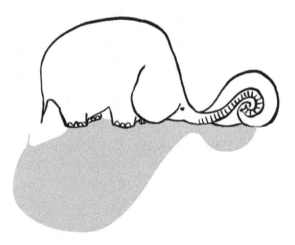

The elephant and the snail

INTRODUCTION

Degrowth

Giorgos Kallis, Federico Demaria and Giacomo D'Alisa

1. The twists and turns of degrowth

The term '*décroissance*' (French for degrowth) was used for the first time by French intellectual André Gorz in 1972. Gorz posed a question that remains at the centre of today's degrowth debate: 'Is the earth's balance, for which no-growth – or even degrowth - of material production is a necessary condition, compatible with the survival of the capitalist system?' (Gorz, 1972: iv). Other Francophone authors then used the term in the follow-up to 'The Limits to Growth' report (Meadows *et al.* 1972). Philosopher André Amar (1973) for example, wrote on *La croissance et le problème moral*[1] for an issue on '*Les objecteurs de croissance*' of the journal *NEF Cahiers*.

A few years later, André Gorz advocated explicitly degrowth in his book *Ecology and Freedom,* writing:

> [O]nly one economist, Nicholas Georgescu-Roegen, has had the common sense to point out that, even at zero growth, the continued consumption of scarce resources will inevitably result in exhausting them completely. The point is not to refrain from consuming more and more, but to consume less and less – there is no other way of conserving the available reserves for future generations. This is what ecological realism is about. [. . . .] Radicals who refuse to examine the question of equality without growth merely demonstrate that "socialism", for them, is nothing but the continuation of capitalism by other means – an extension of middle class values, lifestyles, and social patterns [. . .]. Today a lack of realism no longer consists in advocating greater well-being through degrowth[2] and the subversion of the prevailing way of life. Lack of realism consists in imagining that economic growth can still bring about increased human welfare, and indeed that it is still physically possible.
>
> *(Gorz, 1980[1977]: 13)*

Gorz was a precursor of **political ecology**. For him ecology was part and parcel of a radical political transformation. Nicholas Georgescu-Roegen, who inspired Gorz, was the intellectual pioneer of ecological economics and **bioeconomics**. In 1971 he published his magnus opus 'Entropy Law and the Economic Process'. In 1979, Jacques Grinevald and Ivo Rens, professors at the University of Geneva, edited a collection of the articles of Georgescu-Roegen with the title *Demain la décroissance* (interestingly without prior knowledge of Gorz also using the term). Grinevald chose the book title with Georgescu-Roegen's agreement, translating as décroissance the word 'descent' from G-R's article on a 'Minimal Bio-economic Programme' (Grinevald 1974).

With the end of the oil crisis and the advent of neo-liberalism in the 1980s and 1990s, the interest on limits to growth and degrowth waned; even though in the 1990s the debate thrived again in French. In 1993, the Lyon-based environmental and non-violence activist Michel Bernard got in touch with Grinevald and invited him to write an article for his magazine *Silence* on 'Georgescu-Roegen: Bioeconomics and Biosphere'. The article explicitly referred to degrowth. Later on, in July 2001, Bruno Clémentin and Vincent Cheynet, also based in Lyon, the latter an ex-advertiser and founders with Randall Ghent of the magazine *Casseurs de pub* (the French equivalent of the Canadian Adbusters), launched the term 'sustainable degrowth'. Clémentin and Cheynet registered the term as an intellectual property to mark the date of its invention and playfully warned against its future misuse and conventionalization. The public debate on degrowth in France took off in 2002 with a special issue of *Silence* edited by the two in tribute to Georgescu-Roegen. The issue sold 5,000 copies and was reprinted twice. This was probably the starting point for today's degrowth movement.

In the first phase of the degrowth debate in the 1970s, the emphasis was on resource limits. In the second phase, starting in 2001, the driving force was the criticism of the hegemonic idea of 'sustainable development'. For economic anthropologist Serge Latouche, sustainable development was an oxymoron, as he argued in 'A bas le développement durable! Vive la décroissance conviviale!' In 2002 the conference 'Défaire le développement, refaire le monde' took place in Paris at the premises of UNESCO with 800 participants. The conference marked an alliance between Lyon-based environmental activists, like Bernard, Clémentin and Cheynet, and the post-development academic community to which Latouche belonged (see **development**). In 2002, the Institute for Economic and Social Studies on Sustainable Degrowth was founded in Lyon. A year afterwards, it organized in the city the first international colloquium on sustainable degrowth. The event gathered over 300 participants from France, Switzerland and Italy. Speakers included those who were to become the most prolific authors on degrowth, such as Serge Latouche, Mauro Bonaiuti, Paul Ariès, Jacques Grinevald, François Schneider and Pierre Rabhi. The same year, Bernard, Clémentin and Cheynet edited the book *Objectif décroissance*; this sold 8,000 copies and was re-printed three times and also translated into Italian, Spanish and Catalan.

Décroissance, as a movement of activists, flourished in Lyon in the early 2000s in the wake of protests for car-free cities, communal meals in the streets, food cooperatives and campaigns against advertising. Spreading from France, it became a slogan mobilized by green and anti-globalization activists in Italy in 2004 (as '*decrescita*') and Catalonia and Spain in 2006 (as '*decreixement*' and '*decrecimiento*'). In 2004, degrowth reached a larger audience in France with conferences, direct actions and initiatives like the magazine *La Décroissance, le journal de la joie de vivre*, which today sells 30,000 copies each month. In the same year, researcher-activist François Schneider undertook a year-long walking tour on a donkey to disseminate degrowth through France, receiving widespread media coverage. In 2007, Schneider founded in France the academic collective Research & Degrowth, with Denis Bayon and, later on, Fabrice Flipo, and promoted a series of international conferences. The first was in Paris in 2008 and the second in Barcelona in 2010. The English term 'degrowth' was 'officially' used for the first time at the Paris conference, marking the birth of an international research community. As the Barcelona group from the Institute of Environmental Science and Technology (ICTA) joined the movement by hosting the second conference, the degrowth research community extended beyond its initial strongholds in France and Italy. ICTA provided links to the academic community of ecological economics as well as to Latin American networks of **political ecology** and **environmental justice**. Following the success of the Paris and Barcelona conferences, more conferences were held in Montreal (2011), Venice (2012) and Leipzig (2014), with degrowth spreading to groups and activities in Flanders, Switzerland, Finland, Poland, Greece, Germany, Portugal, Norway, Denmark, Czech Republic, Mexico, Brazil, Puerto Rico, Canada, Bulgaria, Romania and elsewhere.

Since 2008, the English term has entered academic journals with over 100 published articles and at least seven Special Issues in peer-reviewed journals (Kallis *et al.* 2010; Cattaneo *et al.* 2012; Saed 2012; Kallis *et al.* 2012; Sekulova *et al.* 2013; Whitehead 2013; Kosoy 2013). Degrowth is taught at universities around the world, including prestigious schools such as *SciencePo* in Paris. It has been used and misused by French and Italian politicians and has received coverage in many renowned newspapers, including *Le Monde*, *Le Monde Diplomatique*, *El Pais*, *The Guardian*, *The Wall Street Journal* and *Financial Times*.

But what precisely is the meaning of degrowth?

2. Degrowth today

Degrowth signifies, first and foremost, a critique of **growth**. It calls for the decolonization of public debate from the idiom of economism and for the abolishment of economic **growth** as a social objective. Beyond that, degrowth signifies also a desired direction, one in which societies will use fewer natural resources and will organize and live differently than today. 'Sharing', '**simplicity**', '**conviviality**', '**care**' and the '**commons**' are primary significations of what this society might look like.

Usually, degrowth is associated with the idea that smaller can be beautiful. Ecological economists define degrowth as an equitable downscaling of production and consumption that will reduce societies' throughput of energy and raw materials (Schneider *et al.* 2010). However, our emphasis here is on *different,* not only *less.* Degrowth signifies a society with a smaller **metabolism**, but more importantly, a society with a **metabolism** which has a different structure and serves new functions. Degrowth does not call for doing less of the same. The objective is not to make an elephant leaner, but to turn an elephant into a snail. In a degrowth society everything will be different: different activities, different forms and uses of energy, different relations, different gender roles, different allocations of time between paid and non-paid work, different relations with the non-human world.

Degrowth offers a frame that connects diverse ideas, concepts and proposals (Demaria *et al.* 2013). However, there are some centres of gravity within this frame (Figure 1). The first is the criticism of **growth**. Next is the criticism of **capitalism**, a social system that requires and perpetuates growth. Two other strong currents in the degrowth literature are, first, the criticism of **GDP**, and second, the criticism of **commodification**, the process of conversion of social products and socio-ecological services and relations into commodities with a monetary value. However, degrowth is not limited only to criticism. On the constructive side, the degrowth imaginary centres around the reproductive economy of **care**, and the reclaiming of old – and the creation of new – **commons**. Caring in common is embodied in new forms of living and producing, such as **eco-communities** and **cooperatives** and can be supported by new government institutions, such as **work-sharing** or a **basic and maximum income**, institutions which can liberate time from paid work and make it available for unpaid communal and caring activities.

Degrowth is not the same as negative **GDP** growth. Still, a reduction of **GDP**, as currently counted, is a likely outcome of actions promoted in the name of degrowth. A green, caring and communal economy is likely to secure the good life, but unlikely to increase gross domestic activity two or three per cent per year.

FIGURE 1   The keywords of degrowth (size illustrates frequency of appearance of an entry in other entries in this book)

Advocates of degrowth ask how the inevitable and desirable decrease of **GDP** can become socially sustainable, given that under **capitalism**, economies tend to either grow or collapse.

In the minds of most people, **growth** is still associated with an improvement, or well-being. Because of this some progressive intellectuals take issue with the use of the word degrowth. It is inappropriate, they claim, to use a 'negative word' to signify desired changes. However, the use of a negation for a positive project aims precisely to decolonise an **imaginary** dominated by a one-way future consisting only of growth. It is the automatic association of **growth** with better that the word 'degrowth' wants to dismantle. For degrowthers it is the unquestionable desirability of growth in the common sense that needs to be confronted if a discussion for a different future is to open up (Latouche 2009). Degrowth is a deliberately subversive slogan.

Of course some sectors, such as education, medical care, or renewable energy, will need to flourish in the future, while others, such as dirty industries or the financial sector shrink. The aggregate result will be degrowth. We prefer also to use words such as 'flourishing' when we talk about health or education, rather than 'growing' or 'developing'. The desired change is qualitative, like in the flourishing of the arts. It is not quantitative, like in the growth of industrial output.

'**Development**', even if it were to be cleaned of its heavy historical meaning, or beautified with adjectives such as balanced, local or sustainable, is a problematic keyword. The word suggests an unfolding towards a predetermined end. An embryo 'develops' into a mature adult, who then ages and dies. A premise of modern liberal societies, however, is the denial of any ultimate collective end as well as the denial of anything but ascent. Development becomes self-referential: development for the sake of development, the unfolding of a predetermined, not-to-be-questioned arrow of progress with no end in sight (Castoriadis 1985).

A frequent criticism to the degrowth proposal is that it is applicable only to the overdeveloped economies of the Global North. The poorer countries of the Global South still need to grow to satisfy basic needs. Indeed, degrowth in the North will liberate ecological space for **growth** in the South. Poverty in the South is the outcome of the exploitation of its natural and human resources at low cost by the North. Degrowth in the North will reduce the demand for, and the prices of, natural resources and industrial goods, making them more accessible to the developing South. However, degrowth should be pursued in the North, not in order to allow the South to follow the same path, but first and foremost in order to liberate *conceptual* space for countries there to find their own trajectories to what they define as the good life. In the South there is a wealth of alternative cosmovisions and political projects such as **Buen Vivir** in Latin America (or Sumak Kawsay in Ecuador); **Ubuntu** in South Africa; or the Gandhian **Economy of Permanence** in India. These visions express alternatives *to* **development**, alternative trajectories of socio-economic system. They often put forward claims for global **environmental justice**. They only stand to flourish by a retreat of the **growth imaginary** in the Northern countries that have promoted it, if not forced it to the rest of the world.

3. The panorama of degrowth

In what follows, we organize the (old and new) degrowth literature into five themes: the limits of – and the limits to – growth; degrowth and autonomy; degrowth as repoliticization; degrowth and capitalism; and proposals for a degrowth transition.

3.1 The limits of growth

The foundational theses of degrowth are that **growth** is uneconomic and unjust, that it is ecologically unsustainable and that it will never be enough. Moreover, growth is likely to be coming to an end as it encounters external and internal limits.

Growth is uneconomic because, at least in developed economies, "illth" increases faster than wealth (Daly 1996). The costs of **growth** include bad psychological health, long working hours, congestion and pollution (Mishan 1967). **GDP** counts costs, such as the building of a prison or the clean-up of a river, as benefits[3]. As a result, **GDP** may still increase, but in most developed economies welfare indicators such as the Genuine Progress Index or the Index of Sustainable Economic Welfare have stagnated after the 1970s. Above a certain level of national income, it is equality and not growth that improves social well-being (Wilkinson and Pickett 2009).

Growth is unjust, first, because it is subsidized and sustained by invisible reproductive work in the household (see **Care**). **Feminist economics** has shown that this work is gendered, with women doing most of it. Second, growth is unjust because it benefits from an unequal exchange of resources between core and periphery among, and within, nations. The energy and materials that fuel **growth** are extracted from **commodity frontiers**, often in indigenous or underdeveloped territories that suffer the impacts of extraction. Waste and pollutants end up in marginalized territories, communities or neighbourhoods of lower class or of different colour or ethnicity than the majority of the population (see **environmental justice**). However, although **growth** is uneconomic and unjust, it may as well be sustained precisely because the benefits accrue to those who hold power and the costs are shifted to those who are marginalized.

Commodification, which is part and parcel of **growth**, is eroding sociality and mores. **Care**, hospitality, love, public duty, nature conservation, spiritual contemplation; traditionally, these relations or 'services' did not obey a logic of personal profit (see **anti-utilitarianism**). Nowadays they increasingly become objects of market exchange, valued and paid for in the formal **GDP** economy. Profit motivations crowd out moral or altruistic behaviours and social wellbeing diminishes as a result (Hirsch 1976).

Above a certain level, **growth** does not increase **happiness**. This is because once basic material needs are satisfied, extra incomes are devoted increasingly to positional goods (e.g. a house bigger than the neighbour's). Relative, and not absolute, wealth determines access to positional goods. Everyone wants **growth** in order to raise his or her position, but as everyone rises together, no one gets better. This is a zero-sum game. Worse, growth makes positional goods more expensive. These are the **social limits of growth**: growth can never satisfy positional competition; it can only make it worse. **Growth** therefore will never produce "enough" for everyone (Skidelsky and Skidelsky 2012).

Growth is also ecologically unsustainable. With continuous global **growth** most planet ecosystem boundaries will be surpassed. There is a strong and direct correlation between **GDP** and the carbon emissions that change the climate (Anderson and Bows, 2011). The economy could in theory be decarbonized with the advancement of cleaner or more efficient technologies, or by a structural shift to services. However with 2 to 3 per cent global growth per year, the degree of decarbonization required is next to impossible. Global carbon intensity (C/$) by 2050 should be 20–130 times lower than today, when the reduction from 1980 to 2007 was just 23 per cent (Jackson 2008). To date, there are hardly any countries which can claim an absolute reduction in material use or carbon emissions while growing. When they do, this is because they outsourced dirty industrial activities to the developing world. Absolute reductions in energy and material use (see **dematerialization)** are unlikely to come through technological progress: the more technologically advanced and efficient an economy becomes, the more resources it consumes because resources get cheaper (see **Jevons' Paradox**). Service economies also are not materially light. Services have high **emergy** (embodied energy). Computers or the Internet embody lots of rare materials and energy, as well as knowledge and labour also 'produced' with energy and materials (Odum and Odum 2001).

Growth in the developed economies might be coming to an end. This might be due to diminishing marginal returns (Bonaiuti, 2014), the exhaustion of technological innovations (Gordon 2012) or limits in creating effective demand and investment outlets for capital accumulating at a compound interest rate (Harvey 2010). Natural resources also pose a limit to growth. Economic **growth** degrades high-order (low **entropy**) energy stocks, turning them into low-order (high **entropy**) heat and emissions. **Peak oil**, peaks in the extraction rates of essential stocks such as phosphorous, and climate change from carbon emissions, may already restrict **growth**. The new stocks that substitute oil are also exhaustible, such as shale gas, and often dirtier, such as coal or tar sands, accelerating climate change. Renewable energy from solar or wind flows is cleaner, but renewable sources yield lower energy surpluses (energy returns to energy investment – EROI), given the existing technology, compared to fossil fuels. A lot of conventional energy will have to be expended in the transition to renewables. A solar civilization can only support smaller economies, given the low EROI of renewable energies compared to fossil fuels. A transition to renewables will inevitably be a degrowth transition.

From a degrowth perspective, the current economic crisis is the result of systemic limits to growth. It is not a cyclical crisis or fault in the credit system. First, the crisis in the U.S. was triggered by the hike in oil prices; domestic trade suffered and workers' mobility from the suburbs became unaffordable, leading to the house foreclosures that precipitated the subprime mortgage crisis. Second, the fictitious (bubble) economy of finance and personal loans grew because there was no other source of growth and no other way to sustain demand from falling. Private and public **debt** sustained an otherwise unsustainable rate of **growth** (Kallis *et al.* 2009). Stagnation was delayed, but only temporarily.

3.2 Degrowth and autonomy

The fact that there are limits and growth is coming to an end is not necessarily bad. For many degrowthers, degrowth is not an adaptation to inevitable limits, but a desirable project to be pursued for its own sake in the search for **autonomy**. **Autonomy** was a keyword for thinkers such as Illich, Gorz and Castoriadis, but it meant something slightly different to each. Illich (1973) meant freedom from large techno-infrastructures and the centralized bureaucratic institutions, public or private, that manage them. For Gorz (1982) **autonomy** is freedom from wage-labour. Autonomous is the sphere of non-paid work where individuals and collectives enjoy leisure and produce for their own use, instead of money. For Castoriadis (1987) instead, **autonomy** means the ability of a collective to decide its future in common, freed from external ('heteronomous') imperatives and givens, such as the law of God (religion), or the laws of the economy (economics).

Following Illich, degrowthers take issue with fossil fuels not only because of **peak oil** or climate change, but because a high use of energy supports complex technological systems. Complex systems call for specialized experts and bureaucracies to manage them. They unavoidably lead to non-egalitarian and undemocratic hierarchies. **Autonomy** instead requires **convivial** tools, i.e. tools which are understandable, manageable and controllable by their users. An **urban garden,** a bicycle or a Do-It-Yourself Adobe house are convivial and autonomous. A weed-resistant GMO field, a high-speed train or an energy-efficient 'smart building' are not. Degrowthers are critical of such high-tech projects of ecological modernization and green growth not only because they might not turn out to be sustainable, but because they reduce **autonomy**. Projects that signify a degrowth **imaginary** – vacant lot gardening, pirate programming or bicycle repair shops – are convivial, they involve voluntary work and they are governed and shaped directly by their participants (see **nowtopians**).

Rather than *limits to* growth, the literature on **autonomy** emphasizes collective *self-limitations*. Limits, or rather self-limitations, are not invoked for the good of nature or to avoid an impeding **disaster**, but because living simply, and limiting our footprint upon the non-human world that we happen to live in, is how the good life is conceived. Not least, limits also liberate from the paralysis of unlimited choice. And only systems with limited scale can become genuinely egalitarian and democratic, as only they can be governed directly by their users. Limits are therefore 'a social choice . . . and not . . . an external imperative for environmental or other reasons' (Schneider *et al.* 2010, 513). Environmental or social bads and risks – climate change, **peak oil** or uneconomic growth - simply make the case for collective self-limitations stronger.

It is not a coincidence that degrowthers are inspired by the **Neo-Malthusians** anarcho-feminists of Emma Goldman and not by Malthus. Goldman and her companions advocated conscious procreation not in the name of a population bomb but as part of a struggle against the exploitation by **capitalism** of female bodies to produce soldiers and cheap labour. The distinction here is subtle, but crucial. The **Neo-Malthusians** chose consciously to limit their reproduction as part of a project of social and political change. They did not do it for moral reasons, or because 'they had to'. They did not do it to avert a **disaster**. Their act was **political**. It was pre-figuring the world they wanted to produce and inhabit.

3.3 Degrowth as repoliticization

Degrowth was thrown explicitly as a 'missile word' to *re-politicize* **environmentalism** and end the depoliticizing consensus on sustainable development (Ariès 2005). Sustainable development depoliticizes genuine political antagonisms about the kind of future one wants to inhabit; it renders environmental problems technical, promising win-win solutions and the (impossible) goal of perpetuating **development** without harming the environment. The ecological modernization promised by sustainable development evades the core contemporary dilemma, which according to Bruno Latour (1998) is whether 'to modernize or to ecologize'. Degrowth takes sides. Ecologizing society, degrowthers argue, is not about implementing an alternative, better, or greener **development**. It is about imagining and enacting alternative visions *to* modern **development**.

In relation, degrowth calls for the politicization of science and technology, against the increasing technocratization of politics. A neat distinction between science and politics is impossible to sustain when dealing with questions about the global economy or climate change, where 'wars of truth' are waged and values shape the knowledge claims that different actors stake. New models of democratized knowledge production are necessary. **Post-normal science** proposes the extension of the peer-review community that ensures the quality of scientific inputs into decision-making to include all those with a stake, including not least lay people. **Post-normal science** calls for a shift of decisions from 'communities of experts', like scientific committees and advisory councils, to decisions by 'expert communities' (D'Alisa *et al.* 2010).

The apolitical, technocratic discourse of sustainable development is a manifestation of a broader process of **depoliticization** of public debate in liberal democracies, whereby politics have been reduced to the search for technocratic solutions to pre-framed problems instead of a genuinely antagonistic struggle between alternative visions. **Political ecology** attributes this **depoliticization** to the rise of neo-liberalism and the Washington consensus. These subjugated sovereign political choice to the needs of unregulated capital and liberalised markets. Degrowth scholars agree, but trace the origins of **depoliticization** further back in time. Neo-liberal reforms were – and are – justified in the name of **growth,** itself justified in terms of **development**. This **development** consensus, which spans across the left and right political spectrum, and even across the Iron Curtain, evacuated **the political** before neo-liberalism: socialist economies ended up resembling state capitalism, because they remained trapped in the pursuit of **growth** and **development**.

A distinguishing feature of modern, capitalist and socialist economies has been the (institutionalized) investment of a significant part of the social surplus into new production. The consequence of this is the disavowal of what was the exercise *par excellence* of political sovereignty in older civilizations: the decision for the destination of surplus (see theory of **dépense**). In older civilizations, often surplus was dedicated to 'wasteful' expenditures that did not serve a utilitarian purpose (see **anti-utilitarianism**). Expenditures in pyramids, churches, festivals, celebratory fires or **potlatch** were pursued because *they were* what 'the good life' was for these civilizations, not because they contributed to production or growth. In modern industrial civilization, such acts of wasteful **dépense** have been commodified and individualized. In modernity, the meaning of life is to be found by each individual alone. The premise is that each individual has the right to mobilize all resources necessary for this pursuit. At the societal level this translates into a non-negotiable demand for **growth**: only with growth can the demands of all not-to-be-limited individuals be satisfied. However, as individuals search elusively for sense on their own, the genuinely 'political' sphere, where sense could be constructed socially through collective acts of **dépense**, is evacuated and subordinated to the imperative of **growth**.

3.4 Degrowth and capitalism

As the late Eric Hobsbawm (2011: 12) put it very late in his long life, 'there is a patent conflict between the need to reverse or at least to control the impact of our economy on the biosphere and the imperatives of a capitalist market: maximum growth in search for profit'. Two premises underlie this statement. The first was defended in Section 3.1: economic **growth** unavoidably increases throughput and negatively impacts the biosphere (against the argument of proponents of green growth or green capitalism that it is possible to both grow and reduce environmental impact). The second is that growth is an imperative under capitalism.

In theory, capitalism could survive without growth. Indeed, capitalist economies pass involuntary through periods of little, zero or negative growth. However, these have to be temporary periods. Indeed, under **capitalism** the lack of **growth** leads to an increase in the rate of workforce exploitation, if the rate of profit is to be sustained (Blauwhof 2012; Harvey 2010). But, intensifying exploitation cannot be sustained for too long without violence and counter-violence. Lack of growth therefore destabilizes **capitalism** and liberal democracy. A historical example is the rise of fascism after the Great Depression, or of communism in Russia before, political projects that aspired to change or end capitalism. **Growth** avoids redistributive conflict and sustains **capitalism** politically. It is in this concrete sense that **growth** is imperative for capitalism, not in the abstract.

History suggests that is highly unlikely that nations with capitalist economies would *voluntary* choose not to grow. *In theory*, however, one could imagine a scenario under which political forces come democratically in power and enforce resource caps and social minima (e.g. a **job guarantee** for the unemployed), restricting the operation of **capitalism** within environmental and social limits (Lawn, 2005). However for this to happen a radical redistribution of political power would be necessary. Caps, new taxes or income/job security programs harm economically powerful interests with privileged access to governments. Blauwhof (2012) argues that nothing short of a revolution will bring about these institutional reforms. Would a system with such dramatic political and institutional changes be still capitalist? Jackson (2009) responds that it could still be capitalism, but a very different one; he declares his disinterest to semantic debates about the name of the system in a prosperous future without growth. But as Skidelsky and Skidelsky (2012: 6) put it, the end of **growth** 'challenges us to imagine what life after **capitalism** might look like; for an economic system in which capital no longer accumulates is no longer **capitalism**, whatever one might want to call it'.

Degrowth of course is not only about reduced throughput. It is about imagining and constructing a different society – a society that manages to convince itself that it has enough and that it no longer has to accumulate. **Capitalism** is an ensemble of institutions – private property, the corporation, wage labour and private credit and money at an interest rate – whose end result is a dynamic of profit in search of more profit ('accumulation'). The alternatives, projects and policies that signify a degrowth imaginary are essentially non-capitalist: they diminish the importance of core capitalist institutions of property, money etc, replacing them with institutions imbued with different values and logics. Degrowth therefore signifies a transition beyond capitalism.

3.5 The degrowth transition

A degrowth transition is not a sustained trajectory of descent, but a transition to convivial societies who live simply, in common and with less. There are several ideas about the practices and institutions that can facilitate such a transition and the processes that can bring them together and allow them to flourish.

Grassroots economic practices

Eco-communities, online communities (see **digital commons**), communities of **back-to-the-landers**, **cooperatives, urban gardens, community currencies,** time banks, barter markets, associations of child or health **care**. In the context of the crisis and as conventional institutions fail to secure the basic needs of people, there is a spontaneous proliferation of new non-capitalist practices and institutions, in places like Argentina, Greece, or Catalonia (Conill *et al* 2012).

These grassroots practices share five features. First, there is a shift from production for exchange to production for use. Second, there is a substitution of wage labour with voluntary activity, meaning a decommodification and de-professionalization of work. Third, they follow a logic whereby the circulation of goods is set in motion, at least partly by an exchange of reciprocal 'gifts' rather than in search of profit (see **anti-utilitarianism**). Fourth, unlike capitalist enterprise, they do not have a built-in dynamic to accumulate and expand. Fifth, they are outcomes of processes of 'commoning'; connections and relations between participants carry an intrinsic value in and for themselves. These practices are non-capitalist: they diminish the role of private property and wage labour. They are new forms of **commons**.

They are also examples of degrowth in a more restricted sense. They have less carbon content and material throughput when compared to the State or market systems offering the same services. True, per unit of product they might be more inefficient due to a lower degree of specialization and division of labour. An alternative organic food network, for example, might require more workers per unit of product than an agri-business (though also less fertilizers, pesticides and fossil fuels). This is not necessarily bad as far as unemployment is concerned. Decentralized cooperative systems of water or energy production might provide less water or energy output per unit of labour and resource input. However, they are likely to be more environmentally benign precisely because their unproductiveness limits their scale (an inverse **Jevons'** effect): less efficient per unit, smaller as a whole.

Alternative practices of commoning are a source of innovation for renewing public services, averting their privatization. Cooperative health or school systems need not replace public health or education. The otherwise escalating costs of public education and health can be reduced by involving parents in the education of the children, or by developing neighbourhood networks of doctors and patients offering preventive health checks and basic first aid. Preventative health care based on intimate knowledge of the patient is much cheaper than high-tech diagnoses and treatments (these can be reserved for special cases). User-involvement is generally cheaper and more democratic than the expensive outsourcing of public services to private, for-profit providers. Degrowth therefore can bring an improvement, not a deterioration, of public services.

Welfare institutions without growth

In the absence of growth, unemployment increases. In a degrowth transition, new welfare institutions will be needed to decouple paid employment from growth, or else decouple well-being from paid employment. An example of the first is the **job guarantee** scheme, which proposes to make the State an employer of last resort reducing *de facto* unemployment to zero. Another example is the proposal for an unconditional **basic income** granted to all citizens, financed by progressive taxation on wages and profits (while taxation for high incomes can set a **maximum income**) and taxes on consumption. This can secure a basic level of subsistence and security for all without access to paid work. **Worksharing**, i.e. a redistribution of work between the employed and the unemployed via a reduction of working hours in the paid sector, can also reduce unemployment, and redistribute wealth, if hours are reduced without loss of income.

The autonomous sphere voluntary and convivial activity stands to expand if a basic income secures the satisfaction of basic needs or if **worksharing** liberates time from paid work. A **job guarantee** can finance activities in the autonomous sphere, such as **care** and education services, work in urban food gardens, **cooperatives** or free software production. New welfare institutions and grassroots economic practices are therefore complementary.

Care, education, health or environmental restoration services have high social value and provide meaningful employment; they can form the backbone of a **new economy,** prosperous without growth. Such an economy will face less of an unemployment problem, since it will be a labour-intensive economy.

Money and credit institutions

Community currencies, time banks and local exchange trading systems can contribute to downscaling and relocalizing economic activity, constraining circulation within a community. **Community currencies** have served as complements in periods of crisis, allowing continued access to vital services by people who were otherwise left out of the market economy. State money, however, remains the most important locus of intervention in a degrowth transition: first, because taxes, a large part of total circulation, are paid in it; and second, because **community currencies** cannot satisfy the requirements for inter-communal and international trade, which is inevitable in complex economies such as ours.

A transitional degrowth proposal is for the State to take back the control of the creation of new of money from private banks (**public money**). Private banks in effect create new money by issuing loans. While private banks can only issue money as debt through loans, the state could also issue money free of debt to meet public needs. For example, States could issue money to finance a **basic income** or a **job guarantee** or to subsidise **cooperatives**, **care** services, environmental conservation or renewable energy. **Public money** would improve public finances, as states would reclaim seigniorage (the difference between the nominal value of money and the cost of producing it), and as they will no longer borrow from private banks to finance public expenditures.

Money issued as debt creates a growth dynamic. Debts are repaid with an interest, and interest calls for **growth**. Economies cannot be expected to continue growing at the rate necessary to pay a **debt** itself accumulated in the past to sustain a fictitious **growth** (Kallis *et al.* 2009). Debt is a social relation. History is full of examples of societies that excused debts and started afresh. Western societies have maintained a materially affluent lifestyle by shifting promises of payment to the future. A debt jubilee will inevitably cause a decline in the living standards of small creditors and savers. From a degrowth perspective, the goal is not how to re-launch growth and pay off debts, but how to distribute fairly the costs of a jubilee adjustment. Citizen-run **debt audits** are essential for determining which debts are legitimate and which are not. It may be legitimate, for example, to excuse the debts of those whose basic standard of living is threatened, but not pay back debts to those who lent for high profit.

The politics of a degrowth transition

There is no agreement in the degrowth literature about the politics and the political strategies through which alternative institutions, imbued with the values of degrowth, could come to replace the current institutions of **capitalism**. Preferred strategies and political subjects range from non-wage labour **nowtopians**, who share a quasi-class experience of autonomous living and producing, to existing social movements, political parties, or even **Unions**. If there is a consensus in the degrowth community, this is that a transition can only be the outcome of multiple strategies and multiple actors; a movement of movements changing both everyday practices and state institutions (Demaria *et al.* 2013).

D'Alisa *et al.* (2013) classify degrowth strategies and actors into civil and 'uncivil', uncivil defined as those who refuse to be 'governmentalized'. Organized **disobedience** features in the repertoire of degrowth activists. This spans from the occupation of abandoned houses ('squats') to sit-ins against mega-projects and coal plants. This could include land occupations by unemployed landless or poor peasants. Financial **disobedience** includes acts such as that of Enric Duran, a prominent degrowth activist in Barcelona who 'expropriated' 492,000 Euros via loans from 39 banks just before the crisis in 2008, to denounce the speculative credit system dedicating the money to alternative projects.

Latouche (2009) instead sees change coming mainly through parliamentary politics and grassroots action. He posits degrowth as an agenda for parties of the Left, though he is against a 'degrowth party' as such. Others put more faith in social movements such as the **Indignados (Occupy)** to change the parliamentary system into a more direct form of democracy, such as that signified by the assemblies in the occupied squares. And yet others emphasize the transformative potential of non-capitalist grassroots economic practices of education, **care**, food provision, living and producing which are deemed **political**, even if they don't take place in the traditional arenas associated with politics, such as political parties, elections or parliaments. They are **political** because they challenge and develop concrete alternatives to the dominant institutions of **capitalism**, and which can universalised. Interestingly, the practices of the **Indignados (Occupy)** movement – sit-ins, square orchards, communal kitchens, barter exchanges – prefigure the values expressed by alternative projects; the movement may be the incipient political expression of the **nowtopians**.

A hypothesis is that systemic change in the direction of degrowth will follow a similar dynamic with other systemic changes in the past. Capitalism emerged out of feudalism, as connections were forged, first between new economic practices (firms, corporations, trade contracts, banks, investments), and then with institutions that emerged through social struggles to support these practices (abolition of monarchies and feudal privileges, enclosure of the commons, liberal democracy, laws protecting private property). The grassroots practices and the welfare and monetary institutions reviewed in this section might be the seeds of a new transformation emerging from within the system, in the latest crisis of **capitalism** and as the period of **growth** and expansion comes to an end.

4. The future of degrowth

The future of degrowth is open. Research is still necessary to support foundational degrowth claims, claims that are firmly established *within* the degrowth community, providing its shared premises although they are far from being accepted by academia and society at large. Such claims include: the impossibility of dematerialization through technological advance and the inevitability of disastrous climate change if **growth** is to continue; the entry of developed economies into a period of systemic stagnation, partly due to resource limits; or the hypothesis that an abandonment of **growth** will revive politics and nourish democracy, rather than animate catastrophic passions. More research can help us understand how people and nations adapt to the lack of growth, why some grassroots practices succeed while others collapse or get incorporated into the mainstream, or how, and under what conditions, new welfare institutions will produce the outcomes their advocates claim they will.

The political question concerns the social dynamic, the actors, the alliances and the processes that will create a degrowth transition. This question is not just intellectual. Social change is a process of creation, impossible to predict in advance. What academic studies of degrowth can offer are arguments and narratives to animate the politics of transition. The ideas outlined in this entry have already done that. However if degrowth is to remain a concept that is alive and does not stale, there is no reason for these to remain the only narratives. We can use the 'raw material' of the degrowth vocabulary, and constantly create new imaginaries and arguments that escape false dilemmas such as 'austerity versus spending'. This is what we attempt in the last chapter of this book where we frame a new thesis, grounding degrowth in **dépense**.

Notes

1 In this entry we leave the original titles in French, not only for reasons of language pluralism or practicality but also because many of the words involved sound more inspiring in French!
2 In the original translation of the text *Ecologie et liberté* (1977) to English in 1980, the misleading term 'inversion of growth' was used to translate *décroissance*. We replace it here with 'degrowth'.
3 In this chapter, when we do not provide references for the statements we make, this means that the support for the argument can be found in the relevant entry (identified in bold).

References

Amar, A. (1973) 'La croissance et le problème moral'. *Cahiers de la Nef*, « *Les objecteurs de croissance* », 52: 133.
Anderson, K. and Bows, A. (2011) 'Beyond "dangerous" climate change: Emission scenarios for a new world'. *Philosophical Transitions of the Royal Society*, 369: 2–44.

Ariès, P. (2005) *Décroissance ou Barbarie*, Lyon: Golias.

Blauwhof, F. B. (2012) 'Overcoming Accumulation: Is a Capitalist Steady-State Economy Possible?' *Ecological Economics*, 84: 254–61.

Bonaiuti, M. (2014) *The Great Transition*, London: Routledge.

Castoriadis, C. (1985) 'Reflections on "Rationality" and "Development"', *Thesis*, 10/11, 18–35.

Castoriadis, C. (1987) *The Imaginary Institution of Society*, Cambridge: Polity Press.

Cattaneo, C., D'Alisa, G., Kallis, G. and Zografos, C. (eds) (2012) 'Degrowth Futures and Democracy', Special Issue, *Futures*, 44 (6): 515–23.

Conill, J., Cardenas, A., Castells, M., Hlebik, S. and Servon, L. (2012) *Otra vida es posible: prácticas alternativas durante la crisis*, Barcelona: Ediciones UOC Press.

D'Alisa, G., Burgalassi, D., Healy, H. and Walter, M. (2010) 'Conflict in Campania: Waste Emergency or Crisis of Democracy', *Ecological Economics*, 70: 239–49.

D'Alisa, G., Demaria, F. and Cattaneo, C. (2013) 'Civil and Uncivil Actors for a Degrowth Society', *Journal of Civil Society*, 9 (2): 212–24.

Daly, H. (1996) *Beyond Growth: The Economics of Sustainable Development*, Boston: Beacon Press.

Demaria, F., Schneider, F., Sekulova, F. and Martinez-Alier, J. (2013) 'What is Degrowth? From an Activist Slogan to a Social Movement', *Environmental Values*, 22 (2): 191–215.

Georgescu-Roegen, N. (1971) *The Entropy Law and the Economic Process*, Cambridge: Harvard University Press.

Gordon, R. J. (2012) 'Is U.S. Economic Growth Over? Faltering Innovation Confronts the Six Headwinds', *The National Bureau of Economic Research Working Paper* No. 18315.

Gorz, A., (1980) *Ecology as Politics*, Montréal: Black Rosa Books. First published in 1977 as *Écologie et liberté*, Paris: Galilée.

Gorz, A. (1982) *Farewell to the Working Class: An Essay on Post-Industrial Socialism*, London: Pluto Press.

Gorz, A. (M. Bosquet) (1972) *Nouvel Observateur*, Paris, 397, 19 June. Proceedings from a public debate organized in Paris by the *Club du Nouvel Observateur*.

Grinevald, J. (1974) *L'économiste Georgescu-Roegen: intégrer l'économie dans la problématique énergétique et écologique*, Geneva: Uni information, Service de presse et d'information de l'Université de Genève.

Grinevald, J. and Rens, I. (1979) *Demain la décroissance: entropie-écologie-économie*, Lausanne: Pierre-Marcel Favre.

Harvey, D. (2010) *The Enigma of Capital*, London: Profile Books.

Hirsch, F. (1976) *Social Limits to Growth*, Cambridge: Harvard University Press.

Hobsbawm, E. (2011) *How To Change The World: Tales of Marx and Marxism*, London: Little, Brown.

Illich, I. (1973) *Tools for Conviviality*, New York: Harper & Row.

Jackson, T. (2009) *Prosperity without Growth*, London: Earthscan.

Kallis, G., Martinez-Alier, J. and Norgaard, R. B. (2009) 'Paper Assets, Real Debts: An Ecological-Economic Exploration of the Global Economic Crisis', *Critical Perspectives on International Business*, 5 (1/2): 14–25.

Kallis, G., Schneider, F. and Martinez-Alier, J. (eds.) (2010) 'Growth, Recession or Degrowth for Sustainability and Equity?', Special Issue, *Journal of Cleaner Production*, 6 (18): 511–606.

Kallis, G, Kerschner, C. and Martinez-Alier, J. (eds) (2012) 'The Economics of Degrowth', *Ecological Economics*, 84: 172–80.

Kallis, G., Kalush, M., O'Flynn, M., Rossiter, J. and Ashford, N. (2013) '"Friday off": Reducing Working Hours in Europe', *Sustainability*, 5 (4): 1, 545–67.

Kosoy, N. (ed.) (2013) 'Degrowth: The Economic Alternative for the Anthropocene', Special Issue, *Sustainability*, 5. Available online at www.mdpi.com/journal/sustainability/special_issues/degrowth (accessed 3 October 2013).

Latouche, S. (2009) *Farewell to Growth,* Cambridge: Polity Press.

Latouche, S. (2011) *Vers une société d'abondance frugale: Contresens et controverses de la décroissance,* Paris: Fayard/Mille et une nuits.

Latour, B. (1998) 'To Modernize or to Ecologize? That's the Question', In: Castree, N. and Willems-Braun, B. (Eds) *Remaking Reality: Nature at the Millenium,* London: Routledge.

Lawn, P. (2005) 'Is a democratic–capitalist system compatible with a low-growth or steady-state economy?' *Socio-economic Review,* 3 (2): 209-232.

Martinez-Alier, J., Kallis, J., Veuthey, S., Walter, M. and Temper, L. (2010) 'Social Metabolism, Ecological Distribution Conflicts, and Valuation Languages', *Ecological Economics,* 70 (2): 153–158.

Meadows, D.H., Meadows, D.L. and Randers, J. (1972) *Limits to growth.* New York: Universe books.

Mishan, E.J. (1967) *The costs of economic growth,* London: Staples Press.

Odum, H.T., and Odum, E. C. (2001) *A prosperous way down,* Boulder: University Press of Colorado.

Saed (2012) 'Introduction to the Degrowth Symposium', *Capitalism Nature Socialism* 23 (1): 26–29.

Schneider, F., Kallis, G. and Martinez-Alier, J. (2010) 'Crisis or opportunity? Economic degrowth for social equity and ecological sustainability', Special issue, *Journal of Cleaner Production,* 18(6): 511–518.

Sekulova, F., Kallis, G., Rodríguez-Labajos, B. and Schneider, F. (2013) 'Degrowth: From theory to practice', *Journal of Cleaner Production,* 28: 1–6.

Skidelsky, R. and Skidelsky, E. (2012) *How Much is Enough?* New York: Other Press.

Whitehead, M. (2013) 'Degrowth or regrowth?' *Environmental Values,* 22 (2): 141–145.

Wilkinson, R. and Pickett, K. (2009) *The Spirit Level: Why Greater Equality Makes Societies Stronger.* New York, Berlin, London: Bloomsbury Press.

PART 1
Lines of thought

1

ANTI-UTILITARIANISM

Onofrio Romano

DEPARTMENT OF POLITICAL SCIENCES, UNIVERSITY OF BARI "A. MORO"

Anti-utilitarianism is a school of thought that critiques the hegemony of the epistemological postulates of economics in the humanities and social sciences. Anti-utilitarians assert the crucial importance of the social bond when compared to self-interest. They outline a gift exchange paradigm that aims to overstep two major frameworks of the social sciences: holism and methodological individualism.

In 1981, the French sociologist, Alain Caillé, and the Swiss anthropologist, Gérald Berthoud, gave birth to MAUSS – *Mouvement anti-utilitariste dans les sciences sociales* (Anti-utilitarian Movement in the Social Sciences). This brilliant acronym reproduces the surname of the author of *The Gift* (1924), Marcel Mauss. Mauss, together with Karl Polanyi, inspired the work of the group. The two founders made the decision to start up the intellectual venture after having participated the year before in an interdisciplinary debate with philosophers, economists, and psychoanalysts on the topic of "gift exchange". On that occasion they shared the same frustration towards the other participants, who expressed obstinacy in their profound belief that behind every human action, including gift practices and demonstrations of generosity, we must recognize the strategy of egotistical calculation, and nothing more.

The movement was led from the beginning by Alain Caillé and gathered intellectuals from different fields of knowledge: Serge Latouche (economist and philosopher), Ahmet Insel (economist and political scientist), Jean-Luc Boilleau (sociologist and philosopher), Jacques Godbout (anthropologist), Philippe Rospabé (economist and anthropologist) etc. They first created the *Bulletin du Mauss* and, in 1988, the *Revue du Mauss*, printed by the prestigious French publisher *La Découverte* (initially quarterly and, since 1993, half-yearly).

MAUSS is today configured as a large network of researchers located in Europe, North America, North Africa and the Middle East. It is characterized by a wide variety of approaches, subjects, and application fields. Its main theoretical aim is to establish a new epistemological basis for universalism and democracy. This effort – more systematic and accomplished in the works of Alain Caillé – has developed around three main reflection axes: the individual, the social bond, and politics.

Anti-utilitarians challenge the theoretical approaches that interpret any human action as departing from the pivotal axis of the "individual" and thus oriented towards self-satisfaction:

> we qualify as utilitarian any doctrine based on the claim that human subjects are governed by the logic of selfish calculation of pleasures and pains, by their interest only, or by their preferences only; and that this is good because there is no other possible foundation of ethical norms other than the law of **happiness** for individuals and their communities.
>
> *(Caillé 1989: 13)*

The object of criticism of anti-utilitarians is an ideological matrix that cuts across thought and the wider culture:

> utilitarianism is not a philosophical system or a component among others of the dominant ideology in modern societies. Rather it has become that same ideology; to the point that, for modern people, it is largely incomprehensible and unacceptable that what can not be translated in terms of usefulness and instrumental effectiveness.
>
> *(Caillé 1989: 4-5)*

Anti-utilitarians criticize utilitarianism because it reduces the human being. The battle to be waged, they claim, should insist on the recognition of the complexity and the plurality of forms of life. Anti-utilitarianism, far from qualifying itself as anti-modern thought, aims at rediscovering the true meaning of modernity, restoring the scientific spirit against scientism, reason against rationalism, democracy against technocracy. Caillé resumes, in this sense, the Brahmanic classification of man's goals (puruṣārtha): pleasure (*kama*), interest (*artha*), duty (*dharma*), and dissipative liberation from all aims (*moksha*) (Caillé 1989: 89 ff.). According to Caillé, utilitarianism has reduced a multiplicity of goals into the sole kingdom of *artha*. But he also criticizes other schools of thought that translate the ontological multiplicity into one of the three sacrificed motives: the Freudian school devoted to the *kama*, the holistic school pointing to *dharma*, or the existentialist mood (*à la* Bataille) in search of *moksa*. The counter-project proposed by anti-utilitarians is a contemporary citizenship to all Brahmanic levels of existence, i.e. to all "multiple states of the subject." This claim is articulated on both an analytical level (the multi-teleology of the human being has an ontological connotation) and, as we shall see later, on a political level.

The second pole of reflection, the social bond, coincides with the re-evaluation of gift logic. Following Mauss, the gift is here understood as a "total social fact."

Just like the "underlying unconscious structure" envisioned by Lévi–Strauss, the gift becomes the archetypal performer or the universal symbolic matrix of the alliance between individuals and groups. It acts on a micro-sociological level by the device of the triple obligation – "to give, to receive, and to return" – but it can be extended to the meso-sociological scale of the "association" and, finally, to "politics," i.e. the macro-sociological frame. "Each one of these three terms – gift, association and politics – is a metaphor, a symbol and a tool for interpreting the others" (Caillé 1998: 236).

In the second half of the 1990s, the political inclination of the movement gets more accentuated, starting from the "thirty theses for a new and universalist left" (discussed in various issues of the *Revue du Mauss*, starting from n. 9/1, 1997). On the political side, anti-utilitarianism identifies with the project of "democracy for democracy": the democratic ideal can be revitalized only by doing away with any aims or interests, especially egotistic, from the collective discussion. According to Caillé, the main obstacle to democracy, and the main reason for the decline of politics, is a lack of alternate social life patterns so that, for instance, even discussion or selection of said preferences is precluded by the utilitarian ideology (see **depoliticization**). Democracy must enhance diversity by offering a variety of lifestyles, increasing public space for discussion, and pluralizing the possibilities of self-realization. One key proposal in this would be a **basic income** that would become "radically unconditional." It is necessary to decouple income from specific social benefits, as this coupling limits the freedom of citizens to experience the irreducible plurality of human aims. Instead, the largest number of citizens possible should have the chance to realize themselves, and to express who they are and what they want to be.

Due to Serge Latouche, the so-called Anti-Pope of MAUSS (given his differences with Caillé) the anti-utilitarian movement also produced one of the main strands of degrowth. Latouche is less indulgent toward Western **capitalism**, which he approaches mainly through the lens of criticism to **development**. While Caillé aimed to restore the "true" meaning of modernity against its perversions, Latouche pleads for a radical re-thinking of modernity, in order to cut off its genetic link with utilitarianism.

Degrowth is fully part of an anti-utilitarian framework insofar as it pursues the ideal of a society decolonized of the ideology of unlimited **growth**, an ideology that supposes a direct correlation between an increase in **GDP** and collective **happiness**. According to Latouche, there is an explicit inverse correlation between well-having and well-being. Nevertheless degrowth does not mean a deliberate decrease of **GDP**, but merely *a*-growth, i.e. the liberation from a productivist obsession, in order to re-discover other human dimensions, first and foremost the relational one.

Most anti-utilitarians reproach Latouche for the choice of the term "degrowth": the reference to the productive sphere of social life (evoked by the term "**growth**") – even if reversed ("de-growth") – implicitly embeds the alternative into the economic imaginary. So, similar to the ethical discipline that characterizes Western

capitalism as Weber first noted, all alternatives inspired by degrowth entail, in the end, a sober lifestyle and economic restraint. Many anti-utilitarians call, instead, for a "political" critique of boundlessness and excess (Dzimira 2007), uprooting the discourse from an ethical level. Rather, they advocate a political project that metabolizes the principles of "reversibility" (i.e., against the externalities of progress that threaten collective existence) and of "reciprocity" (i.e., against the power of most developed societies, which limits and threatens the chances for life and action of less developed societies and future generations). The risk they see in the degrowth discourse is that the emphasis on the imperative of the preservation of life stands as yet another translation of the "neutralitarian" root of utilitarian political philosophy: politics becomes a mere function for preserving citizens' "biological" life ("life for life's sake"). To them, this does not differ too much from the main goal of the development age, i.e. fertilizing life ("growth for growth's sake"). In both cases, assuming that it is the exclusive domain of individuals and their networks, the political and collective construction of the meaning of life is not on the agenda. The strategy changes but the goal is always the same: life, without any political meaning.

Mutual charges between anti-utilitarians and their degrowther descendants are all well-grounded. Both may fail, but for different reasons, in their attempt to produce an epistemological discontinuity with the utilitarian foundations of our society. A more solid path towards anti-utilitarianism and degrowth might be built, on the one hand, by integrating the theoretical stream opened by Bataille with his notion of **dépense**, and, on the other hand, by a wider look on the numerous and unnoticed anti-utilitarianist practices and experiences that go on inside and outside Western societies (Romano 2012).

References

Caillé, A. (1989) *Critique de la raison utilitaire. Manifeste du MAUSS*, Paris: La Découverte.

Caillé, A. (1998) *Il terzo paradigma. Antropologia filosofica del dono*, Torino: Bollati Boringhieri.

Dzimira, S. (2007) «Décroissance et anti-utilitarisme», *Revue du Mauss permanente*, 26 mai. Available online at www.journaldumauss.net/./?Antiutilitarisme-et-decroissance (accessed October 4 2013).

Mauss, M. (1954) *The gift. Forms and functions of exchange in archaic societies*, London: Cohen and West.

Romano, O. (2012) "How to rebuild democracy, re-thinking degrowth," *Futures*, 44(6): 582–9.

2

BIOECONOMICS

Mauro Bonaiuti

DEPARTMENT OF ECONOMICS, UNIVERSITY OF TURIN

Bioeconomics is a field of study mainly connected to the figure of Nicholas Georgescu-Roegen (hereafter G-R), who first and most radically enquired into the consequences of an integration of the physical and biological sciences into economics (Bonaiuti 2011: 1–48). As far as its field of studies is concerned, bioeconomics is no different from ecological economics, although some of the *preanalytic premises* that characterise G-R's bioeconomics are significantly different from those that prompted the founders of ecological economics (Daly, Costanza etc.). These premises explain the considerable differences between G-R's standpoint and that of most ecological economists, particularly as far as the paradigm of sustainable development is concerned his statements against the new formula are so forceful that there can be no doubt about what he thought: "sustainable development is one of the most toxic recipes" (Bonaiuti 2011: 42).

His sharp criticism to sustainable development explain also why G-R's bioeconomics was taken from the very outset as a pillar of the basis for degrowth. Opposing this neoclassical reductionist approach, in the second half of the 1960s, G-R opened up economics to twentieth-century developments in physics and natural sciences, starting with the thermodynamic revolution (Georgescu-Roegen 1971).

The term 'bioeconomics' was used for the first time at the end of the 1960s by Jiři Zeman, of the Czechoslovakian Academy, who adopted this expression in a letter to mean a 'new economics' in which precisely 'the biological substance of the economic process in almost every respect' should be adequately acknowledged (Bonaiuti 2011: 158). Georgescu liked the term and, from the early 1970s made it the banner summing up the most important conclusions he had come to in a lifetime of research.

The first insight is that the economic process, having physical and biological roots, cannot ignore the limitations imposed by the laws of physics: in particular, the law of **entropy**. This leads to the consideration that the fundamental aim of economic activity, unlimited **growth** of production and consumption, being based on finite sources of matter/energy, is not compatible with the fundamental laws of nature. The community of ecological economists today accepts this conclusion, however shocking it may have been at the time when it was first announced.

The second insight concerns methodology: the circular, reversible representation of the economic process, presented at the beginning of any textbook on economics, showing how demand stimulates production, which in its turn provides the income necessary to feed new demand, in a reversible process apparently capable of reproducing itself indefinitely. This must be replaced by an evolutionary representation, in which the economic process interacts with its biophysical roots, on the one hand, and with values and institutional frames, on the other. The latter aspect must be stressed: the reciprocal interactions that the economic process sets up with 'socio-cultural organisations' and the qualitative transformations (emergence) connected to leaps in scale in the process of **growth** explain some of the fundamental differences that characterise G-R's standpoint compared to that of the founders of **steady-state economics**. For G-R **development** is not (as it is for Daly) an abstract process that merely implies 'more utility' but a concrete historical process that cannot 'be separated from economic **growth**' (Bonaiuti 2011: 46). The inevitable reduction in matter and energy consumption (oil, etc.), the related urgency to move towards renouncing all luxury goods, the decrease in population and the social control over technological innovations that constitute the core of the 'minimal bioeconomic programme', indeed, cannot be attained simply through policies of *governance* (as most ecological economists suggest): the entire institutional framework of today's economies must be questioned.

Although Georgescu did not use the term 'degrowth' in his works, he authorised the use of this expression in the French translation of his works on bioeconomics, edited by Jacques Grinevald in 1979 and entitled *Demain la Décroissance*. The slogan 'degrowth' was revived in 2002, in the monograph issue of the review *Silence*, and in the international conference *Défaire le développement, refaire le monde* held in Paris in the same year. It immediately became evident that two lines of thought were unified under the new slogan: that of the 'cultural/institutional' criticism of the society of **growth**, supported throughout the years in particular by Ivan Illich (1973), Cornelius Castoriadis (2010) and Serge Latouche; and that of the bioeconomic criticism.

The former, taking the failure of **development** policies in the southern hemisphere, in particular in Africa, as a starting point, came to radically criticise the very concept of **development**, both in its imaginary presuppositions (**anti-utilitarianism** etc.) and in its historical and social manifestations. The two lines of thought met, and to a certain extent felt as if they already knew each other, in their criticism of sustainable development (Latouche, Foreword to Bonaiuti 2014: xiv).

Ten years later, it might be interesting to ask what the reasons for the success of this union may have been. The fundamental reason for this may be the fact that bioeconomics and cultural criticisms of development share similar (pre-analytical) premises. In particular, even before he developed his bioeconomic theory, Georgescu became convinced that 'economic laws – far from having a natural and universal foundation' take shape within specific cultural premises and institutional frameworks. In his works of 1960-6 on overpopulated peasant economies, undoubtedly inspired by his memories of Romania, and then corroborated by his stays in India (1963) Brazil (1964, 1966 and 1971) and Ghana (1972), Georgescu had already become lucidly aware that prescriptions valid for capitalist economies can be devastating when applied, for example, to peasant economies. In other words, Georgescu's bioeconomics was open to the idea, developed more rigorously by critics of **development** (Illich 1973; Castoriadis 2010), that the fundamental reasons for the social and ecological unsustainability of the Western model must, in the final analysis, be attributed to cultural premises and their corresponding institutional mantle. For this reason, Georgescu was vehemently opposed to the paradigm of sustainable development, which, like that of the **steady state**, does not radically question the anthropological and institutional foundations of the market economy. After attempting a criticism of the dominant model on a purely phisical and rational basis (the 'fourth law of thermodynamics') in the last years of his life, G-R intuited that ecological unsustainability was only the final consequence of the cultural and institutional premises that characterise **growth** economies.

It is not hard to imagine that if Georgescu had read the works of Marcel Mauss and Karl Polanyi or, perhaps, met Ivan Illich in Mexico in the 1970s, the main outline of a degrowth society might have been formulated 30 years earlier. However, the silence that in the final 25 years of the last century surrounded Georgescu's 'minimal bioeconomic programme', like the proposals of André Gorz (who actually did meet Illich in Cuernavaca), reveal that the time was not yet ripe.

What has changed? From the 1970s onwards, with the oil crisis and the transition from the Keynesian-Fordist system of accumulation to that of flexible accumulation, founded on the tertiary sector, the rates of **growth** and productivity in advanced capitalist societies have gradually decreased. In contrast, social and ecological costs, connected to the hyper-complexification of the bureaucratic and economic-financial '*mégamachine*' increased. The crisis of the 1970s marked the passage to a second phase of an *S shaped* cycle of accumulation: the phase of 'declining marginal returns' (Bonaiuti, 2014). This phase is accompanied by a reduction in social well-being, which has become even more acute with the 2007 financial crisis.

References

Bonaiuti M. (ed.) (2011) *From Bioeconomics to Degrowth: Georgescu-Roegen's 'New Economics' in Eight Essays*, London, New York: Routledge.
Bonaiuti, M. (2014) *The Great Transition*, London, New York: Routledge.
Castoriadis, C. (2010) *A Society Adrift – Interviews and Debates 1974–1997*, New York: Fordham University Press.

Georgescu-Roegen, N. (1971) *The Entropy Law and the Economic Process*, Cambridge, MA: Harvard University Press.

Georgescu-Roegen, N. (1979). *Demain la décroissance: entropie-écologie-économie*, preface and translation by Ivo Rens and Jacques Grinevald. Lausanne: PierreMarcel Favre.

Illich, I. (1973) *Tools for Conviviality*, New York: Harper & Row.

3

DEVELOPMENT, CRITIQUES OF

Arturo Escobar

DEPARTMENT OF ANTHROPOLOGY, UNIVERSITY OF NORTH CAROLINA

It is impossible to provide a single definition of development. For many, development is the ineluctable strategy by which poor countries need to modernize; for others, it is an imperial imposition by the rich capitalist countries on the poor ones, and as such it should be opposed; for yet others, it is a discourse invented by the West for the cultural domination of non-Western societies that needs to be denounced as such, beyond its economic effects; for many common people the world over, finally, development has become either a reflection of their aspirations to a dignified life, or an utterly destructive process with which they have to coexist, and not infrequently both at the same time. Taken as a whole, it can be said that development is a recent historical process that involves social, economic, political, and cultural aspects.

The concept of development did not exist in its current connotation until the late 1940s, when "economic development" became associated with the process to pave the way for the replication in "under-developed areas" of the conditions characterizing industrialized nations (broadly, agricultural technification, urbanization, industrialization, and the adoption of modern values). The genesis of the concept can be traced back to the late colonial period in some contexts (as in the British Colonial Development Act of 1929 and some "community development" schemes in Southern Africa in the 1930s), as an explicit and often planned process for the eradication of poverty. However, the concept of development was a product of the great realignments that took place at the end of the Second World War and the creation of the vast institutional apparatus that included the Bretton Woods Institutions and planning agencies in most Third World capitals. "Development" and the "Third World" were thus the product of the same historical conjuncture, with development as the strategy par excellence to bring about the modernization of the so-called Third World (Escobar 1995; Rist 1997). The resurgence of the classical concern with capital accumulation in the late 1940s with the **growth** economics of Harrod and Domar relating **growth** to savings and investment (through the so-called capital-output ratio) was another important pillar of the process by which development became firmly established and associated with growth ever since. For a handful of philosophers such as Vatimo or Dussel, development and progress are pivotal aspects of modernity, whether in the form of the inevitable privilege accorded to "the new" or the "developmentalist fallacy" that asserts that all countries have to travel the same historical stages, if necessary by force.

Over the past six decades, the conceptualization of development in the social sciences has seen three main moments, corresponding to three contrasting theoretical orientations: modernization theory in the 1950s and 1960s, with its allied theories of **growth**; Marxist-inspired dependency theory and related perspectives in the 1960s and 1970s; and critiques of development as a cultural discourse in the 1990s and 2000s. Modernization theory inaugurated a period of certainty in the minds of many theorists and world elites, premised on the beneficial effects of capital, science, and technology. This certainty suffered a first blow with dependency theory, which argued that the roots of underdevelopment were to be found in the connection between external dependence of poor countries on the rich ones, and internal exploitation of the poor by the rich within countries, not in any alleged lack of capital, technology, or modern values. For dependency theorists, the problem was not so much with development as with **capitalism**, and they thus advocated for socialist forms of development, while maintaining the assumption of **growth** intact. Starting in the 1980s, a growing number of cultural critics in many parts of the world questioned the very idea of development. They analyzed development as a discourse of Western origin that operated as a powerful mechanism for the cultural, social, and economic production of the Third World (Escobar 1995; Rist 1997). These three moments may be classified according to the root paradigms from which they emerged: liberal, Marxist, and poststructuralist theories, respectively. It is fair to say that despite overlaps and eclectic combinations, some version of the modernization paradigm continues to inform most positions at present. This is the case of the overarching framework of neoliberal globalization, with its continued core assumptions of **growth**, progress, modern values, and rational policy action, even if of course the market has become more central than in previous development decades. Marxist and culturalist perspectives have by no means disappeared; this is clearly the case in Latin America, where debates on twenty-first century socialism (for the Marxist-inspired perspectives), and **buen vivir** (for the culturally oriented perspectives) pose veritable challenges to liberal and neoliberal frameworks.

While the poststructuralist analyses were less known than the Marxist critiques, it is important to highlight them here, given that they entailed a radical questioning of the core cultural assumptions of development, including **growth**, and as such were important in early degrowth theories in Italy and France. These critiques came of age with the publication in 1992 of a collective volume edited by Wolfgang Sachs, *The Development Dictionary*. The book started by making the startling and controversial claim, "The last forty years can be called the age of development. This epoch is coming to an end. The time is ripe to write its obituary" (Sachs, ed. 1992: 1). If development was dead, what would come after? Some started to talk about a "post-development era" in response to this question, and a second collective work, *The Post-development Reader*, launched the project of giving content to this notion (Rahnema and Bawtree 1997). Some degrowth theorists, notably Latouche, contributed to disseminate this perspective in the North. Reactions on all sides of the scholarly-political spectrum have continued since, resulting in a vibrant, albeit at times somewhat acrimonious, debate, bringing together practitioners and academics from many disciplines and fields.

Postdevelopment was generally meant as an era in which development would no longer be the central organizing principle of social life. In this way, it is related to two other emerging imaginaries, that of postcapitalism (questioning **capitalism**'s ability to fully and naturally occupy the economy, with the concomitant visualization of an array of diverse economic practices) and post- or degrowth (decentring **growth** from the definition of both the economy and social life). There is a certain geographical unevenness, however, in how these frameworks are seen and cultivated in the Global North versus the Global South. Whereas in the Global North the scholarly and political debate on degrowth is receiving increasing attention, in the Global South this is not the case yet. On the one hand, some argue that at least some sectors need to grow (e.g., health, education, even livelihoods). On the other, critical debates in the South are more directly concerned with redefining development. To this extent, there has been a significant reactivation of the debate over development, particularly in Latin America, over the past five years. The current mood is "to search for alternatives in a deeper sense, that is, aiming to break away from the cultural and ideological bases of development, bringing forth other imaginaries, goals, and practices" (Gudynas and Acosta 2011: 75). Whereas the wave of progressive regimes in Latin America over the past decade created a context conducive to these debates, the main impetus behind them have been social movements. Two key areas of debate and activism are the notions of **buen vivir** (collective well-being) and the Rights of Nature. This debate parallels discussions on change of civilization model and transitions to postextractivist models. It seems a good moment to build more explicit bridges between degrowth and transitions narratives in the North and alternatives *to* development, civilizational change, and transitions to postextractivism in the South. In building these bridges, however, it is important to resist falling into the trap of thinking that while the North needs to degrow, the South needs "development." There is an important synergy to be gained from discussing degrowth and alternatives to development in tandem, while respecting their geopolitical and epistemic specificities.

World-wide, economic globalization has taken on a tremendous force (especially in Asia), seemingly relegating critical debates over "development" to the back burner. These debates are also carefully domesticated within the discourses of the Millennium Development Goals [MDGs]) and, after 2015 when the MDGs expire, the "sustainable development goals." However, global movements and the deepening of poverty and environmental destruction continue to keep critical conversations alive, connecting development debates to questions of epistemic decolonization, social and environmental justice, the defense of cultural difference, and transition to postcapitalist and postgrowth frameworks. For most of these movements, it is clear that conventional development of the kind offered by neoliberalism is not an option. In this context, the return of the alternatives to development discussions in Latin America is a beacon of hope. At the very least, it is becoming clear that if "Another World is Possible," to appeal to the slogan of the World Social Forum, then alternatives to development should also be possible. At least for many social movements and for transition advocates, whatever form "development" or alternatives to development take will have to involve more radical questionings of **growth**, extractivism, and even modernity than ever before.

References

Escobar, A. (1995) *Encountering Development*, Princeton: Princeton University Press.

Gudynas, E. and Acosta, A. (2011) 'La renovación de la crítica al desarrollo y el buen vivir como alternativa', *Utopía y Praxis Latinoamericana*, 16 (53), 71–83. Available online at www.gudynas.com/publicaciones/GudynasAcostaCriticaDesarrolloBVivirUtopia11.pdf (accessed February 12 2014).

Rahnema, M. and Bawtree, V. (eds.) (1997) *The Post-Development Reader*, London: Zed Books.

Rist, G. (1997) *The History of Development*, London: Zed Books.

Sachs, W. (ed.) (1992) *The Development Dictionary: A Guide to Knowledge as Power*, London: Zed Books.

4

ENVIRONMENTAL JUSTICE

Isabelle Anguelovski

ICTA (INSTITUTE ENVIRONMENTAL SCIENCE AND TECHNOLOGY),
AUTONOMOUS UNIVERSITY OF BARCELONA

Environmental justice is about the right to remain in one's place and environment and be protected from uncontrolled investment and growth, pollution, land grabbing, speculation, disinvestment, and decay and abandonment.

In the late 1970s, the first visible and widely reported environmental justice (EJ) mobilizations emerged and took place in the US: Love Canal, NY (1978) and Warren County, NC (1982). They had clear targets: environmental contamination and its impacts on human health. Love Canal embodied the struggles of white working-class residents fighting against 20,000 tons of toxic chemicals sitting underneath homes and schools and winning the relocation of 833 households. Warren County added a racial dimension to environmental burden impacting historically marginalized groups, as African American residents became the target of 10,000 truckloads of contaminated soil to be spread in a landfill that the Environmental Protection Agency had authorized. Their resistance brought to light the disproportionate exposure and harm that populations of color suffer from toxic waste sites, hence the close relationship between environmental inequalities and environmental racism.

Since the 1980s, an extensive literature in sociology, environmental policy, and environmental health has examined inequities between groups in exposure to contamination and health risks from waste sites, incinerators, refineries, transportation, and small-area sources (Sze 2007). Exposure to harm and risk also exists in the workplace as farm or chain employees, for instance, are obliged to be in close contact with pesticides and hazardous waste. Similarly, in the Global South, mercury spills from gold mines, open cast copper and coal mining, oil and timber extraction, deforestation and erosion from mono-cultural farming, and hydroelectric dams are devastating millions of hectares and disrupting poor residents' health. In addition, tons of toxic waste from industry, agriculture and electronic products, and ships to be dismantled, are also being exported to poorer countries (Carmin and Agyeman 2011).

Activism around environmental injustices has been strong in the Global North, particularly in the US. Residents, accompanied by environmental NGOs, community organizations, scientists, and lawyers, have organized against refineries, waste sites, recycling facilities, basically against locally unwanted land uses (LULUs). Demands to address environmental racism were initially rooted in a civil rights framework before becoming framed through a human rights perspective and even gender lens. The EJ movement in the US became global in the mid-1990s. From their Northern origin, the words "environmental justice" spread to the world, and especially to the Global South, linking to what has been called the **environmentalism** of the poor and to the conflicts that were already taking place in Latin America, for instance, around land struggles and environmental disasters. Robert Bullard, a scholar and founder of the Environmental Justice movement in the US, was influential in Brazil in the 1990s and also in South Africa, pushing national EJ movements. Today, conflicts around natural resources explode every week around the world, in which poor and indigenous residents defend their land from natural resource extraction and contamination. In the many resource extraction and waste disposal conflicts, the poor defend their interests, their livelihoods, and their cultural values and sense of territorial identity against a dominating economic language of valuation.

Environmental inequalities exist not only in the distribution of environmental bads and in the extraction of natural resources, but also in the allocation of environmental goods and services, which is particularly manifest in cities. Deprived communities have generally poor environmental services such as green spaces, street cleaning, and waste collection, while wealthier and white ones enjoy environmental privileges – parks, coasts, open space – in a racially exclusive way (Park and Pellow 2011). These conditions are often combined with neighborhood decay. Similarly, in the South, mega cities such as Mumbai or Djarkata present drastic inequalities – between lush secluded communities that benefit from environmental amenities and unauthorized slums that are not connected to city services such as waste collection or water provision.

Consequently, over the past ten years, the environmental justice agenda has expanded, become more multi-faceted, and also includes just sustainability dimensions (Agyeman et al. 2003). Today, urban EJ groups in the North mobilize for well-connected, affordable, and clean transit systems in cities, for healthy, fresh, local, and affordable food, for green, affordable, and healthy housing, along with recycling practices and green spaces inside housing structures, and for training and jobs in the green economy. Environmental initiatives, such as **urban gardening**, in marginalized neighborhoods are often a direct response to years of direct or indirect destruction and decay, to what residents perceive as urban war and environmental violence. Beyond offering a medium for socializing and building stronger ties, projects such as community farms help repair fragmented communities and overcome environmental trauma. For instance, in the 1980s the neighbourhood of

Dudley in Boston was ravaged by arson and abandonment, and had 1,500 empty lots. Today, projects such as community gardens, farms, and parks and playgrounds remediate the insecurity that residents have experienced from being exposed to neglect, environmental degradation, and poverty. Residents can regain a sense of home and place. Some of these EJ initiatives are also part of degrowth because they foster a smaller, simpler, and alternative form of economy based on the **commons**.

Scholars such as Logan and Molotch have used the image of the **growth** machine to point to elites, rentiers, and the economic and political coalition around them as being the motor of unregulated **capitalism**, private capital accumulation, and spatial inequalities. The argument is that because investments move from place to place in cycles of growth, devaluation, destruction, reinvestment, and mobilization, development ends up being uneven throughout the city. In other words, the treadmill of production benefits investors, elites and decision-makers while negatively impacting those at the bottom of the social pyramid (Schnaiberg et al. 2002). Wealthier groups live in neighborhoods with resources, and are able to reap the benefits from environmental goods and amenities while shifting environmental burdens to marginalized neighborhoods. In rural areas, the growth in resource extraction conflicts is largely explained by increasing social **metabolism** and the need for new supplies and resources by corporations, which must be obtained from the expansion of **commodity frontiers**.

In other words, in cities and rural regions, in the North and South, land is a matter of private appropriation, speculation, and exploitation. **Growth** is thus part of the process that creates injustices. As progress in technology drives the expansion of production and consumption in a synergetic way, and since states, investors, and workers are dependent on economic **growth** to achieve job creation and revenues, cycles of unstopped production, extraction of material resources, waste accumulation, and uneven spatial development perpetuate. Thus, today the most recent aspect of EJ mobilization – and maybe, its most fundamental one – is the defense of the right to place. In rural areas, poor farmers resist land grabbing for agrofuel production, mining, or oil and gas extraction and value their land and also their water as commons to preserve. In Northern cities, many EJ groups have moved their work from waste sites and degraded spaces' rehabilitation to fights for housing affordability and ensuring that residents can afford living in their revitalized space. In Southern cities such as Bangalore or Mexico City, many mount resistance to protest as airports and highways or gated communities because they affect their territory. Others, such as the Alliance of Indian Wastepickers (AIW), organize to secure a living collecting, sorting, recycling, and selling materials that individuals and industries have discarded, and they protest that incinerators that would take away their source of income.

As a result, many EJ activists are involved in fights around the right to the city, which is connected to degrowth discourses. Using Lefebvre's discourses about the right to the city and the importance of not only controlling spaces of production but also of using and shaping the city, coalitions such as the "Right to the City Alliance" in the US demand economic and environmental justice and greater democracy, together with the end of real estate speculation, community space privatization, and gentrification. As they resist the replacement of their community space and gardens by luxury housing, they question projects that maximize exchange value while beautifying and sanitizing the city. In the South, resistance against displacement is often connected to land rights movements such as Via Campesina (International), Landless Workers' Movement (Brazil), or the Bhumi Uchhed Pratirodh Committee (India).

From an organizing and political standpoint, such movements frame transformative claims – the need to remain autonomous from the state and construct more spontaneous and direct forms of democracy and decision-making. From an outcome standpoint, EJ movements are split between some groups demanding a more radical transformation of the economic system and a move away from a fixation on **economic growth** (i.e., indigenous groups pushing for the concept of *Sumak Kawsay* in Ecuador, **Buen Vivir**), and those who want to improve free-market capitalism without proposing a true alternative to the current system – they do not make the link with the long-term and broader implications of increased production and consumption, resource extraction, and unequal environmental siting.

In sum, environmental justice movements act as a reminder that consuming and producing less is not enough per se. The "less" needs to be distributed more equally, with people controlling production processes so that cities and rural spaces become more equal.

References

Agyeman, J., Bullard, D. and Evans, B. (2003) *Just sustainabilities: development in an unequal world*. Cambridge, MA: MIT Press.

Carmin, J. and Agyeman, J. (2011) *Environmental inequalities beyond borders: local perspectives on global injustices*. Cambridge, MA: MIT Press.

Park, L. S.-H. and Pellow, D. (2011) *The slums of Aspen: immigrants vs. the environment in America's Eden*. New York: New York University Press.

Schnaiberg, A., Pellow, D., and Weinberg, A. (2002) "The treadmill of production and the environmental state." In Mol, A. and Buttel, F. (eds.) *Research in social problems and public policy*. Greenwich, CT: Emerald.

Size, J. (2007) *Noxious New York: the racial politics of urban health and environmental justice, environmental justice in America: A new paradigm*. Cambridge, MA: MIT Press.

5

ENVIRONMENTALISM, CURRENTS OF

Joan Martinez-Alier

RESEARCH & DEGROWTH AND ICTA (INSTITUTE OF ENVIRONMENTAL SCIENCE
AND TECHNOLOGY), AUTONOMOUS UNIVERSITY OF BARCELONA

There are three main currents of environmentalism. These three currents could be named as, first, the Cult of Wilderness, second, the Gospel of Eco-Efficiency, and third, the Mantra of **environmental justice** or the Environmentalism of the Poor. They are as three big branches of a single tree or three crosscutting streams of the same river.

In the United States, the Cult of Wilderness has its origin in the work of Scottish-American naturalist John Muir and the creation of Yosemite and Yellowstone National Parks. There were similar movements in Europe and other continents. Even in India, where the doctrine of the "environmentalism of the poor" was put forward in the 1980s in opposition to the "cult of wilderness," there are great local traditions of bird watching and other forms of upper and middle class nature conservation.

In terms of the human and economic resources available, this movement is indeed large. Its main concern was historically, since the nineteenth century, the preservation of pristine nature by setting aside natural areas from where humans would be excluded, and the active protection of wildlife for its ecological and aesthetic values and not for any economic or human livelihood value. The world conservation movement has been increasingly drawn to an economic language. Although many of its members claim to believe in "deep ecology" (the intrinsic value of nature) and revere nature as sacred, the mainstream movement decided to join the economists. The TEEB reports ("The Economics of Ecosystems and Biodiversity", a project supported by the World Wildlife Fund [WWF] and indeed the whole IUCN) in 2008–11, published under the United Nations Environment Programme (UNEP)'s auspices, follows this leitmotiv: to make the loss of biodiversity visible, we need to focus not on single species but on ecosystems, and then on ecosystem services to humans, and finally we must give economic valuations to such services because this is what will attract the attention of politicians and business leaders towards conservation. The TEEB enthusiastically praises mining corporation Rio Tinto's principle of "net positive impact." This principle suggests that nation-states or corporations can engage in open cast mining anywhere provided that the state or business support a natural park there or replant a mangrove yonder. John Muir would have been horrified by such proposals.

The second current of environmentalism is perhaps, then, the most powerful today. Its name recalls Samuel Hays' 1959 book *Conservation and the Gospel of Efficiency: The Progressive Conservation Movement, 1890–1920*, which explains the early efforts of federal environmental policy in the United States to reduce waste, and also to conserve forests (or turn them into tree plantations). One main public figure of eco-efficiency was Gifford Pinchot, who trained in forestry in Europe.

The concept of "sustainability" (*Nachhaltigkeit*) had been introduced in nineteenth century forest management in Germany, not to denote respect for pristine nature but, on the contrary, to indicate how monetary profits could be made from nature by obtaining optimum sustainable yields from tree plantations. This idea can be seen in today's panoply of recipes on sustainable technologies, environmental economic policies (taxes, tradable fishing quotas, markets in pollution permits), optimal rates of resource extraction, substitution of manufactured capital for lost "natural capital," valuation and payment for environmental services, dematerialization of the economy, habitat and carbon trading, and, in summary, sustainable development. The "Gospel of Eco-efficiency" goes together with doctrines of "ecological modernization" and belief in so-called "environmental Kuznets curves." The words "sustainable development" became widely known in 1987 with the publication of the Brundtland report.

Degrowthers are against "sustainable development" on two counts. First, they do not believe that economic **growth** is or can be environmentally sustainable. Second, many of them are also against the very idea of **development**, because as Arturo Escobar, Wolfgang Sachs, and others explained in the 1980s, it has meant a pattern of uniform change towards an American way of life which is very different from today's emphasis, in some countries of the South, of a **Buen Vivir** or Sumak Kawsay (Vanhulst and Beling 2014).

The degrowth movement often emphasizes that the benefits of increased eco-efficiency can easily be nullified through the operation of the **Jevons' Paradox** or rebound effect. Nevertheless, most governments and the United Nations align themselves with the "Gospel of Eco-Efficiency." Meanwhile, the **environmental justice** movement (which is certainly not as well organized as the IUCN) is an assortment of local resistance movements and networks. These movements combine livelihood, social, cultural, economic, and environmental issues (Martinez-Alier et al. 2014). They set their "moral economy" in opposition to the logic of extraction of oil, minerals, wood, or agrofuels at the **"commodity frontiers,"** defending biodiversity and their own livelihood. This includes claims for climate justice and for water justice.

In mounting resistance to environmental injustices, there are many people around the world who are killed while defending the environment.

Poor people do not always think and behave as environmentalists. To believe this would be blatant nonsense. The environmentalism of the poor arises from the fact that the world economy is based on fossil fuels and other exhaustible resources, going to the ends of the earth to get them, disrupting and polluting both pristine nature and human livelihoods, encountering resistance by poor and indigenous peoples who are often led by women. Poor and indigenous peoples sometimes appeal for economic compensation but more often they appeal to other languages of valuation such as human rights, indigenous territorial rights, human livelihoods, and the sacredness of endangered mountains or rivers.

The conservation movement has ignored the environmentalism of the poor. But also the degrowth movement (and the **steady state economics** movement), with their European or North American roots, have downplayed until recently the intensity of the fight for resources around the world. However, one main hypothesis in political ecology is that there are more and more resource extraction conflicts and waste disposal conflicts because of the increase in the global societal **metabolism**. Many such environmental conflicts around the world, classified by country and commodity, are gathered in an open access database by the EJOLT project (www.ejatlas.org, accessed September 15 2014).

There have been attempts to bring the conservation movement closer to the environmentalism of the poor and indigenous people who fight against deforestation, agrofuels, mining, tree plantations, and dams. For instance, mangroves can be defended against shrimp aquaculture because of the livelihood needs of women and men living there, but also because of their biodiversity and their beauty. Despite opportunities for bringing together the conservation movement with environmental justice, this is often difficult not only because the conservation movement, consorts too closely with the second current, the engineers and economists, but also because the conservation movement has sold its soul to companies like Shell and Rio Tinto.

On the other hand, the degrowth movement could easily connect to the movement for **environmental justice** and the environmentalism of the poor. However, the political left (e.g. presidents Lula and Roussef in Brazil, the Communist Party in West Bengal in India, or presidents Evo Morales in Bolivia or Rafael Correa in Ecuador) does not like the environmentalism of the poor and the indigenous that explicitly fights against the inroads of the generalized market system and the growth of societal **metabolism**, in order to have an economy that sustainably fulfills the food, health, education, and housing needs for everybody.

Despite the deep cleavages we have noticed between the three main currents of environmentalism, there is hope of a confluence among conservationists concerned with the loss of biodiversity, the many people concerned with the injustices of climate change who push for repayment of ecological debts and promote changes in technology towards solar energy, eco-feminists, some socialists and trade unionists concerned about health at work and who moreover know that one cannot adjourn economic justice through promises of economic **growth** forever. There is also hope of confluence between urban squatters who preach "autonomy" from the market, agro-ecologists, neo-rurals or **back-to-the-landers**, the degrowthers and the partisans of "prosperity without growth" in some rich countries, the large international peasant movements like Via Campesina, the pessimists (or realists) on the risks and uncertainties of technical change, the indigenous populations who demand the preservation of the environment at the **commodity frontiers,** and the world **environmental justice** movement.

In terms of policies, the degrowth movement often advocates "resource caps." This already exists in some countries as limits to emissions of carbon dioxide (and therefore on the burning of fossil fuels). It could be extended to minerals and to the use of biomass. Proposals such as the Yasuni ITT initiative from Ecuador and similar attempts in Nigeria to leave "oil in the soil" fit perfectly with the degrowth perspective (Martinez-Alier, 2012).

The **environmental justice** movement including the environmentalism of the poor coincides with another main platform of the degrowth movement, which is to downgrade the social relevance of the economy (in the sense of chrematistics). This means to take the generalized market system out of the collective imagination as a principle of social organization, by showing that many people around the world defend their right of access to natural resources for livelihood through systems of communal management i.e. **commons**.

References

Hays, S. (1959) *Conservation and the gospel of efficiency: the progressive conservation movement, 1890–1920,* Cambridge: Harvard University Press.

Martinez-Alier, J. (2002) *The environmentalism of the poor: a study of ecological conflicts and valuation,* Cheltenham: Edward Elgar.

Martinez-Alier, J. (2012) "Environmental justice and economic degrowth: an alliance between two movements," *Capitalism Nature Socialism,* vol. 23/n.1, pp. 51–73.

Martinez-Alier, J., Anguelovski, I., Bond, P., Del Bene, D., Demaria, F., Gerber, J. F., Greyl, L., Haas, W., Healy, H., Marín-Burgos, V., Ojo, G., Porto, M., Rijnhout, L., Rodríguez-Labajos, B., Spangenberg, J., Temper, L., Warlenius, R., and Yánez, I. (2014) Between activism and science: grassroots concepts for sustainability coined by environmental justice organizations, *Journal of Political Ecology,* 21: 19–60.

Vanhulst, J. and Beling, A. E. (2014) "Buen vivir: emergent discourse whithin or beyond sustainable development," *Ecological Economics,* 101: 54–63.

6

METABOLISM, SOCIETAL

Alevgül H. Şorman

ICTA (INSTITUTE ENVIRONMENTAL SCIENCE AND TECHNOLOGY)
AUTONOMOUS UNIVERSITY OF BARCELONA

Societies metabolize energy and material flows in order to remain operational. This process is referred to as societal metabolism. Similar to that of living organisms, which require a certain series of complex chemical reactions within their systems to function, societal metabolism is used to characterize the pattern of energy and material flows that can be associated with the expression of functions and reproduction of structures of human societies. The metabolism of human societies is based on exosomatic energy use (energy metabolized under human control, outside the human body), an extended form of endosomatic energy (energy metabolized inside the human body).

The concept of "metabolism" arose in the nineteenth century in the writings of Moleschott, von Liebig, Boussingault, Arrhenius, and Podolinski, denoting the exchange of energy and substances between organisms and the environment, and the totality of biochemical reactions in living systems. To give examples, these systems could be: a biological cell, a legal system, and/or the capitalist state. They are referred to as autopoietic systems, meaning that they are capable of reproducing and maintaining themselves. Marx and Engels were among the first to utilize the term "metabolism" to grapple with the dynamics of socio-environmental change and evolution. Today, there are various perceptions of the term metabolism. The Vienna school of *social* metabolism conducts material and energy flow analyses (MEFA) of economies, focusing on historical transitions between agricultural and industrial economies and the quantification of such flows (Fischer-Kowalski and Haberl 2007). In **political ecology**, the notion of metabolism has been invoked to signal the "rift" between humans and nature under capitalism, the social power relations that govern the flow of materials and resources in the production of urban spaces, or the increase in the global flows of energy and materials that cause conflict in the world's **commodity frontiers**. This entry however focuses on a different approach, called *"societal"* metabolism, developed by Mario Giampietro and Kozo Mayumi (Giampietro et al., 2012, 2013).

Societal metabolism does not focus only on the quantification of flows but in establishing a relation between flows and the agents that transform input flows into outflows, while maintaining and preserving their own identity (these elements are referred to as fund elements originating from the definition of **bioeconomics** of Georgescu-Roegen [1971]). So, for example, in the production of automobiles, the materials (aluminium, steel), energy (consumed in assemblage and in the extraction of the raw materials) and the water used in these process would be the "flows," whereas the human activity (the workers), the land, and the capital machinery would be the "funds." Societal metabolism, therefore, connects funds (the agents and transformers of a process) and flows (the elements that are utilized and dissipated), to generate indicators characterizing specific features of the system. Examples of such metabolic indicators are: energy input per hour of labor or water consumed per hectare of land in production.

Societal metabolism focuses on the biophysical processes that guarantee the production and consumption of goods and services: what is produced, how it is produced, the purpose for which it is produced, and by whom it is consumed. This is then linked to the analysis of the production of added value (in relation to the investments of production factors). Hence, the analysis marks an approach that establishes a link between monetary representations of the economic process and a representation of the biophysical transformations associated with the production and consumption of goods and services. This is an integrated analysis, taking into account multiple dimensions such as demographic factors and the issue of multiple-scales (co-existence of different space and time scales) of the economies analyzed.

The characterization of the societal metabolism of a country, for instance, is based on typical quantitative indicators used as points of reference called "benchmarks" against which the biophysical or economic performance of a system may be assessed. Depending on their organization and the specific functions that they carry out, different societies exhibit different metabolic profiles. Such benchmarks may refer to the socio-economic side (e.g., energy consumption per hour of activity in the service sector) or to the ecological side (e.g., consumption of water in the agricultural sector per hectare) of sustainability.

There is great variation among the metabolism of European countries in terms of energy flow rates per hour of work in the productive sectors. For example, in the energy, mining, construction, and manufacturing sectors, energy throughput per hour can range from 130 to 1,000 MJ/hour. Likewise, there is a great variation of labour productivity in these sectors ranging from 10 to 50 €/hour (Giampietro et al., 2012, 2013). Accordingly, the metabolic profiles of economies with a well-developed extractive industry, such as Finland and Sweden, generally show higher rates of energetic throughput with higher labour productivity in the productive sectors. These differences originate from a combination of external and internal constraints and manifest the historic pathways of different countries.

Societal metabolism has had a long history in the literature of energetics since the 1970s, focusing on the analysis of biophysical constraints acting upon societies. However, it was left aside in the discussions over sustainability, mostly due to the abundance of cheap oil and the loss of interest in the limits of growth and energy. Energetics and the analysis of societal metabolism have regained momentum in the last decade as academics once again seek for innovative conceptual tools capable of analyzing society-environment interactions from a biophysical perspective.

In light of degrowth, analysis of societal metabolism comes as an approach useful for assessing the feasibility and desirability of proposed alternative modes of development and the viability of economic downscaling from an energetic and material perspective. From a metabolic standpoint, there are several challenges that remain to be addressed within degrowth proposals (Sorman and Giampietro, 2013).

Primarily, it is important to note that current societal functions (service and government, production of food etc.) and their associated metabolic patterns (joules of fossil fuels used for the maintenance of the health system, the hours of human activity used for producing a certain quantity of food) are based on the exploitation of fossil fuels as a principal energy source. Fossil fuels are a source with a high output yield and quality. The advent of fossil fuels has dramatically reduced the amount of energy, labour, and technical capital going into the actual production of useful energy itself. Thus, modern societies have been able to achieve their current level of complexity with the surplus of time that cheap sources of energy yield. However, as we reach **peak oil**, a switch to lower quality energy alternatives directly implies a dramatic requirement for and increase in the amount of energy, labor, and technical capital diverted to energy production itself (renewable or other) in order to sustain the metabolic patterns of societies and the complex structures they have attained. To meet the requirements of socio-economic systems such as the contemporary ones in the Global North, which operate with high economic diversity, high dependency ratios (due to a rising proportion of elderly persons and a higher average age of schooling) and high percentage-wise contribution of the service sector in the economy, it is likely that more workers and more working hours will be required to maintain the current metabolic patterns of societies as fossil fuels dwindle. This points to a contradiction with the degrowth proposal, which calls for reducing work hours (**worksharing**). In a future scarce in energy we will have to work more, not less.

Additionally, even if voluntary reductions of affluence are achieved, as degrowthers want, there are no robust studies showing that this will lead to a global reduction in energy or material consumption, given a rising global population and their affiliated levels of growing consumption patterns. As countries such as China, India, and Brazil and their populations acquire a higher level of prosperity, their material and energetic requirements will increase considerably, possibly outpacing the gains from energy efficiencies or voluntary reductions of consumption in the Global North.

Moreover, the phenomenon of the **Jevons' Paradox** challenges the efficacy of the voluntary reductions that degrowthers espouse. A voluntary reduction of energy consumption in some activities or by some people will tend to be compensated by an (voluntary or involuntary) increase in energy consumption in other activities or other people. The biophysical view of societal metabolism warns about the limitations of degrowth strategies based on voluntarily consuming fewer resources, less energy, or less capital. These will not suffice on their own.

References

Fischer-Kowalski, M. and Haberl, H. (2007) *Socioecological Transitions and Global Change: Trajectories of Social Metabolism and Land Use*, Cheltenham, UK: Edward Elgar.

Georgescu-Roegen, N. (1971) *The Entropy Law and the Economic Process*, Cambridge, MA: Harvard University Press.

Giampietro, M., Mayumi, K., and Sorman, A. H. (2012) *The Metabolic Pattern of Societies: Where Economists Fall Short*, London: Routledge.

Giampietro, M., Mayumi, K., and Sorman, A. H. (2013) *Energy Analysis for a Sustainable Future: Multi-Scale Integrated Analysis of Societal and Ecosystem Metabolism*, London: Routledge.

Sorman, A. H. and Giampietro, M. (2013) "The Energetic Metabolism of Societies and the Degrowth Paradigm: Analyzing Biophysical Constraints and Realities," *Journal of Cleaner Production*, 38, 80–93.

7

POLITICAL ECOLOGY

Susan Paulson

CENTRE FOR LATIN AMERICAN STUDIES, UNIVERSITY OF FLORIDA

This entry focuses on an approach to research and practice that is applied throughout the world and identified in Anglophone literature as 'political ecology'.

The number of researchers and practitioners engaging in political ecology has increased exponentially since the 1980s, broadening the field and opening new possibilities. Little energy goes into establishing orthodoxy or debating who should be labeled 'political ecologist', a term used here to refer to all participants in what Paul Robbins (2011: xix) describes as a community of practice advancing the field 'as an intellectual investigation of the human–environment interaction, and as a political exercise for greater social and ecological justice'. In contrast to certain 'isms' and 'ists', political ecologists share with degrowth advocates an eagerness to explore a plurality of knowledges and a diversity of practical actions, including those of non-dominant groups.

Geographers Piers Blaikie and Harold Brookfield (1987: 17) marked political ecology as an approach that combines ecology and political economy to address relations between society and land-based resources, and between social groups and classes with differing access to and use of those resources. Theirs and other rural studies in the Global South were later complemented by studies in northern contexts and in cities, conceived as 'dense networks of interwoven sociospatial processes that are simultaneously local and global, human and physical, cultural and organic' (Swyngedouw and Heynen 2003: 899). In their 2011 volume *Global Political Ecology*, Richard Peet, Paul Robbins and Michael Watts integrate these strands into an environmental politics of production, consumption and conservation world-wide.

While degrowth and political ecology both address the destruction of specific socioecologies, the latter has pushed further to explore the ongoing production of natures and cultures. Arturo Escobar (2010: 92) describes the field as evolving in three overlapping stages: the first analyses political economic factors in environmental degradation; the second explores epistemological processes through which cultural, scientific and political conceptualizations and discourses impact human-nature relations; and the third raises ontological questions about processes through which a multiplicity of socionatural worlds are produced and reproduced.

These epistemological and ontological explorations can help degrowth scholars to think in new ways about the concept 'mode of production', not conceptualizing natural resources as finite givens (in danger of being exhausted), but as aspects of socioecological environments that are continually constructed through cultural and historical processes. In this view, humans manufacture not only food, shelter and clothing, but also biophysical landscapes, together with regimes of production, consumption and environmental knowledge and governance. Most amazingly, we humans produce ourselves: human bodies socialized with skills, visions and desires, including appetites for consumption. This leads to more sophisticated understandings of consumption that do not separate putative 'physical necessities' from 'cultural choices'. For humans, all aspects of life are inseparably material and meaningful: the most basic 'physical' desires, such as eating and sex, are always imbued with symbolic meaning and value, while even our subjective fantasies and political visions depend on the biochemical character and physical size of the human brain.

One of degrowth's biggest challenges is the narrow cultural scope and shallow historical depth that circumscribe contemporary environmental discourse, constraining our potential to visualize alternatives to currently dominant human-environment relations. In response to this challenge, political ecologists have drawn on research documenting arrangements not based on **growth**, some of which endured over centuries, even millennia. Anthropologists, archaeologists and geographers working in the Andes and Amazon, for example, have shown how surprisingly large populations have been sustained through raised field agriculture, terracing, swidden, vertical archipelagos and other strategies based on elaborate systems for organizing reciprocity and managing the **commons**. They have also asked what disturbed certain systems in given periods. Political ecologists, such as Bina Agarwal, working in South Asia, and Anna Tsing in Indonesia, continue to ask these questions with attention to the production and maintenance of common wealth such as forests.

Challenges to ethnocentric parameters of economic science are vital. Starting in the 1970s, for example, critical interpretation of data from a range of 'primitive' societies enabled Marshall Sahlins to argue in *Stone Age Economics* that hunter-gatherers conceive and achieve affluence in different ways from Western societies: the former by desiring little and enjoying leisure, the latter by producing and consuming much. Hunter-gatherer systems have endured for 150,000 years of human history and agriculture-based ones for around 8,000; in contrast, industrial/fossil fuel economies seem to be in jeopardy after only a few centuries. The purpose of deeply historical approaches to political ecology, like those compiled by Alf Hornborg, Brett Clark and Kenneth Hermele (2012), is not to promote a return to primitive life. On the contrary, cross cultural and (pre)historical knowledge helps to relativize currently dominant systems among many possible modes of human existence, and to widen horizons for imagining unprecedented futures in answer to questions like: 'How can non-expanding economies sustain human societies?' and 'How can humans live without the motivation and joy provided by consumer culture?'

Environmental scientists and policy makers need more powerful ways of conceptualizing and operationalizing multi-scale analysis, social differentiation and, most vitally, power. How do we link together phenomena ranging in scale from individual voluntary simplicity to global markets, national economies, socio-political institutions, and biophysical characteristics of local ecosystems? By locating environmental phenomena at the crossroads of multiple relations of power, political ecologists have expanded the scale of environmental analysis to transcend geographic locales and local populations. It is now recognized that transnational factors ranging from climate change and fish-stock depletion to markets and media affect even the most isolated socioecologies. Also, new awareness is dawning that people involved in local environmental struggles engage global forces and ideas in innovative and sometimes transformative ways, such as the concept of **Buen Vivir** expressed at the People's Climate Summit in Bolivia.

From the start, political ecology was grounded in analysis of socioeconomic and spatial inequalities, and early on it foregrounded the environmental interests, knowledge and practices of diverse actors. With time, political ecologists like Juanita Sundberg and Dianne Rocheleau developed deeper analyses of the ways in which ethnoracial, gender and other social systems interact with environment, moving beyond a focus on the identities of marginalized people to study identity systems that work through time and space to engineer and justify inequitable access to and exchange of resources. A more systemic grasp of the role that hierarchical identity systems play in the constitution of economies, landscapes and environmental governance is needed to deepen dialogue among degrowth, political ecology, ecofeminism, **environmental justice** and related movements, and to strengthen the impact of their work.

How do power and politics function in the production of commodities, discourses and socioecologies? During a tumultuous period in intellectual history, political ecology developed in tandem with critical explorations of colonialism, international development, environmental history, race, ethnicity and gender. These new areas of study interrogated key foundations of Western academia: the dichotomy between nature and culture, the universality of reason (and of *homo economicus*), the adequacy of conventional disciplines and the neutrality of Western scientific categories and findings. Their investigations of power in unanticipated places, notably in the production of knowledge, provoked considerable strife in academia. It also enabled political ecologists such as Alf Hornborg to theorize power as both material and meaningful, expressed through unequal control of resources, including human labour and energy, and exercised in the formation of social systems through which these inequalities are maintained, notably via cultural mystifications that naturalize social constructs such as the power of the machine and the representation of labour and nature as commodities.

Among all the creatures interacting in the earth's ecosystems, humans are unique in their use of politics in attempts to meet their needs and to assure their descendants' survival. These politics influence how power circulates in particular regimes of knowledge, technology and representation, and how those dynamics influence social and biophysical outcomes. Political ecology's multi-scale analysis of power and politics, together with its awareness of the magnitude of variation in human-environment relations, are vital arms in the struggle to decolonize imaginations confined to business as usual.

Degrowth evolved out of the multidimensional philosophical and sociopolitical Franco-European movement called '*l'ecologíe politique*', which has debated the relations between politics and ecology since the 1970s and included the likes of André Gorz, Ivan Illich and Bernard Charbonneau, all foundational degrowth thinkers. Degrowth today flourishes further through its alliance with the second variant of political ecology described here. Both degrowth and political ecology challenge dominant interpretations of the causes of environmental problems. Both contest the prevalent technocratic and economistic responses. Both are critical of sustainable development, and the promotion of **commodification** in its name. And both motivate political and practical action toward more equitable distribution of economic and ecological resources and risks.

References

Blaikie, P.M. and Brookfield, H. (1987) *Land Degradation and Society*. London: Methuen.

Escobar, A. (2010) 'Postconstructivist Political Ecologies'. In M. Redclift and G. Woodgate (eds) *International Handbook of Environmental Sociology*, Second Edition. Cheltenham: Edward Elgar.

Hornborg, A., Clark, B. and Hermele, K. (2012) *Ecology and Power: Struggles over Land and Material Resources in the Past, Present and Future*. London and New York: Routledge.

Peet, R., Robbins, P. and Watts, M. (eds) (2011) *Global Political Ecology*. London and New York: Routledge.

Robbins, P. (2011) *Political Ecology: A Critical Introduction*, Second Edition. Chichester: Wiley-Blackwell.

Swyngedouw and Heynen (2003) 'Urban Political Ecology, Justice and the Politics of Scale'. *Antipode* 35(5): 898–18.

8

STEADY STATE ECONOMICS

Joshua Farley

COLLEGE OF AGRICULTURE AND LIFE SCIENCES, UNIVERSITY OF VERMONT

A stable human population and a constant rate of throughput characterize a steady state economy, where throughput is defined as the extraction of raw materials from nature and their return to nature as waste (see **metabolism**). For any given set of technologies, a steady state economy will imply a constant stock of human made artefacts maintained by a constant flow of throughput. The laws of physics make it impossible to create something from nothing or nothing from something. The economic process is a matter of **bioeconomics**. It transforms energy and raw materials provided by nature into economic products that generate service to humans before eventually returning to nature as waste. Durable capital stocks, such as factories, houses, and other infrastructure require a steady flow of mainten-ance throughput to counteract the forces of **entropy** and decay. Finite stocks of non-renewable fossil fuels account for 86 percent of the energy used in economic processes, and consumption dramatically exceeds new discoveries (see **peak oil**); finite flows of renewable energy account for 2 percent, less than the annual growth rate of total energy use. Fossil fuel combustion is a one-way process that transforms useful energy into dispersed energy and waste by-products, such as carbon dioxide and particulate matter. In summary, the economy is a physical sub-system of a finite planetary system, so endless economic **growth** is impossible.

Humans, like all species, depend for their survival on life support functions of ecosystems, including their capacity to sustain the flow of renewable raw materials required for economic production and to absorb wastes.

A steady state economy must obey five rules. First, renewable resource extrac-tion cannot exceed regeneration rates without eventually driving resource stocks to zero. Second, waste emissions cannot exceed waste absorption capacity, or else waste stocks and the harm they cause will continuously increase. Third, with cur-rent technologies it would likely be impossible to meet the basic needs of current populations without certain non-renewable resources, such as fossil fuels. The rate at which society consumes these resources therefore cannot exceed the rate at which it develops renewable substitutes. Fourth, neither resource extraction nor waste emissions can threaten the ecosystem functions essential to human survival. Finally, human populations must be stable. The most obvious approach to achieving the first four of these goals is to mandate limits on throughput. How to achieve a stable human population is more controversial (see **neo-malthusianism**).

These rules describe what is possible, but do not specify what is desirable: we might achieve a steady state economy with large human populations, low but stable stocks of renewable resources, and subsistence levels of consumption, or with a much small population, larger resources stocks, and higher levels of per capita consumption. A basic premise in economic analysis is that the more one has of something, the less an additional unit is worth. The marginal benefits from economic **growth** are declining, and the marginal ecological costs are rising. **Growth** should stop before marginal costs exceed marginal benefits, or it becomes uneconomical. This is true even if we cannot precisely or objectively measure costs and benefits.

Many advocates of a steady state economy argue that society must achieve a stable Gross Domestic Product (**GDP**), the most common measure of economic activity. But increases in **GDP** are not inextricably linked to increases in throughput. For example, imposing caps on throughput then auctioning off access could potentially increase the number of economic transactions and hence **GDP** while simultaneously reducing throughput. Alternatively, many economists believe that the **dematerialization** of the economy is possible, breaking the link between **GDP** and throughput. Though **GDP** is arguably the best proxy for throughput, targeting steady state throughput is less controversial and more important than ending **growth** in **GDP**.

For most of human history, **growth** of the economy and of human populations were scarcely measurable from one generation to the next, and the steady state economy was the accepted status quo. This changed dramatically with the emergence of the fossil fuel powered market economy during the eigteenth century. Since then, several distinct views have emerged on the steady state economy.

Early philosophers such as Thomas Malthus and Adam Smith equated **growth** with progress, but recognized that **growth** could not continue indefinitely on a finite planet. From this perspective, the steady state economy is inevitable but unfortunate. Later economists, including John Stuart Mill and John Maynard Keynes, viewed the eventual end of economic **growth** as a desirable state that would allow society to focus on mental, moral, and social progress, rather than simply amassing more material wealth at the expense of nature. These philosophers focused more on the desirability of a steady state economy than its inevitability.

The dramatic increase in population growth and per capita consumption beginning in the 1950s, followed by growing awareness of its environmental impacts, generated considerable research on the limits to growth. Ecologists, environmentalists, systems thinkers, and ecology-minded economists sounded alarms about the potentially catastrophic impacts of resource depletion, waste emissions, and population growth. Applying the laws of thermodynamics to the field of economics, Georgescu Roegen concluded that even a steady state economy was not viable on a finite planet (see **bioeconomics**). Herman Daly more optimistically called for a transition to a steady state economy in which quantitative growth in throughput must end, but qualitative improvements in human welfare could continue. Working with like-minded academics, Daly helped found the field of ecological economics in the 1980s, which prioritizes a steady state economy as a central goal.

The need for a steady state economy forces attention to the issue of distribution as well. The primary beneficiaries of a steady state economy are likely to be future generations who otherwise might have insufficient resources to meet their basic needs. From an ethical perspective, it makes little sense to care about the needs of the unborn while ignoring the basic needs of those alive today. Furthermore, if we must limit throughput, we must consider who is entitled to use it, and the starting point of the ethical debate should be equal distribution of our shared inheritance. From a practical viewpoint, those who have a hard time meeting basic needs today will not further reduce their consumption to meet the needs of future generations. We cannot grow our way out of poverty, and must therefore accept redistribution.

Conventional economists continue to reject the need for a steady state economy however, assuming that technological progress will allow **growth** to continue indefinitely. An end to growth would result in misery, poverty, and unemployment. As a result, exponential economic **growth** remains the dominant goal in virtually all countries and among almost all politicians, regardless of political and economic ideology.

Advocates of a steady state economy however increasingly call for a period of degrowth in the transition to a steady state.

A growing number of studies now suggest that the global economy has exceeded critical planetary boundaries, ranging from biodiversity loss to climate change. Throughput currently exceeds all the limits compatible with a steady state economy. Humanity is no longer living off the regenerative capacity of the global ecosystem, but is actively reducing natural capital stocks and future capacity to sustain economic activity. The question is no longer when to stop economic **growth**, but rather how much degrowth is necessary before we transition to a steady state. The longer we delay the transition, the greater the level of degrowth that will be required.

While degrowth is essential for the planet as a whole, there are nearly a billion people living in dire poverty, unable to meet basic human needs. The marginal benefits of **growth** to the poor are immense. Within developed nations, there is little evidence that doubling per capita income in recent decades has improved life satisfaction, but abundant evidence that the world's poorest regions will suffer the most from climate change and other unintended but inevitable consequences of that income doubling. Furthermore, the rich and poor compete for finite resources in an economy that weights preferences by purchasing power, resulting in simultaneous crises of obesity and malnutrition. Greater equality is strongly correlated with a reduction in social and health problems. This empirical evidence suggests that it would be possible to dramatically reduce consumption in the wealthiest countries without reducing quality of life, freeing up the resources required to meet basic human needs in the poorest nations.

A failed growth economy results in misery, poverty, and unemployment now, while endless **growth** threatens ecological catastrophe accompanied by misery and poverty in the future. These are unacceptable trade-offs. The solution is a carefully planned transition to a steady state economy via a process of socially equitable and environmentally sustainable degrowth.

References

Czech, B. (2013) *Supply Shock: Economic Growth at the Crossroads and the Steady State Solution*, Gabriola, BC, Canada: New Society Publishers.

Daly, H. E. (1991) *Steady State Economics: 2nd Edition with New Essays*, Washington, DC: Island Press.

Dietz, R. and O'Neill, D. (2013) *Enough is Enough: Building a Sustainable Economy*, San Francisco: Berret-Koehler and London: Routledge.

Farley, J., Burke, M., Flomenhoft, G., Kelly, B., Murray, D. F., Posner, S., Putnam, M., Scanlan, A., and Witham, A. (2013) "Monetary and Fiscal Policies for a Finite Planet." *Sustainability*, 5: 2, 802–26.

Victor, P. (2008) *Managing Without Growth: Slower by Design, not Disaster*, Cheltenham: Edward Elgar Publishing.

PART 2

The core

9

AUTONOMY

Marco Deriu

DEPARTMENT OF ARTS, LITERATURE, HISTORY AND SOCIAL STUDIES, UNIVERSITY OF PARMA

Cornelius Castoriadis defines autonomy as the ability to give laws and rules to ourselves independently and conciously. Heteronomy, on the other hand, refers to conditions in which laws and rules are imposed by others (mainly meant as the discourse and the imaginary of the others inside of us). Addressing the distinction between autonomy and heteronomy, Castoriadis makes clear that the Other (or Others) should not be understood, as is often done, as an external obstacle, or as a curse suffered, but as constitutive of the subject, because "human existence is an existence with others" (Castoriadis 1987: 108). His clarification is especially important given that, in the philosophical tradition, men generally tend to hide, minimize, or devalue the **care** and services given them by other people – especially by women – so as to present as part of their image, autonomy, and independence.

By projecting the image of "the independent man" in the public realm, we obfuscate a large area of **care** and service in the domestic sector. We also ignore care and service received in the work "back office," or public office. In this light, autonomy should not be seen as a synonymous with independence. Autonomy opposes closure and fear of the Other, but here it can also be said to oppose symbiotic relationships that stifle distance and difference. To clarify, and for the sake of definition, autonomy should necessarily promote a sense of self that includes a conscious recognition of the relationships that bind us to life. Human existence is not simply inter-subjective, it is social and historical, as well. Autonomy, for Castoriadis, remains both interconnected and in tension with society's institutions. It can only be conceived of as a collective project.

Reflecting on the expansion of Nazism in Europe and the inertia of the populations threatened by Hitler's roundups, the psychoanalyst Bruno Bettelheim noted that people were slowed in their efforts to escape by the difficulty of abandoning their goods. Bettelheim points to a conflict central to our times. Contemporary human beings suffer from the inability to choose between basic alternatives.

Freedom and individual subjectivity appear at odds with material comforts offered by modern technology and a consumer society:

> [N]obody wishes to give up freedom. But the issue is much more complex when the decision is: how many possession am I willing to risk to remain free, and how radical a change in the conditions of my life will I make to preserve autonomy.
>
> *(Bettelheim 1991: 268).*

Bettelheim's reflections indicate a basic operation of the **growth** society. **Capitalism** and consumer culture produce an acceptant populace, uncritical of elements and decisions made by others. This concerns initially trivial things – material aspects, organizational, and technical – but gradually it involves the acceptance of patterns of behavior and social meanings that underlie the materialism. In theory, our society produces technologically and economically powerful individuals. But reality is exactly the opposite. The more powerful a society is – in its facilities and its technological means – the more an individual feels powerless and experiences anxiety about his condition and therefore has to find someone, or better yet something, to lend himself to.

Bettelheim, in the early 1960s, had already detected this change of mentality:

> [W]hat is so new in the hopes and fears of the machine age are that savior and destroyer are no longer clothed in the image of man; no longer are the figures that we imagine can save and destroy us direct projections of our human image. What we now hope will save us, and what in our delusions we fear will destroy us, is something that no longer has human qualities.
>
> *(Bettelheim1991: 53–4)*

Even today, many believe that the only answer to the socio-ecological crisis lies in technology. Yet the more we rely on external tools for solutions, the less we trust changes we implement independently as part of our subjective choices adherent to our values.

Modern society threatens individual autonomy through addiction and dependence on goods and convenience. It also threatens autonomy in two other key ways: it reduces the possibility of action and creation by imposing market conditions, and it limits our personal ability to make decisions.

With regard to the first aspect, Ivan Illich has developed the concept of radical monopoly: "I speak about radical monopoly when one industrial production process exercises an exclusive control over the satisfaction of a pressing need and excludes non-industrial activities from competition" (Illich 1975: 69). Personal responses and personal production are systematically being replaced with standardized industrial products. Eventually, even the simplest needs cannot be met outside of the market: "Radical monopoly imposes compulsory consumption and thereby restricts personal autonomy" (Illich 1975: 67). Radical monopoly restricts autonomous organization and self-determination, and in the medium-term, it results in a net loss of practical skills because these can no longer be exercised.

The second issue is a progressive disinclination to make autonomous decisions in the face of concrete problems. The fact of the matter is that, as Bettelheim notes about the contemporary individual:

> scientific and technical progress has relieved him of having to solve so many problems that he once had to solve by himself if he meant to survive, while the modern horizon presents so many more choices than it used to. So there is both: less need to develop autonomy because he can survive without it, and more need for it if he prefers not to have others making decisions for him. The fewer meaningful decisions he needs for survival, the less he may feel the need, or the tendency to develop his decision making abilities.
>
> *(Bettelheim 1991: 71)*

This trend does, however, have an end. If the logic of capitalist **growth** is based on the need to create and continuously meet new needs and aspirations, the fact remains that such a dream is also an illusion. Its underpinnings ironically relieve us of the right to determine for ourselves the content of our own needs and desires. It postulates the extreme dream of retaining the consumer from the cradle to the grave. Beyond a certain limit of productivism and consumerism, frustration begins to exceed gratification. According to Illich, our need for autonomous initiative limits industrial expansion with its requirement for mandatory consumption.

From this point of view, we now understand how autonomy and degrowth are deeply entangled. On one hand, degrowth is an attempt to adopt new rules and values in a society that is otherwise dependent on the rules and priorities dictated by finance, the market and techno-science. On the other hand, it is hard to imagine any real form of autonomy and self-government without questioning the central imperative of economic **growth**. For Serge Latouche, the project of degrowth society effectively completes Castoriadis' vision of a society that is self-instituted or self-regulating (Latouche 2010). **Conviviality** and autonomy complement one another; the pleasure of **conviviality** is an alternative to the enjoyment sought in consumerism or the subjugation and exploitation of other people. There is not only manipulation on a large scale (which also happens), but, above all, a voluntary submission to a certain kind of lifestyle.

The path toward degrowth can be thought of as a journey of integration to restore autonomy as well as a process of liberation from dependence on alienating and heteronomous systems. It is as important that we discuss this transition process as it is we achieve the objective of degrowth; and, the process must be convivial and based on a call for autonomy. Illich is extremely opposed to the idea of entrusting experts with the task of setting limits to growth: "Faced with these impending disasters, society can stand in wait of survival within limits set and enforced by bureaucratic dictatorship. Or it can engage in a political process by the use of legal and political procedures" (Illich 1975: 115). According to Illich, the (heteronomous) bureaucratic management of human survival would not only be unacceptable; more importantly, it would be unnecessary. Delegating the multivalent task to technocrats would imply an attempt to keep the industrial system at the highest level of sustainable productivity in order to force down the threshold of tolerance by any means available. As Illich writes, "only an active majority in which all individuals and groups insist, for their own reasons, on their own rights, and whose members share the same convivial procedures, can recover the rights of men against corporations" (Illich 1975: 114). In this light, it would be safe to assume that Illich would claim only an active majority could strip the power of the leviathan that frames **growth** as the only means to survive.

The proposal of degrowth is therefore a political objective and an example of what Castoriadis called new "social **imaginaries** and meanings." This change produces and is produced (in a circular logic) through a revolution in technologies that are more convivial, and through the transformation of individuals and forms of social organization. The project for a society of degrowth is a proposal of self-limitation, one sought consciously and democratically organized. It is the establishment of a common world that foregrounds the ideals of autonomy, **conviviality**, and regeneration, and that rejects the ideology of limitless economic **growth**.

References

Bettelheim, B. (1991) *The Informed Heart*, London: Penguin Books.
Castoriadis, C. (1987) *The Imaginary Institution of Society*, Cambridge: Polity Press.
Illich, I. (1975) *Tools for Conviviality*, Glasgow: Fontana/Collins.
Latouche, S. (2010) *Pour sortir de la société de consommation. Voix et voies de la décroissance*, Paris: Les liens qui liberent Editions.

10

CAPITALISM

Diego Andreucci[1] and Terrence McDonough[2]

[1]RESEARCH & DEGROWTH AND ICTA (INSTITUTE OF ENVIRONMENTAL
SCIENCE AND TECHNOLOGY), AUTONOMOUS UNIVERSITY OF BARCELONA;
[2]DEPARTMENT OF ECONOMICS, NATIONAL UNIVERSITY OF IRELAND

Capitalism is a historically specific mode of social and economic organisation. There is disagreement as to the date of its origin, depending on whether one places capitalism's distinctiveness in the sphere of exchange or in the sphere of production. Most commentators, however, following Marx, have identified its emergence in the qualitative changes in the productive system and associated social relations which emerged in England in the latter half of the sixteenth and early seventeenth century and were ultimately consolidated in the Industrial Revolution.

Capitalism is distinguished from other socio-economic systems, such as feudalism or socialism by five essential features. First, a capitalist system must concentrate the means of production into relatively few hands. Second, 'freed' of the means to make their own living, a substantial portion of the population must be forced to exchange their labour in return for a wage. Third, capitalists retain ownership of the products of the production process and must bring them for sale on markets to realise profits. In this way, capitalist production is the production of commodities, that is, goods and services produced for sale, not immediate use. Fourth, capitalism relies on a monetary system for the production of money through bank credit, and on market exchange as a key coordinating mechanism. Prices of production and consumption are determined by competition in the markets; money, labour, production and consumption goods are all exchanged in markets, as are financial assets. Finally, in capitalist economies, production is primarily motivated by profit. In the absence of the expectation of profit, production will not be undertaken.

These institutional arrangements have been subject to conflicting interpretations (Watts 2009). Liberal theorists such as Hayek, following Adam Smith, have understood the market as a rational and self-regulating mechanism, a source of social harmonisation and integration, ultimately capable of promoting individual freedom and welfare. Critics such as Marx and Polanyi, on the other hand, have tended to see the 'free market' as a politically enforced – rather than spontaneous – institution, the extension of which has been predicated upon the coercive subsumption of land, labour and the social **commons** under capitalist relations. Similarly, while mainstream economists see labour as a commodity freely sold in the market, for critical scholars from Marx onwards the formal freedom enjoyed by the labourer obscures the highly unequal and exploitative character of this relationship (Watts 2009).

Two further clarifications are in order. First, 'accumulation' refers to the dynamic of reproduction of capital on an expanding scale through the reinvestment of surplus value. In this sense, accumulation is understood as a *process*, and it is thus distinct from economic **growth**. Resulting from accumulation, '**growth**' simply indicates the overall increase in the production of goods and services at the aggregate level, commonly measured as the change in a nation's **Gross Domestic Product (GDP)**. Second, from a Marxist perspective, the term 'capital' does not denote a quantity of money or a stock of assets, but their mobilisation in production with the expectation of increased profits. In this sense, capital is 'value that aspires to valorise itself', the core economic engine of capitalism. As De Angelis (2007) argues, while capital tends to increasingly colonise socio-economic relations in a capitalist system (see **commodification**), it never conquers them completely. This is a central point. The different degrees to which capital penetrates social relations, as well as the different sets of social, political and ideological institutions which sustain accumulation, largely account for the historico-geographical variety of capitalism. By and large, however, a society can be said to be capitalist as long as capital thus defined remains its predominant logic of (re)production.

A relevant question for degrowth is whether expansion is a necessary or contingent (hence modifiable) feature of capitalism. The consensus among critical scholars is that capitalism is inherently compelled to grow. Continuous self-expansion – 'accumulation for accumulation's sake' – is regarded as a structural feature of capitalism. For Marx, while 'simple reproduction' is conceivable in the abstract, the capitalist's quest for survival in competitive markets underpins the necessity of 'accumulation through expanded reproduction'.

The argument can be summarised as follows: capitalists compete for access to money, labour, raw materials and markets. This competition is conducted through the reinvestment of profits. Thus to survive firms must strive to maximise profitability. This is achieved through the more effective extraction of 'surplus value' driving the intensification of work, the investment in technological improvements and expanding the scale of operations. This draws ever more areas of social activity, ever larger areas of the globe and ever greater quantities of resources into the ambit of capitalist relations of production. This expansion, in turn, heightens competition, thereby reproducing capitalism's **growth** dynamic.

Beyond the strictly economic, expansion is also served by the cultural and political deployment of profit. According to Max Weber's classical position, the 'Protestant ethic' of Western Europe, through promoting work, savings and investment rendered a logic of continuous accumulation dominant (Ingham

2008: 25–30). Today, while this religious element has largely lost its significance, new needs and limitless wants are stimulated through marketing (see **social limits of growth**). Moreover, given the socially disruptive effects of recession, a depoliticising representation of **growth** as a 'common good' has become a dominant discourse. Political challenges to growth are also consistently countered by capitalists' financial dominance of political systems.

There is no agreement among degrowth theorists concerning the inevitability of capitalist expansion. For some commentators, such as steady-state economist Philip Lawn, capitalism and negative or no **growth** can be reconciled by devising institutions capable of countering the disruptive social effects of recession, most notably unemployment. Marxist critics, on the other hand, insist that while temporary fixes can be found to sustain capitalist profits in the absence of **growth**, these further aggravate crises and undermine the system's legitimacy. Furthermore, they point out, political institutions cannot be naively treated as external to and independent of the requirements of accumulation.

Despite these discussions, the existence of a strong connection, historical or contingent, between capitalism and **growth** is unquestionable. A central point, made within all the intellectual currents which inform the degrowth movement today, is that limitless accumulation is neither desirable nor sustainable in a finite world. Critics of different traditions have highlighted the existence of both 'internal' and 'external' limits to capital accumulation. First, there are increasing difficulties in reinvesting large surpluses. As Harvey (2010) has pointed out, the recurring problem of capital 'overaccumulation' (lack of further profitable outlets for investment), particularly dramatic since the 1970s, has been mainly addressed through a) aggressive privatisation (an instance of 'accumulation by dispossession') and b) the expansion of debt and financial speculation. Neither of these solutions is sustainable in the long run. Financialisation in particular, while restoring profits of some capitalist sectors, has rendered the economy increasingly unstable and crisis-prone.

A second set of limits is more forcefully highlighted by ecological economists, namely, 'external' or absolute biophysical limits to **growth**. While some Marxist-inspired commentators are suspicious of the Malthusian undertones of the 'absolute limits' discourse, there is widespread agreement that capitalist expansion is increasingly running up against ecological barriers and undermining the biophysical bases of society and life itself. As James O'Connor (1991) has argued, the need for endless expansion creates a fundamental contradiction for capitalism: the drive to increasingly reduce nature and humans alike to commodities in order to sustain accumulation undermines the very conditions for the system's reproduction.

Degrowth is in full agreement with other radical ecologist traditions regarding the impossibility of 'greening' capitalism. As climate change policy best exemplifies, the possibility of successfully adopting market-based solutions to solve ecological problems is often unrealistic. Similarly, the search for 'technical fixes', as proposed by ecological modernisation advocates, is strongly disputed. A typical example of this is 'energy efficiency': against mainstream environmentalists and policy makers who have proposed it as a panacea, critics have convincingly shown that relative efficiencies enable expanded consumption and investment and do not necessarily reduce absolute material and energy consumption levels. This is the so-called 'rebound effect' or '**Jevons' paradox**'.

If capitalism is compelled to grow, and if **growth** is incompatible with social and ecological sustainability, is degrowth feasible in a capitalist context? In some form or other, most degrowth advocates would concede that there is a fundamental incompatibility between capitalism and degrowth (e.g. Latouche 2012), but are reluctant to explicitly position themselves against capitalism. This reluctance has been a point of contention with Marxism and an object of debate within degrowth itself. There are at least three reasons for such reluctance. First, for degrowth theorists such as Latouche (2012), capitalism should not be fetishised as the principal object of critique: it is rather the economistic and 'productivist' imaginary which underpins it that should be targeted. Second, degrowth as a social movement is inspired by principles of voluntary association and decentralised, horizontal self-organisation, whereby the promotion of specific alternative projects replaces large-scale, revolutionary forms of struggles clearly positioned against capitalism. Finally, in academic debate, many degrowth advocates are primarily concerned with the acceptability of the degrowth project; such a willingness to engage, and seek the approval of, economists and social scientists within the mainstream discourages the adoption of an explicitly anti-capitalist discourse.

Due to these concerns, degrowth has so far largely renounced a critical engagement with the political economy of capitalism and the possibility of its transformation. This remains a crucial intellectual and political task which degrowth scholars and activists cannot avoid confronting in the future.

References

De Angelis, M. (2007) *The Beginning of History: Value Struggles and Global Capital*. London: Pluto Press.

Harvey, D. (2010) *The Enigma of Capital and the Crises of Capitalism*. Oxford: Oxford University Press.

Ingham, G. (2008) *Capitalism*. Cambridge: Polity.

Latouche, S. (2012) 'Can the Left Escape Economism?' *Capitalism, Nature, Socialism*. 23(1): 74–8.

O'Connor, J. (1991) 'On the Two Contradictions of Capitalism'. *Capitalism Nature Socialism*, 2 (3): 107–9.

Watts, M. (2009) 'Capitalism'. In D. Gregory, R. Johnston, G. Pratt, M. Watts and S. Whatmore (eds). *The Dictionary of Human Geography* (5th ed.). Oxford: Wiley-Blackwell, pp. 59–63.

11

CARE

Giacomo D'Alisa[1], Marco Deriu[2] and Federico Demaria[1]

[1]RESEARCH & DEGROWTH AND ICTA (INSTITUTE OF ENVIRONMENTAL SCIENCE AND TECHNOLOGY), AUTONOMOUS UNIVERSITY OF BARCELONA
[2]DEPARTMENT OF ARTS, LITERATURE, HISTORY AND SOCIAL STUDIES, UNIVERSITY OF PARMA

Care is the daily action performed by human beings for their welfare and for the welfare of their community. Here, community refers to the ensemble of people within proximity and with which every human being lives, such as the family, friendships or the neighbourhood. In these spaces, as well in the society as a whole, an enormous quantity of work is devoted to sustenance, reproduction and the contentment of human relations. Unpaid work is the term used in **feminist economics** to account for the free work devoted to such tasks. Feminists have denounced for years the undervaluation of work for bodily and personal care, and the related undervaluation of the subjects delegated to undertake it, i.e. women (Jochimsen and Knobloch 1997). Feminists continue to affirm the unique role that care has in the wellbeing of humans. This is not simply because this unpaid work exceeds the total quantity of paid work performed in the market space (Picchio 2003). It is because care is fundamental in the support the mental, physical and relational integrity of each and every human being.

Nevertheless, the dominant streams of political and economic thought obscure this hidden flux of hours and energies devoted to sustenance, reproduction and relations, as these are not directly consistent with productivity, the only variable that, in theory, capitalist societies value for the remuneration of labour.

Historically there have been strong connections between the distribution of care work and the distribution of power across hierarchies of gender, class and ethnicity. Eco-feminists have revealed these connections and the magnitude of the care-time that is needed for a man to sell his productive work in the market each day. Feminists denounce the virile male labour force, which renders them invisible by passing production costs on to women and nature.

Hierarchies, conflicts and forms of dominance become visible when we juxtapose production time (by 'productive men') with the biological reproduction time assigned to women. The contemporary economic imaginary speaks about time as a scarce resource to be allocated efficiently, keeping in mind costs and opportunities. In the spaces of domestic economy and care, on the other hand, the use of time is not directed toward efficiency, but proceeds according to the rhythm of life. Feminist criticism focuses on the chronological time of production as disembodied from the daily cycles of the body and the cycle of life, and further disengaged from the ecological time of seasons and the regeneration of ecosystems, as well as the biological time of reproduction (see **bioeconomics**). The time of emotional support and care is strongly conditioned by the necessities of nourishment and rooted in the space of proximity (Mellor 1997).

Under **capitalism**, where markets are subjected to the imperative of constant **growth**, there seems to remain little time to dedicate to oneself, to family, friends or civil and political activities. Yet relationships are fundamental to a good life, as Aristotle teaches in the *Nicomachean Ethics*. Indeed, Martha Nussbaum (1986) reminds us that there are three beneficial relationships for the self, according to Aristotle: love, friendship and political commitment. These spheres of life constitute ends in themselves and cannot be instrumental. They can only be enjoyed through reciprocity. This characteristic renders them particularly fragile – a fragility that is put to a tough test by the profit logic of the market. For example, love, as such, exists only when it is mutual; when buying sex, you can only enjoy a surrogate of physical, psychological and emotional support, but certainly not love. Taking care of your own children implies an enormous amount of hours; paying a babysitter to assist, on the other hand, is a surrogate of parenting.

Economic **growth** is unable to sustain the **happiness** that it promises through increased income. Easterlin's paradox shows that as societies get richer, individuals do not necessarily get happier. Production and the market constantly expand, occupying spaces of care, social life and reciprocity, leading inevitably to the disintegration of relationships and engendering negative consequences on well-being. Care is outsourced outside the family sphere to the state or the market (e.g. child or elderly care) debasing its essence, which is reciprocity. **Happiness** literature argues that an allocation of time with priority on family life and health (and thus care) increases subjective well-being.

In its strong claim for socio-**environmental justice**, degrowthers cannot ignore the feminist claim for a fairer distribution of care work; the impossibility of cancelling such necessary work has to face its inextensible redistribution across gender and class. In their commitment to fight productivity – the obsession of modernity – degrowthers have to account for the continuous re-emergence of reproductive activities; the care of the other is a step towards emancipation from the individual excesses of contemporary human being living in an industrialized society. If these assumptions are true then the inescapable question is how might it be possible to reinstate the dignity of care in a degrowth society?

Putting care at the centre of a degrowth society requires, first, a radical rethinking of human relations and the ways in which these may correspond to human needs and overcome oppositions, dualisms and hierarchies. Joan Tronto (1993) has noted that the process of care is composed of four phases:

1. *caring about*: implies the perception of a need and the personal as well as social recognition for the need of care;
2. *taking care of*: contemplating the assumption of some responsibility relative to the identified need and a choice as to how to respond to it;
3. *care-giving*: implies commitment and concrete work for the satisfaction of the needs of care and generally requires a direct relationship between the person who gives care and the person who receives it.
4. *care-receiving*: represents the final movement in which the receiver can respond by showing that the care is indeed for her/his benefit or, alternatively, to show the inefficiency or inappropriateness of the care offered.

Tronto shows how the expression 'taking care of' is often associated with masculine and public roles and that when men 'care about' this refers almost universally to public questions. On the other hand, the expressions 'care-giving' and 'care-receiving' are associated with women; and when the actor is a woman, the expression 'cares about' refers to real persons with flesh and blood in intimate and private space. Clearly this distinction is founded in the dualistic approach to care in our patriarchal society. The man occupies the public sphere with his interest in the important questions society has to face. The woman occupies the private sphere with her responsibilities for the daily necessity of the family. Two separate spheres, hierarchically predetermined, institute and reinforce asymmetrical power between man and woman. Overcoming this schism is an important goal for a degrowth society. This would allow women to express their passion for the world, participating in creating the public definition of what society should care about and take care of. Transcending this schism would allow men to learn what it really means to care for persons in concrete terms of time-consumption and emotional burden. In this way, degrowthers will be able to bring back the experience of the vulnerability of bodies' needs and of people and relocate these at the centre of politics and of the economy.

It is easy to imagine why re-centring a society around care would pave the way to degrowth. It responds first to the idea of equity among genders by shar-ing care work within the sphere of the community as well as within society as a whole. Secondly, it re-instates the importance caring has on the well-being of the self, the family, the neighbourhood and the society as whole. It would persuade people to work less and devote less time to the economic sphere. As a consequence the unequal burden of care work on immigrants (normally women) could also diminish. Third, because fewer hours of work would be available for the market, this would promote **work-sharing**, allowing most people to find paid work. Last but not least, working to lessen the vulnerability of others allows everybody to experience their own vulnerability and reflect on its characteristics. This is a first important step toward abandoning narcissistic affirmations of the self as a guard against weakness, or in other words, abandoning the anthropological essence of growth society.

References

Jochimsen, M. and Knobloch, U. (1997) 'Making the Hidden Visible: the Importance of Caring Activities and their Principles for an Economy', *Ecological Economics*, 20: 107–12.

Mellor, M. (1997) 'Women, Nature and the Social Construction of 'Economic Man', *Ecological Economics*, 20(2): 129–40.

Nussbaum, M. (1986) *The Fragility of Goodness: Luck and Ethics in Greek Tragedy and Philosophy*, Cambridge: University Press.

Picchio A. (ed.) (2003) *Unpaid Work and the Economy. A Gender Analysis of the Standards of Living*, London and New York: Routledge.

Tronto, Joan, (1993) *Moral Boundaries: A Political Argument for an Ethic of Care*, New York, NY: Routledge.

12

COMMODIFICATION

Erik Gómez-Baggethun

NORWEGIAN INSTITUTE FOR NATURE RESEARCH (NINA), RESEARCH & DEGROWTH AND
ICTA (INSTITUTE OF ENVIRONMENTAL SCIENCE AND TECHNONLOGY), AUTONOMOUS
UNIVERSITY OF BARCELONA

The reach of markets into aspects of life traditionally governed by nonmarket values and norms is one of the most significant developments of our time. The notion
of commodification describes this phenomenon and can be defined as the symbolic, discursive and institutional changes through which a good or service that
was not previously meant for sale enters the sphere of money and market exchange.

Commodification has been often criticized on the grounds that some things
ought neither to be for sale nor governed through the market logic. Much of
the controversy stems from the historically grounded observation that commodification transforms the values that govern the relationships between people and
between people and nature as these adopt the form of market transactions. An early
observer of the social effects of commodification was Marx, who used the notion
of *commodity fetishism* to note how, in the marketplace, producers and consumers
perceive each other by means of the money and goods that they exchange. Mauss
(1954), a reference thinker of degrowth that inspired French **anti-utilitarianism**,
observed that, as commodity exchange unfolds, symbolic ties and reciprocity logics
that traditionally accompanied economic transactions tend to erode and eventually disappear. Mauss' thesis was taken up by Polanyi (1957), who claimed that
commodification in market societies had a tendency to dissolve all social relations
into one of monetary exchange. He critically scrutinized commodification of land,
labor, and money in the rise of liberalism, noting that, unlike traditional commodities, such *fictitious commodities* were not human-made or intended for sale.

Historically, commodification has been part and parcel of common property
enclosures. Pioneer analysis of enclosures by Proudhon (1840) and Marx (1842)
famously portrayed the private appropriation of the commons as theft. In *Capital*,

Marx suggested that *enclosures* of common lands in Europe in the early days of modernity, were at the root of the so-called "primitive accumulation" that allowed capitalist relations to unfold. Thinkers like Federici (2004) and Harvey (2003) expanded his thesis, noting that enclosures on the commons extend until the present day with accumulation of wealth by dispossessing the public of their land and resources. Contemporary enclosures include land grabs in Africa and the commodification of nature through biodiversity offsets and carbon trading schemes.

Degrowth is as much a critique of **growth**, as it is a critique of the colonizing expansion of market values, logic, and language into novel social and ecological domains. It demands the de-commodification of social relations and of the human relationship with nature and challenges the "new environmental pragmatism" that sees market based instruments as the solution for environmental protection. Environmentalists (see **environmentalism**) are both victims and villains of the commodification of nature. Disappointed by the failure to reverse the ecological crisis, many are focusing on monetary valuation and market incentives as a pragmatic short-term strategy to communicate and capture the value of biodiversity in a language that reflects dominant political and economic views. This well-intentioned strategy oversees the broader sociopolitical processes through which markets expand their limits and monetary value colonizes new domains. Within the prevailing institutional setting in market societies, a focus on monetary valuations and incentives paves the way, discursively and sometimes technically, for the commodification of human-nature relations and can crowd out intrinsic motivations for conservation by inducing a logic of short-term economic calculus. Such is the tragedy of well-intentioned valuation.

Commodification – and the fight against it – is a core theoretical and practical component in the struggle of the defense and re-appropriation of the **commons**. This struggle is an inevitable part of a broader struggle against **capitalism**. With the structural tendency to decline with market competition, capitalist economies constantly seek to expand the frontiers of commodification into new social and ecological domains (Luxemburg 1951, Harvey 2003). The **commons** constitute the natural playing field where capital seeks fresh space for accumulation. Yet, their colonization is always incomplete. In its expansion, commodification encounters limits of biophysical, institutional, and social nature. Biophysical limits stem from the non-fungible character of ecosystem processes and components, meaning that they may not be separable into discrete tradable units. Bakker (2007) suggests that this uncooperative nature of environmental commodities explains the failure to achieve higher levels in the commodification of water in the United Kingdom in recent decades. Institutional limits stem from the public good nature of many ecological commons, meaning low capacity to prevent others having access to them, which is a precondition to set up effective markets. This explains why well-developed markets of ecosystem services are still relatively rare despite being actively promoted by economists and intergovernmental organizations. Finally, social limits stem from the fierce opposition commodification can encounter when it affects essential goods to cover basic needs. For example, in the 2000 conflict known as the *Water War* in Cochabamba, Bolivia, an attempt to privatize water encountered contestation that scaled up to an insurrection.

As these cases illustrate, commodification is a contested and transient phenomenon, contingent on the power relations that prevail at each historical moment between possessors and dispossessed. Contrary to what is often assumed, the process of commodification is not necessarily unidirectional or irreversible. Objects move in and out of commodity status and history offers many cases of de-commodification. These range from the abolition of the medieval practice of selling indulgence letters to the formal abolition of slavery in many countries worldwide during the nineteenth and twentieth centuries. Indulgencies and human beings were externalized from markets and (re)regulated following non chrematistic values such as spirituality and human rights. Examples of institutions that limit the commodification of nature include the Convention on International Trading with Critically Endangered Species (CITES) and the constitutions of countries like Bolivia and Ecuador, which are permeated – if timidly – by values and ontologies of non-capitalist indigenous societies. These constitutions formally recognize rights to nature, and the latter declares ecosystem services as public goods that may not be subject of private appropriation (see **Buen Vivir**).

To keep their hands away from the mud of real life politics, many social movements and contemporary critics shelter themselves in the distant and morally safe position of opposing every form of commodification. But despite its ubiquitous character under **capitalism**, commodification is a millenary and pre-capitalist phenomenon, and markets stand among the most enduring institutions of humanity. Re-embedded within proper social and ecological boundaries, markets will certainly have a role to play as a coordination mechanism in any realistic political project able to organize exchange and provision on our increasingly complex and vastly populated planet.

The critical question is thus to define where to put the limits to commodification, a dilemma hinted at by Emanuel Kant in his famous statement "In the kingdom of ends everything has either a price or a dignity." Thus, if technical aspects such as the feasibility of producing equivalent substitutes, or the level of rivalry and excludability exhibited by the affected good can be important practical criteria, the question of where to put the limits to commodification is most fundamentally an ethical and political one. Sacredness, uniqueness, rareness, intrinsic value, human rights, **environmental justice**, and basic needs are some of the notions and criteria that can help us delineate what may or may not be commodifiable. Such delineation needs to be addressed from multiple angles, ranging from the enactment of international treaties for the protection of the global **commons**, to national constitutions protecting public goods, to local rules, norms, and taboos which ban on specific forms of commodification. Many ingredients for this institutional assemblage can be found in current institutional diversity. Others can be rescued from the vast laboratory of institutional arrangements developed by human societies over millennia and swept away by modernity and capitalist globalization. Many other new forms of still to be collective action will be necessary to secure an effective defense of the global commons in an era of unprecedented world interconnectedness.

Only once the sphere of markets and commodities has been tentatively defined will environmentalists, growth objectors, and society at large be ready to decide which *externalities* are to be internalized in markets and which *internalities* are to be externalized and governed by non-market norms and values.

References

Bakker, K. (2003) *An Uncooperative Commodity: Privatizing Water in England and Wales*, Oxford: Oxford University Press.

Federici, S. (2004) *Caliban and the Witch. Women, The Body and Primitive Accumulation*, New York: Autonomedia.

Harvey, D. (2003) *The New Imperialism*, Oxford: Oxford University Press.

Luxemburg, R. (1951) *The Accumulation of Capital*, Monthly Review Press.

Marx, K. (1975/1842) "Proceedings of the Sixth Rhine Province Assembly. Debates on the Law of the Theft of Wood." In Karl Marx and Frederick Engels, *Collected Works, Volume I*, New York: International Publishers, pp 224–63.

Mauss, M. (1954) *The Gift*, New York: Free Press.

Polanyi, K. (1957) *The Great Transformation: The Political and Economic Origins of Our Time*, Boston: Beacon Press.

Proudhon, P-J. (1840) *Qu'est-ce que la propriété?* Paris: Chez J.-F. Brocard.

Sandel, M. (2012) *What Money Can't Buy: The Moral Limits of Markets*, New York: Farrar, Straus and Girou.

13

COMMODITY FRONTIERS

Marta Conde and Mariana Walter

RESEARCH & DEGROWTH AND ICTA (ENVIRONMENTAL SCIENCE AND
TECHNOLOGY INSTITUTE), AUTONOMOUS UNIVERSITY OF BARCELONA

In the Barcelona School of Ecological Economics and Political Ecology, we understand and analyze 'commodity frontiers' as the locus where extraction geographically expands, colonizing new land in search for raw materials (oil, minerals, biomass etc.). This makes it possible to feed the expanding demand associated with the increase of the social **metabolism** of industrialized economies (MartinezAlier *et al.* 2010). The expansion of commodity frontiers fosters conditions of social and environmental degradation and conflict.

The term 'commodity frontier' can also be traced to the theory first introduced by Jason W. Moore (2000) to describe how **capitalism** initiated its expansion with the sugar complex in the fifteenth century. He argues that going beyond existing frontiers is the main strategy for expanding the scope and scale of the **commodification** process. Further expansion is possible as long as there remains un-commodified land, products and relations. Here, land should be seen as equivalent to the space to grow food or to extract minerals, or the sea for oil or gas exploration.

Moore's (2002, 2003) definition of commodity frontiers combines Immanuel Wallerstein's world-system theory with the Marxist concept of metabolic rift. The world-system theory's concept of a 'commodity chain' explores the labour and production processes that result in a finished commodity. Instead of focusing on the finished product, the task in a commodity frontier analytical framework is to track the frontier of expansion by looking at the different raw materials that constitute it. The concept of metabolic rift gives light to the social and ecologic rupture that occurred with the development of **capitalism**. With the displacement of small-scale agriculture and industrialisation, peasants lost their traditional forms of subsistence. Disconnected from the soil, their social **metabolism** and their production, they became alienated from their natural environment. At the same time, flows of products (and nutrients) were taken from the countryside to the cities, causing degradation at points of extraction and pollution at points of consumption (Moore 2003). The rise of wage labour through the **commodification** of land and labour is at the core of this rift. The dispossession of subsistence farmers and herders from common land resulted in the proletarianisation of rural populations, who flooded to urban centres in search of work (Marx 1976). According to Moore (2003), those still in possession of land generally became highly indebted, fostering instability and overexploitation by capitalists. This process led to declining productivity, driving the frontier further in search of fresh supplies of labour and land.

The sugar complex expansion from Madeira in the late fifteenth century, to Brazil in the sixteenth century and the Caribbean in the seventeenth century, showed an industrialization pattern that transformed the land and labour of these countries profoundly. The sugar industry required high quantities of wood, not only for its production, but also for the construction of infrastructures and ships for transportation, causing massive forest clearance and land erosion. Ecological exhaustion at the production point and the environmental destruction that followed pushed capitalist expansion to other lands through a process of cyclical fluctuations. As land was being exhausted, fresh land was being occupied. Moore sustains that local ecosystems that might have otherwise been allowed to regenerate were destabilized, leading to falling productivity and profitability. This renewed the search for fresh land, often found outside the boundaries of the capitalist world-economy (Moore 2000). From a social point of view, labour transformations did not succeed in the case of sugar production. Existing indigenous labour in the Caribbean rapidly died off, so Africans were then imported to work on sugar slave islands (Moore 2003).

An important implication of commodity frontiers is that they set in motion a vast complex of economic activities that imply the expansion towards new frontiers. For instance, consider modern gold mine extraction; this activity requires inputs, such as chemical reagents, machinery, fuel, construction materials and food for the workers, that need to be extracted and processed, thereby pushing other frontiers further.

What happened with sugar in America later happened (and is still happening) with minerals, fossil fuels, timber and crops (i.e. cotton, soy bean, agrofuels). In such extractive activities, labour is organized in ways that often exclude local populations from qualified job opportunities and benefits. The ecological implications are vast; topsoil vegetation is removed, generally implying deforestation and huge biodiversity loss that is pushed and further encroached into smaller areas. Fertilizers and pesticides are produced to feed the expansion of industrialized crops, polluting land, water and bodies. Water is extracted and used in large quantities, competing with local uses, affecting its availability and quality. The extraction of minerals produces irreversible changes in hydro-geological structures. **Environmental Justice** and Ecological Economics have explored the incommensurable implications for local populations that live at these commodity frontiers. Indigenous and peasant communities, whose livelihood and culture is tied to their territory, have seen how their land is enclosed, removed or polluted (Martinez Alier *et al.* 2010).

Indeed, one of the features of the 2000s has been the significant increase of socio-environmental conflicts involving communities that oppose extractive and other high-impact activities in their lands (Martinez Alier *et al.* 2010). In Latin America, these contestations have triggered proposals based on alternative views of what **development** can be that question **growth** as a social aim and reframe the meaning of wellbeing and Nature. In Africa there has been a call for a return to **Ubuntu**, an African socio-cultural framework that rests on values such as solidarity, consensus and autonomy. Martinez- Alier (2012) has suggested that there is an opportunity to generate alliances between the movements promoting **Buen Vivir** in the South and degrowth in the North.

However, the advance of extraction frontiers and their impact are not only a matter of concern for the South. The crisis and subsequent structural adjustments that have recently affected Europe have brought a devaluation of labour costs and the elimination of health and environmental regulations. Extraction projects that were not possible in the past are now increasingly more feasible. Coal and gold mining is returning to Europe, creating violent conflicts such as the one in Chalkidiki in northern Greece. This tendency is accentuated by the advent of new technologies such as gas fracking, which has expanded rapidly in the US and now in Europe and both deep, and not so deep, sea drilling.

As physical frontiers become saturated, new modes of expanding capital not tied to geography have taken shape. The **commodification processes** of indigenous knowledge, environmental services and CO_2 emissions (through the carbon market) are examples of the new frontiers of accumulation.

Commodity frontiers and degrowth are linked in four ways. First, the presence of commodity frontiers is rooted in the inherent and ceaseless drive of **capitalism** to expand.

Second, commodity frontiers reminds us that **growth** comes at a high cost to people far from the location in which it is delivered. The commodities that supply our growing global economy come from particular places, where people live and whose lives are transformed at a high social and environmental cost in incommensurable ways. The intent of degrowth should be not only to reduce human consumption at the point of delivery but also to challenge the structures of production at the point of extraction. Contesting successfully the imperative of endless economic **growth** can have direct and positive impacts in the lives of communities at these frontiers.

Third, the social and environmental impacts of extracting resources are increasing as the quality and availability of resources decreases. In the case of mining, a much larger amount of waste and pollution is generated today to obtain the same quantity of metal ores than was generated a decade ago. The question is no longer whether there are available resources but rather what the social and environmental cost will be if they continue to be extracted.

Fourth, in Europe and the Americas, economies that in the very recent past mostly imported raw materials are now promoting extraction within their own borders, fostering new industries, dynamics and conflicts. Thus, the expansion of the extraction frontier is extending from the South to the North, and to the core of capitalist societies.

Finally, opportunities can rise to form alliances between the movement for degrowth and the movements that contest extraction and frame innovative alternatives to growth-laden development formulas.

References

Martinez-Alier, J. (2012) 'Environmental Justice and Economic Degrowth: An Alliance between Two Movements', *Capitalism Nature Socialism*, 23(1): 51–73.

Martinez-Alier, J., Kallis, G., Veuthey, S., Walter, M., and Temper, L. (2010) 'Social metabolism, ecological distribution conflicts, and valuation languages', *Ecological Economics*, 70: 153–8.

Marx K. (1976) *Capital: A Critique of Political Economy, vol. 1*, London: Penguin Classics.

Moore, J. W. (2000) 'Sugar and the Expansion of the Early Modern World-Economy: Commodity Frontiers, Ecological Transformation, and Industrialization', Review: *A Journal of the Fernand Braudel Center,* 23(3): 409–33.

Moore, J. W. (2003) 'The Modern World-Systems Environmental History? Ecology and the Rise of Capitalism', *Theory and Society*, 32(3): 307–77.

14

COMMONS

Silke Helfrich and David Bollier

COMMONS STRATEGIES GROUP

The commons consists of a vast array of self-provisioning and governance systems that flourish mainly outside of both the market and the State, on the periphery of mainstream politics and economics. While functioning as a social glue and embodying a different logic than that of market fundamentalism, commons are essentially invisible. They generally are not based on money, legal contracts, or bureaucratic fiat, but on self-management and shared responsibility.

The commons is usually understood in two primary senses: as a paradigm of governance and resource-management, and as a set of social practices in virtually all fields of human endeavor. As a system of governance, the term refers to the norms, rules, and institutions that enable the shared management of specific resources. As social practices, the commons is better understood as a verb (a social process) than a noun. It is more accurate to talk about "commoning" or "making the commons" than "the commons" as a thing. Commons don't just fall from the sky. They aren't simply material or intangible collective resources, but processes of shared stewardship about things that a community (a network or all of humankind) possesses and manages in common or *should* do so. These things we are entitled to use collectively may be gifts of nature or collectively produced resources like knowledge and cultural techniques, urban spaces, landscapes, and countless others.

A resource *becomes* a commons when it is taken care of by a community or network. The community, resource, and rules are all an integrated whole.

This definition of the commons poses enormous conceptual challenges to conventional economics and even to traditional commons scholarship. Both tend to see the commons as inhering in the resource itself. In conventional economics it is customary to call a resource a commons if excludability is difficult and the resource is "rivalrous" (my use of a resource diminishes your capacity to use the same resource). Yet, culture or code does not get used up if someone uses them. They are "non-rivalrous." And still, many people talk about them as commons (such as Wikipedia and free software). This suggests, that it is impossible to base a coherent commons approach on resource-categories. What matters most in the commons are the social commitments, knowledge, and practices to manage the resource, whatever it may be. A source of freshwater can be stewarded as a commons – with non-discriminatory but limited use by all – or it can be fenced, converted into a commodity and sold as bottled water (see **commodification**). The centre of the commons and of commoning is not a "common pool resource," but the active process of "pooling common resources." Both, rivalrous (water, land, fish, etc.) and non-rivalrous resources (knowledge, code, etc.) can be pooled – or not. It is mainly up to us. Thus, the commons is primarily about the ways we relate to each other when using something in common.

Before a commons can be created, however, a problem of collective ideation has to be overcome. Everyone must share a clear vision of what is to be shared and how. Commons may fail because of bad leadership, inappropriate governance structures, or simply because of the power relations in a marketized world.

According to the International Land Coalition (ILC), an estimated two billion people in the world *directly* rely on the commons as a provisioning model. Even though it has been around for millennia as the default mode of social reproduction, its strength as a pattern for change has only recently been rediscovered. Much of the academic interest grew out of research on "common property regimes" by Vincent and Elinor Ostrom, who in 1973 founded the Workshop in Political Theory and Policy Analysis at Indiana University. Elinor Ostrom would win the Nobel Prize in Economics in 2009. The commons also got a boost when new communication and information technologies arose in the 1980s (see **digital commons**).

Most commons have little to do with individual property rights, markets, or geo-political power. They are focused on solving concrete problems and meeting people's needs by providing effective self-governance of a shared resource or space. Hence, the commons are constantly and continuously being overwhelmed and destroyed by market forces, parliaments, and governments. This process is called *enclosure*. Throughout history, enclosures have been justified by a narrative that also underlies one of the most quoted essays in social sciences of the last 45 years – "The Tragedy of the Commons," published in 1968 by Garrett Hardin. Its misleading message continues to hold sway in the popular mind. Hardin makes his readers picture "a pasture open to all . . . ." He argues that if everybody can graze cattle on common land, no single herder will have a rational incentive to hold back. Instead, he will put as many cattle as possible. Thus, the pasture will *inevitably* be overexploited. The practical solution, Hardin suggests, would be individual property as a way to protect exclusivity or top-down control and coercion by authorities.

Hardin was not in fact describing a commons but an open-access regime, a free-for-all situation without boundaries, rules, and communication among users. But a commons has boundaries, rules, monitoring systems, punishment of free-riders, and social norms – all of which are typically developed by the users themselves according to their circumstances. The conditions in which self-management can thrive were summarized in the design principles that Elinor Ostrom published in the 1990 book, *Governing the Commons*. They include clearly defined boundaries, effective exclusion of unauthorized parties, locally adapted rules regarding the appropriation and provision of resources, collective-choice arrangements that allow most users to participate, monitoring, graduated sanctions for rules violations, easily accessible mechanisms of conflict resolution, and recognition by higher-level authorities.

Many commoners continuously points to the generative side of the commons as a form of wealth creation. In Yochai Benkler's (2006: 63) description of the so-called **digital commons**, we are seeing "the emergence of more effective collective action practices that are decentralized but do not rely on either the price system or a managerial structure." The commons out-compete by out-cooperating. Benkler's term for this is "commons-based peer production," meaning systems that are collaborative, non-proprietary, and based on "sharing resources and outputs among widely distributed, loosely connected individuals" (ibid.)

Over the past few years, a fledgling commons movement – working alongside scholars – has developed a discourse of the commons as a political philosophy and policy agenda. This network is fighting moral and political justifications for enclosures, today justifying individual (corporate) ownership of ethno-botanical knowledge, genes, life-forms, and synthetic nano-matter. Degrowth strategies must confront these (new) enclosures, which sweep aside people's bonds, impose an extreme individualism, and convert citizens into mere consumers. This is the ground on which an alliance with the commons movement is emerging.

In fact, both discourses reinterpret the notion of wealth while linking it to an idea of "enhanced liberty in connectedness." A critique of **growth** sets the frame (what to do?), while the commons develops a narration for *how* to live and structure our social relationships within this frame. Degrowth helps us to understand the urgency of getting out of the "iron prison of consumerism," while commoning shows what a "beyond-consumerist-culture" looks and feels like. Commoners tend to set forth a "logic of abundance," the proposition that there will be enough produced for all if we can develop an abundance of relationships, networks, and forms of co-operative governance. This kind of abundance can help us develop practices that respect the limits of growth *and* enlarge everybody's freedom to act in a self-determined way.

Furthermore, commoning *can* actively contribute to the **dematerialization** of production and consumption in three ways. First, it can re-localize production (many commons are tied to a geographic territory); second, commoning can intensify use through co-use and collaborative and complementary use, which in turn can either prevent or intensify rebound effects (see **Jevons' paradox**); third, commoning can foster "prosumption," the combining of production and consumption into one process. It is important to note, however, that strengthened social bonds in itself spur **dematerialization**, because they are needs-based instead of needs-creating.

In short; the commons and degrowth are complementary to each other. The commons suggests radically democratic solutions that don't pit environmental concerns against social justice. The principles of commoning don't need **economic growth** to thrive. Instead, they help replace the cultural imperative "to have more" with alternative social spheres that demonstrate that "doing together" can trump "having" – and thus bring "degrowth" and "quality of life" into closer alignment. Furthermore, the commons movement's focus on (intellectual) property rights has the virtue of undermining a fundamental pillar of capitalism and thus growth.

If "the economy" is re-imagined through key commons notions like distributed production, modularity, collective ownership, and stewardship, it is possible to embrace the idea of a high-performance economic system while rejecting capitalist notions and institutions (corporation, global markets, competition, labor) (see **capitalism**).

References

The Commoner, A web journal for other values. Available online at www.commoner.org.uk (accessed September 4 2013).

Benkler, Y. (2006) *The Wealth of Networks: How Social Production Transforms Markets and Freedom*, New Haven: Yale University Press.

Bollier, D., Helfrich, S., and Heinrich Böll Foundation (eds.) (2012) *The Wealth of the Commons: A World Beyond Market and State*, Amherst, Massachusetts: Levellers Press. Available online at hwww.wealthofthecommons.org (accessed March 3 2013).

Linebaugh, P. (Jan.8–10, 2010) "Some Principles of the Commons," *Counterpunch*, available online at www.counterpunch.org/2010.01/08/some-principles-of-the-commons (accessed July 1 2013).

Ostrom, E. (1990) *Governing the Commons: The Evolution of Institutions for Collective Action*, Cambridge: Cambridge University Press.

Weber, A. (2013) "Enlivenment: Toward a Fundamental Shift in the Concepts of Nature, Culture and Politics," *Series on Ecology, No. 31*, Berlin, Germany: Heinrich Boell Foundation. Available online at http://commonsandeconomics.org/2013/05/15/a-new-bios-for-the-economic-system (accessed 3 February 2014).

15

CONVIVIALITY

Marco Deriu

DEPARTMENT OF ARTS, LITERATURE, HISTORY AND SOCIAL STUDIES, UNIVERSITY OF PARMA

Ivan Illich derives his idea of conviviality from *Physiologie du goût ou méditations de gastronomie transcendante*, an 1825 text by Jean Anthelme Brillat-Savarin. Illich's reflection nevertheless unfolds with complexity and moves far beyond a reminder of the importance of the social bond. To Illich, the word 'conviviality' does not mean joy or light-heartedness; it refers to a society in which modern tools are used by everyone in an integrated and shared manner, without reliance on a body of specialists who control said instruments.

Illich's reflections on conviviality come from an awareness that industrial **growth** forces us to recognize: that there exist certain 'thresholds' of wellbeing that cannot be crossed. As institutions related to medicine, education or economics grow beyond a certain point, the ends for which they were originally designed change. Institutions become a threat to society itself.

For Illich, conviviality is the 'opposite of industrial productivity'. In reality, the apparent freedom the growth of industrially produced devices guarantees impoverishes humankind and limits possibility. In fact, industrial tools often introduce what Illich calls a 'radical monopoly'. Monopoly does not refer here to alternatives within a specific category, but to the fact that the supply of commodities or services, produced industrially, ends up depriving people of the freedom to produce goods on their own, or to exchange and share what they need outside the market.

As our needs are transformed into commodities, new commodities create new needs (see **commodification**). So the measure of wellbeing is not equivalent to a disproportionate increase in production, but in a reasonable balance between goods and commodities, allowing a synergy between use value and exchange value. This line of reasoning distinguishes Illich's contribution from traditional ecological thought, which focuses primarily on the environmental effects of production.

Even with more eco-efficient products, Illich points out, an affluent society generates, through radical monopoly, the paralysis of its people and eliminates their **autonomy**: 'This radical monopoly would accompany high-speed traffic even if motors were powered by sunshine and vehicles were spun of air' (Illich 1978: 73).

It is therefore in a social sense – not just an environmental one – that the instruments society has created prove inadequate in guaranteeing the sustainability of our society. Unfettered industrialization produces tools that are seemingly indispensable, but which, primarily, devalue individual **autonomy** and force people to become increasingly dependent on commodities for which they have to work more and more. The result, argues Illich, is that the rate in growth of frustration exceeds the rate of production, resulting in a form of 'modernization of poverty'. Convivial tools for Illich are a condition for the realization of **autonomy** understood as the power to control the use of resources and on the satisfaction of our own needs.

One detects a connection here with the theme of alienation in Marx. But the alienation that Illich describes does not depend on the ownership of the means of production. It is not an issue of property or redistribution, but of the inherent logic embedded in the instrument. Certain tools are inherently destructive, maintains Illich, no matter who owns and uses them. According to Illich, some tools are designed to produce new demands and new forms of slavery so as to make an industrial society with an intensive market economy indispensable.

On the other hand, the tool is convivial if it can be used and adapted with ease and for a purpose chosen by the individual, and if it has the result of expanding freedom, **autonomy** and human creativity. Illich cites the motorway networks, aircrafts, open pit mines and the school as examples of tools that are not convivial; he cites the bicycle, sewing machine, telephone and radio as convivial tools. But the conviviality of other devices is more complicated. Consider, for example, the computer and the Internet– would they be considered convivial according to Illich?

In his work *Tools of Conviviality* (1973), Illich views the computer, information technologies, and more generally what can be called the digital civilization and cybernetics, as controversial. In other essays, too, the author wonders if the computer encourages 'disembodied' thinking. He emphasizes his fear that humans may become more and more dependent on computers in order to talk and think – just as we have become dependent on cars. In the work *Deschooling Society* (1973), Illich identifies computer networks and the ability to create connections between peer groups based on similar interests in the same city, or even in distant lands, as an alternative means of meeting, creating and having social relationships and learning, when compared to traditional forms of standardized education (Illich 1971). For this reason, Michael Slattery (http://convivialtools.org, accessed 3 November 2013), who runs the site *Convivial Tools*, claims that Illich was a precursor of the digital revolution. He recalls how the computer engineer Lee Felsenstein, a designer of the Osborne 1, the first industrially produced laptop, had read Illich's text and considered his computer a convivial tool. One could counter that critical considerations of the change of the perception of speed, time and image and the value of face-to-face relationships hardly make Illich's position tantamount to that of the so-called network society enthusiasts.

In any case, the discussion reveals the ways in which Illich's definition of the convivial demonstrates a degree of uncertainty and ambiguity. It is true that Illich expressly refers to the structure of the instrument and not to the structure of the character of the individual and the community; yet, too rigid a separation between convivial and non-convivial tools risks losing sight of two crucial aspects of his argument.

The first is that technical tools do not exist in a vacuum but, rather, are immersed in networks of social and gender relations. Illich seems to put the structure of the object first, or above the structure of relations. From one point of view, it is a certain structure of relations that led to the invention of the first firearms, car, jet or the atomic bomb. On the other hand, in the structure of a non-convivial relation the use of any instrument, even a seemingly convivial one, will work against the **autonomy** and freedom of choice of men, women and children. Any tool therefore fits into an ambit of social and gender relations, and to a certain extent, expresses the structure of these relationships. So the structure of social relations and the structure of the instrument are codetermined and develop in a circular and non-unidirectional fashion.

From here, we arrive at the second consideration. Some tools – the Internet probably among them – seem to fall into a grey area and demonstrate a certain degree of malleability and dynamism and, depending on the context, can be tilted more towards their use value or their exchange value. To a certain extent, if the structure of social relations can change, so too can the convivial or non-convivial character of an instrument. It is worth noting that Valentina Borremans (1979: 4), has expressed the need for a new discipline of research on convivial instruments and cultural, social and political conditions that could defend their use value.

Illich points out in several places that there is no reason to ban from a convivial society any powerful tool or any form of centralized production. What matters is that the society ensures a balance between the instruments that it produces to meet the demands for which they were conceived, and tools that will foster invention and personal fulfilment. 'Convivial reconstruction demands the disruption of the present monopoly of industry, but not the abolition of all industrial production' (Illich 1975: 88). The convivial society is not motionless or frozen. 'A changeless society would be as intolerable for people as the present society of constant change. Convivial reconstruction requires limits on the rate of change' (Illich 1975: 91).

The transition to a post-industrial society is a potential opening toward a model of society in which the ways and means of production are diversified and favourable to personal initiative. While industrial production is standardized in the long run, convivial production encourages personal creativity and collaborative innovation. The transition from productivity to conviviality is, in some ways, the transition from economic scarcity to the spontaneity and extravagance of a gift economy.

Without doubt, the contribution of Ivan Illich on 'conviviality' has been a major source of inspiration for degrowth theorists, starting with Serge Latouche (2010). From the perspective of degrowth, conviviality constitutes one of its core anthropological constructs; it represents faith in the possibility of space for relationships, recognition, pleasure and generally living well, and thereby, reduces the dependence on an industrial and consumerist system.

However, Illich did not use the term 'degrowth'. He believed that the inverse of a progressively modernized poverty was a form of 'modern existence', which he called 'convivial austerity'. This would be one process of political choice, 'to safeguard the freedom and use of convivial tools', and is very close to what we now mean by the prospect of voluntary degrowth:

> [L]et us call the modern subsistence the style of life that prevails in a post-industrial economy in which people have succeeded in reducing their market dependence, and have done so by protecting – by political means – a social infrastructure in which techniques and tools are used primarily to generate use-values that are unmeasured and un-measurable by professional need-makers.
>
> *(Illich 1978: 52)*

References

Borremans, V. (1979) *Guide to Convivial Tools*, Library Journal Special Report, 13, Preface by Ivan Illich, New York: R.R. Bowker Company.

Brillat-Savarin, J. A. (1825) *Physiologie du goût ou méditations de gastronomie transcendante*, Paris: A. Sautelet.

Illich, I. (1971) *Deschooling Society*, New York: Harper & Row.

Illich, I. (1973) *Tools for Conviviality*, Glasgow: Fontana/Collins.

Illich, I. (1978) *The Right to Useful Unemployment*, London: Marion Boyars.

Illich, I. (1978) *Toward a History of Needs*, New York: Pantheon.

Latouche, S. (2010) *Pour sortir de la société de consommation. Voix et voies de la décroissance*, Paris: Les liens qui libèrent Editions.

16

DEMATERIALIZATION

Sylvia Lorek

SUSTAINABLE EUROPE RESEARCH INSTITUTE

The term "dematerialization" refers to a reduction (in fact a tremendous reduction) in the quantity of materials used to serve the production and consumption needs of our planet. Dematerialization indicates how (much) our social **metabolism** has to decrease. Dematerializsation is an input-oriented strategy, which, in contrast to traditional 'end-of-pipe' measures, intends to tackle environmental problems at their source. The concept of dematerialization argues that current environmental problems (such as climate change and biodiversity loss) are closely related to the volume of material and energy used for the production of goods and services: if the input decreases the overall environmental impact will decrease as well.

Dematerialization is also intended as a response to the fact that the availability of non-renewable resources are coming to an end and that some important renewable resources, like fish and timber, show higher rates of consumption than their reproduction rate. Some indicative data:

- Extraction of "conventional" crude oil peaked in 2006; most major fields were discovered in the 1960s and production from them is declining at 4–6 percent per year (and "new" oil cannot keep up) (see **peak oil**).
- Sixty-three of the 89 non-renewable resources that enable high-tech industrial society had become globally scarce by 2008.
- Eighty-two percent of monitored fish-stocks were fully exploited or over-exploited by 2008 (32 percent are overexploited, up from 10 percent in the 1970s)
- Thirty percent of the world's arable land has become unproductive; soil erosion/ degradation continues at 10–40 times the rate of natural replenishment.

Dematerialization is often used in relation to the term decoupling and gets mixed up with it. Resource decoupling means reducing the rate of resource use per unit of economic activity measured in **GDP**. Decoupling generally refers to the economy and its activities while dematerialization takes the Earth's capacity and its limitations as the reference point. A general distinction exists between relative and absolute decoupling. Relative decoupling is achieved when resource use grows less then GDP. Absolute decoupling means that the economy grows but resource use remains at least stable or decreases. Dematerialization, as defined here, would show up as absolute decoupling, i.e. an absolute reduction in material and carbon use. The possibility of an absolute decoupling is often invoked, for example, in the visions of a "Factor 4"or "Factor 10" decline in the material or carbon intensity of the economy.

Such declines in resource use are expected by their advocates to happen through a significant increase in resource productivity compensating for any increase in resource consumption due to economic **growth**. Strategies to achieve an absolute decoupling include a variety of approaches like the development of new technologies and materials, resource productivity standards in construction, increasing durability and recycling of goods, and new, so-called "resource-extensive lifestyles." These developments require specific policy measures such as support for research and development, fostering of eco-efficient public procurement, and active support for the establishment of markets for dematerialized products and services. Other common proposals by advocates of decoupling are the internalization of external environmental costs, in particular through market-based instruments such as energy taxes or taxes on raw materials.

Some nations like Germany or the US claim to have managed an absolute decoupling of their economy (i.e. stabilizing resource use despite growing GDP) as a result of their resource efficiency programs. In reality, the consumption of materials and carbon in these countries increases. It is only that it takes place in countries from which they increasingly import material goods.

The impression of absolute decoupling results from the way material flows are accounted for. There is an ongoing global shift, whereby developed economies substitute domestic material extraction and processing as well as production processes with imported embodied material resources from developing and emerging countries (Peters et al, 2011). This raises a question of **environmental justice**. Regarding such physical trade balance between regions, Europe is the biggest shifter whereas Australia and Latin America are the largest takers of environmental burden. It is this shift that has created the impression of absolute decoupling in Europe.

To improve its data on material use, the European Environmental Agency has developed programs that calculate economies' material use not on the basis of production but on the basis of consumption. This means accounting the total material required (TMR) in all final products consumed within a nation and involves following resource consumption back all along the production chains – including investments in machinery and infrastructure as well (European Environment Agency 2013).

Most countries, however, do show a relative decoupling which means that material consumption is still increasing but at a pace slower than economic output. Globally material productivity increased by 37 percent from 1980 to 2008. **GDP** grew 147 percent, while material consumption grew by "only" 79 percent. Such relative decoupling, however, involved a tremendous further materialization of the global economy. Indicatively, during this same period, the global use of biomass increased by 35 percent, mineral extraction grew by 133 percent, fossil fuels went up 60 percent, and metals 89 percent. GHGs rose by 42 percent (Dittrich et al. 2012).

The technological and market-based solutions raised by the proponents of decoupling remain far from adequate for the scale of the challenge faced if population and income continue to grow. The sheer scale of action implied by continuous growth is daunting. In a world of 9 billion people all aspiring to Western lifestyles, the carbon intensity of every dollar of output must be at least 130 times lower in 2050 than it is today if we are to stay within the 350 ppm limit that scientists claim is necessary for avoiding dangerous climate change. By the end of the century, economic activity will need to be taking carbon out of the atmosphere not adding to it. This is made even more difficult if one considers the **Jevons' Paradox** and the possibility that money saved by efficiency gains are spent on other material/energy intensive goods. Efficiency gains might lead to more, rather than less, resource use.

In this context, more appropriate mechanisms for absolute dematerialization are carbon and resource caps, since these reduce the possibility of "leakages" and rebounds (see resource cap coalition). The aim of cap agreements is to realize an absolute reduction in resource use through resource allowances that get progressively lower year by year. This can constantly transform production and consumption patterns and prove incentives for innovations towards products and services with low material input. A planned resource cap can also contribute to re-localizing the economy with shorter economic cycles and higher self-sufficiency, favoring initiatives covered in this volume, such as **nowtopias**, **urban gardening**, or **back-to-the-landers**.

Slight adjustments within the system will not be enough to foster the radical reductions in the use of materials and carbon that are necessary, according to the precautionary principle, for staying within Earth's safe capacity. Dematerialization is unlikely in an economy that continues to grow. Instead a substantial degrowth is necessary to reduce our social **metabolism** to a sustainable **steady state** level. Caps are one politically sanctioned way to push for such degrowth.

References

Clugston, C. (2012) *Scarcity – humanity's final chapter?* Port Charlotte: Booklocker.

Dittrich, M., Giljum, S., Lutter, S., and Polzin, C. (2012) *Green economies around the world? – Implications for resource use for development and the environment.* Vienna: SERI.

European Environment Agency (2013) "Environmental pressures from European consumption and production." EEA Technical Report No 2/2013. Copenhagen.

Peters, G. P., Minx, J. C. Weber, C. L., and Edenhofer, O. (2011) "Growth in emission transfers via international trade from 1990 to 2008." Proceedings of the National Academy of Sciences, 108(21): 8903–8.

17

DÉPENSE

Onofrio Romano

DEPARTMENT OF POLITICAL SCIENCES, UNIVERSITY OF BARI "A. MORO"

Energy consumption consists of two parts. The first is necessary for the conservation and the reproduction of life. The second is used for non-productive expenditures: luxury, mourning, war, religion, games, spectacles, the arts, perverse sexual activity. All told, these activities – qualified as *dépense* – are ends in themselves. Any society has an excess of energy, defined precisely as all that energy that is not needed for the mere reproduction of life.

In a wider sense, which includes nature, *dépense* indicates that share of energy which cannot be employed by living organisms, owing to their physiological limits. This portion continues to circulate aimlessly in the environment up until the point where it extinguishes itself.

George Bataille introduces this definition of excess energy in his essay "The Idea of *Dépense*" appearing for the first time in *La Critique Sociale* (1/1933). As with all of Bataille's theoretical constructs, the contents and contours of *dépense* are flexible and never defined in axiomatic categories. There are seven different versions of this essay alone. Bataille eventually attempted to construct a theoretical project for a "general economy" departing from the notion of *dépense*. The first fragmentary versions of it appear in the essays *L'Économie à la mesure de l'univers* (1946) and *La limite de l'utile* (posthumously published in the complete works, 1976). The project was fully born in the work *La part maudite* (1949). A second part to this work followed with the title *Histoire de l'érotisme* (1957) and then a final third part entitled *La Souveraineté* (Bataille 1976). Some resonances with *dépense* can be found in the Freudian concepts of *Vergänglichkeit* (transience) and the death impulse (Freud 1990) but mainly in Marcel Mauss' analysis of *potlach* in *The Gift* (1925). All these works deal with a perturbing tendency of human beings and societies toward loss, reversing their alleged "natural" vocation to self-advance.

From an anthropological framework, energy could be redefined as the fuel of action, that is, the fuel that calls us to act. The portion of energy that a living being employs for either sustenance or biological growth, Bataille terms "servile." In fact, mere biological sustenance can be achieved spending only a miniscule portion of the total amount of available energy. The basic problem relates to the residual energy that exceeds the share devoted to such servile use. Excess energy requires a "sovereign" use: it is necessary to choose a destination for the fuel of action on the basis of the philosophical intent of a political prospect (Romano 2014). It is the sovereign employment of excess energy that qualifies us as "humans." The different patterns of excess energy use characterize and distinguish different types of societies across space and time. Excess can be spent on sacrifice or festival, in war or in peace. The Tibetan society, for example, almost entirely employs excess energy to support a specific class of monk.

The human encounter with excess energy is a crucial moment. In this sense, excess energy is an "accursed share": it forces human beings to question the meaning of life and their path in the world. The non-use of excess energy would signal the incapacity of human beings to exercise their own freedom. For this reason, all human societies have designed forms of ritual for *dépense* – that is, forms of destruction of that energy which lies beyond the servile.

These forms of ritual have different degrees of sophistication and respond to different functions:

- They serve to humanize excess waste, bringing it from the dominion of uncontrolled natural processes into the realm of culture and the symbolic.
- They release energy from the utilitarian dimension (the biological-functional) to access the sacred – in fact, the destruction of the objects is aimed to destroy their servile status as useful things, in order to relocate them in the realm of the sacred (this is the true meaning of sacrifice: producing sacred things through their ritual destruction).
- They physically delete the stressful presence of excess and therefore, the call to be and to act.

The concept of *dépense* helps identify a main hole in the "society of **growth**." How should we go about the removal of the problem of energy and excess? The worship of the servile moment is in fact at the foundation of this society. Modernity arose in a context of existential emergency and fear for the survival of the species, unleashed by an unexpected demographic explosion (and therefore an increase of social needs) that was incompatible with the productive capacities of the communities of the time. This imbalance resulted in the deconstruction of traditional communities whose symbolic codes did not permit them to confront the new challenge. In order to satisfy their unfulfilled needs, individuals tried to break bonds with their communities and to autonomously take up new and more effective, **growth**-oriented, courses of action. For Europe, Riesman (1950) dates this crucial demographic shift, and its social consequences, to the seventeenth century.

The process of individualization deprived communities of their ability to manage energy. This included *dépense* rituals that burned off excess energy. Still imprinted by this "original emergency" of survival, modern society continues its **growth** momentum without stopping. Making permanent the original emergency situation removes the problem of excess energy, so we avoid confronting the "meaning" of action. Perpetually in pursuit of survival (which requires continuous **growth**), we are liberated from the state of paralysis when faced with the necessity of "being," which arises from the emergence of excess energy. In other words, remaining animal frees us from the fatigue of becoming human. At the same time, we expunge *dépense* from the "official" public forum. Instead it is "privatized" and hidden in shame (as any "wasting" activity becomes morally incompatible with the alleged perpetual state of emergency).

Given the individualization of society, single individuals take on the burden of waste through small trade-offs: from perverse sexuality to alcoholism, gambling and flashy consumption – what Bataille called the "vulgar eructation" of the petty bourgeoisie. In the era of **growth** there is no longer sumptuous and collective *dépense*, only its private dissolution informally consumed. Hence modern societies try to solve the problem of energy with a twofold strategy: they first expand to an unprecedented level their servile use (i.e. the **growth** obsession), and second they privatize *dépense*. But this strategy appears inadequate for the crucial cause of putting the available energy to work. A large amount of energy remains unused; it continues to circulate and to stress human beings. Lacking tools of deliberate and symbolic catastrophe (i.e. the ritual collective *dépense*), the inhabitants of **growth** societies begin to dream and to desire a "real" natural catastrophe.

Dépense is a key concept, then, for theorizing a way out of the **growth** society. Yet, paradoxically, it does not figure among the epistemological pillars of mainstream theories of degrowth, nor is it a source of inspiration for the movement of growth objectors. This is perhaps because truly embracing *dépense* would entail the dismantling of a cognitive frame of catastrophe and scarcity that is at the basis of the degrowth paradigm. In light of *dépense*, the catastrophe threat haunting Western societies is only a symptom of the failed disposal of excess energy. For degrowth supporters it is a "real" risk. Degrowth thought is therefore implicitly subordinated to the dominant culture, one that justifies neoliberal capitalist restructuring. It denounces a shortage of resources necessary to sustain contemporary lifestyles and indeed acts out a mere reversal of the foundational problem of the **growth** society. According to Bataille:

> [A]s a rule, *particular* existence always risks succumbing for lack of resources. It contrasts with *general* existence whose resources are in excess and for which death has no meaning. From the *particular* point of view, the problems are posed *in the first instance* by a deficiency of resources. They are posed *in the first instance* by an excess of resources if one starts from the *general* point of view.
>
> *(Bataille 1988: 39)*

The individualized being is bound by the precarious nature of its existence and therefore obsessed with the problem of its survival. When isolated, it embraces a fundamentally servile position and reverts to the status of an animal, in which obtaining resources is central. The challenge of excess energy becomes visible only if we are able to relocate our point of view to a systemic level. Degrowth supporters do little more than transfer the servile position typical of the individualized subject to the general system; humanity's complexity becomes subject to "the rule of needs," supported by a utilitarian logic of survival. The individual point of view that emphasizes the insufficiency of resources gets applied to the general collective.

As a result, the theory of degrowth risks to reanimate and give new momentum to the basic precept of economics, that is, the principle of scarcity. It risks mirroring the myth of **growth** by using the same imaginary from a reversed viewpoint, an imaginary that entails the employment of all the energy in circulation for the preservation of existence, this time round by means of "virtuous" lifestyles and efficient techniques. The degrowth project could gain a wider breath and appeal by emphasizing instead its concern towards the collective construction of meaning in life and the restoration of political sovereignty. That is the only way for us moderns to face the challenge of excess energy.

References

Bataille, G. (1933) "La notion de dépense." *La Critique Sociale*, 1: 7.

Bataille, G. (1946) "L'Économie à la mesure de l'univers." In *Œuvres complètes* (1976), vol. 7. Paris: Gallimard.

Bataille, G. (1949) "La Part maudite." In *Œuvres complètes* (1976), vol. 7. Paris: Gallimard.

Bataille, G. (1957) "Histoire de l'érotisme." In *Œuvres complètes* (1976). vol. 8. Paris: Gallimard.

Bataille, G. (1976) *Oeuvres completes, Tome VIII.* Paris: Gallimard.

Bataille, G. (1988) *The accursed share. An essay on general economy vol. I Consumption.* New York: Zone Books.

Freud, S. (1990) *Beyond the pleasure principle.* New York: W. W. Norton & Company.

Riesman, D. (1950) *The lonely crowd.* New Haven: Yale University Press.

Romano, O. (2014) *The sociology of knowledge in a time of crises. Challenging the phantom of liberty.* London & New York: Routledge.

18

DEPOLITICIZATION ('THE POLITICAL')

Erik Swyngedouw

DEPARTMENT OF GEOGRAPHY, SCHOOL OF ENVIRONMENT, EDUCATION, AND DEVELOPMENT,
UNIVERSITY OF MANCHESTER

'The political' is the contested public terrain where different imaginings of possible socio-ecological orders compete over the symbolic and material institutionalization of these visions. Indeed, the terrain of struggle over political-ecological futures – a terrain that makes visible and perceptible the heterogeneous views and desires that cut through the social body – and how to achieve this is precisely what constitutes the terrain of 'the political'. The political refers, therefore, to a broadly shared public space, an idea of living together, and signals the absence of a foundational or essential point (in nature, the social, science, the cultural, or in political philosophy) on which to base a polity or a society. The political is an immanent domain of agonistic practice.

Transformative politics in the direction of 'de-growth' therefore require particular forms of politicization adequate to the situation the world is currently in.

However, while the normative view of the need for 'de-growth' substantiates its claims on the basis of the analysis of the entropic energetic imbalances of capitalist metabolisms of nature, and the socio-ecological inequalities and conflicts that inhere in these processes, the transformation of a 'growth' to a 'de-growth' based socio-ecological configuration has to extend its concern from 'scientific' and social arguments to consider the political.

I consider politics or policy-making, in contrast to the political, to refer to the power plays between political actors and the everyday choreographies of negotiating, formulating, and implementing rules and practices within a given institutional and procedural configuration in which individuals and groups pursue their interests. Politics, then, in the forms of the institutions and technologies of governing, and the tactics, strategies, and power relations related to conflict intermediation and the furthering of particular partisan interests, contingently institute society and give society some (instable) form and temporal coherence.

Politics as public management stands in contrast to the political as the sphere of agonistic dispute and struggle over the environments we wish to inhabit and on how to produce them. There is a tendency for the first to suture, and ultimately disavow or foreclose, the former. This process is marked by a colonisation of the political by politics or the sublimation of the political by replacing it with 'community' (as an imagined undivided unity), a particular sociological **imaginary** of 'the people' (as nation, ethnic group, or other social category), 'organization', 'management', 'good governance'. In the current de-politicizing neoliberal climate, the public management of things and people is hegemonically articulated around a naturalization of the need for **economic growth** – the unquestioned mobilization of market relations and forces as the only possible mode of accessing, transforming, and distributing (transformed) nature – and **capitalism** as the only reasonable and possible form of organization of socio-natural metabolism. This foreclosure of the political in terms of at least recognizing the legitimacy of dissenting voices and positions constitutes a process of de-politicization. In other words, de-politicization takes the form of the increasing domination of a series of inter-related managerial and technical forms of governance aimed at maintaining and nurturing **growth** and understood as the uninterrupted accumulation of economic wealth (see Swyngedouw, 2011). For example, the dominant ecological concern today is one whereby sustainable development refers primarily to the mobilisation of technical and institutional configurations, like the Kyoto protocol to mitigate climate change, whereby the aim is to make ecological concerns compatible with a capitalist growth-based economy 'so that nothing really has to change' (Swyngedouw 2010: 222). The wider framework of neoliberal **growth** is in itself not contestable. Consider, for example, how the post-2008 crisis was governed by the assembled national and international elites in ways that permitted the survival and ultimate strengthening of the accumulation process and restoration of **economic growth**. It is precisely this condition that disavows, or rather, forecloses the agonistic appearance of dissenting voices or alternative visions that many have come to identify with post-democratic forms of managing the existing order. It is a process marked by the twin imperatives of the de-politicization of the economy (i.e. neoliberal **capitalism** cannot be disputed within the existing registers of dominant politics) and the economization of politics (i.e. rendering every domain of public concern subject to market rule and economic calculus).

The challenge for politicizing de-growth, then, is to think and practise the re-emergence of the political in an age of post-democratic de-politicization. The political cannot be suppressed indefinitely. It returns invariably as an immanent practice that revolves around the tropes of emergence, insurrection, equality, and theatrical staging of egalitarian being-in-common. The re-emergence of the political unfolds through a procedure of interruption in the state of the situation: a riot, a rebellion, an insurgency, or the politicized staging of new practices of being-in-common. It is always specific, concrete, particular, but stands as the metaphorical condensation of the universal. This procedure implies the production of new egalitarian material and discursive socio-ecological spatialities within and through the existing spatialities of the existing order. It asserts dissensus as the base for politics, and operates through the (re-)appropriation of space and the production of new socio-ecological qualities and new socio-ecological relations (Wilson and Swyngedouw 2014).

Examples of such emergent forms of embryonic re-politicization can be discerned in the variegated insurgent activism and proliferating manifestations of radical discontent, such as the **Indignados** in Spain, the **Occupy!** movement, and a range of other insurgencies as well as by the fledgling de-growth movement and assorted other activist mobilisations articulated around more equitable, socially inclusive, and ecologically more appropriate sensibilities. What marks these hesitant returns of 'the political' is precisely that these movements operate outside the registers of actually existing (democratic or otherwise) policy-making or politics. In other words, politicization operates, as Miguel Abensour argues, at a distance from the state. Moreover, the claims and demands voiced by such new political agents stage a claim for equality in a context whereby unequal socio-ecological conditions prevail.

In a context of neoliberal de-politicization, a re-politicization of socio-ecological matters requires urgent and strategic thought. First, rather than embracing the postmodern obsession with identitarian politics and celebrating the diversity of possible modes of being, or celebrating the micro-politics of dispersed resistances and individualized alternative practices, it is important to foreground division and exclusion, and emphasize 'the political act' and a fidelity to a political truth procedure that necessitates taking sides while aspiring to universalization. The latter refers to a politicizing process whereby everybody is invited in (although by no means all will accept the invitation). Insurgent egalitarian performances, if they are to be effective, transgress the fantasy of the sort of acting that calls upon 'resistance' as a positive injunction. The act of resistance ('I have to resist the process of, say, unlimited **growth**, neoliberalization, globalization, or **capitalism**, or otherwise the city, the world, the environment, the poor will suffer') just answers the call of power in its post-democratic guise. Resistant acting is actually what is invited, but leaves the police order intact. Politics understood merely as rituals of resistance is doomed to fail politically. Resistance and nurturing conflict, as the ultimate horizon of many social movements, has become a subterfuge that masks what is truly at stake, i.e. the inauguration of a different socio-ecological, post-capitalist order.

Therefore, and second, attention needs to turn to the modalities of re-politicization. Re-politicization as an intervention in the state of the situation that transforms and transgresses the symbolic orders of the existing condition marks a shift from the old to a new situation, one that cannot any longer be thought of in terms of the old symbolic framings. Politicization is thus about inaugurating practices that lie beyond the symbolic order of the existing post-democratic arrangement and, therefore, would necessitate transformation in and of the existing order to permit symbolization to occur. The most promising politicizing moments of the de-growth movement reside precisely in sustaining and nurturing such tactics.

Third, the proper response to the injunction (by the elites) to undertake action, to design the new, to be creative (in a neoliberal sense), to be different, is the refusal to act. Time after time, the population is invited to act in certain ways, to recycle waste, to reduce ecological footprints, sustaining the myth that such individualized consumer practices will nudge the socio-ecological order in a more equitable and ecologically sensible direction, while, in fact, making sure that nothing really happens. Such refusal to act is also an invitation to think or, rather, to think again. There is an urgent task that requires the formation of new egalitarian **imaginaries** or fantasies and the resurrection of emancipatory thought that has been censored, scripted out, suspended.

All this centres on re-thinking equality politically, i.e. thinking equality not as a sociologically verifiable concept or procedure that permits opening a policy arena which will remedy the observed inequalities (utopian/normative/moral) some time in a utopian future, but as the axiomatically given and presupposed, albeit contingent, condition of the democratic political; equality appears in its performative staging. One should insist on the equality of each and all in their capacity to take active part in the production of life-in-common in an egalitarian and free manner. Achieving this requires, foremost, the radical politicization of the manner through which we organize access, transformation, and distribution of socio-ecological things and services. Indeed, traversing consensual elite fantasies requires the intellectual and political courage to imagine radically the collective production of equitable and common socio-ecological spatialities. It also requires the inauguration of new political trajectories of living life-in-**common**, and, most importantly, the courage to choose, to take sides, to declare fidelity to the egalibertarian practices already pre-figured in some of the place-moments that mark the emergent political landscapes of which the de-growth movement is an integral part. In that sense, we have to reclaim socio-ecological egalibertarian practices as an utmost necessity for today. De-growth and egalitarian democratization are indeed, of necessity, interlinked.

References

Abensour, M. (2011). *Democracy Against the State*. Cambridge: Polity Press.
Badiou, A. (2012). *The Rebirth of History*. London: Verso.
Rancière, J. (1998). *Disagreement*. Minneapolis: University of Minnesota Press.
Swyngedouw, E. (2010). 'Trouble with Nature: Ecology as the New Opium for the People'. in Hillier, J. and P. Healey (eds). *In Conceptual Challenges for Planning Theory*, Farnham: Aldershot.
Swyngedouw, E. (2011). 'Interrogating Post-Democracy: Reclaiming Egalitarian Political Spaces'. *Political Geography*, 30, 370–80.
Wilson, J. and E. Swyngedouw (2014). *The Post-Political and its Discontents: Spaces of Depoliticization, Specters of Radical Politics*. Edinburgh: Edinburgh University Press.

19

DISASTER, PEDAGOGY OF

Serge Latouche

FACULTÉ DE DROIT, ÉCONOMIE ET GESTION JEAN MONNET, UNIVERSITÉ PARIS-SUD

Denis de Rougemont, one of the early pioneers of ecology, wrote in 1977:

> [I] feel it coming, a series of disasters created through our diligent yet
> unconscious efforts. If they're big enough to wake up the world, but not
> enough to smash everything, I 'd call them learning experiences, the only
> ones able to overcome our inertia.
>
> *(de Rougemont cited in Partant 1979)*

Partant's idea expressed in their citation, based on the popular concept that
experience provides lessons, is both shockingly radical and fatalistic. At the same
time, one might doubt its effectiveness. Yet, with the publication of Jean-Pierre
Dupuy's book, *For a Crystalizing Catastrophe* (2002), it has experienced a revival.

Dictionaries define disasters as a sudden and fateful misfortune to a person or
people. An example of a disaster would include an accident that causes the death
of many people: a rail or air disaster. Literally this would be: "a decisive event
that brings about a tragedy." The catastrophes or disasters that concern us here are
those of the Anthropocene, that is, those generated by the dynamics of a complex system, the biosphere, in co-evolution with human activity and altered by it:
Chernobyl or Fukushima, but also climate change or the collapse of biodiversity.
To bring about the decolonization of the **imaginary** needed to change the fatal
path we are on we can hardly rely on such "disaster lessons." Yet François Partant,
guru of the French alternatives and a harbinger of degrowth, counted on such
threats for a "jump start" out of the madness of the productivist society. It is not by
chance that he titled one of his books, provocatively, *May the Crisis Deepen!* In this
1978 book he argued that a profound crisis would be the only way to prevent the
self-destruction of humanity.

Is this vision catastrophic? Worshipers of progress immediately accuse anyone who reflects on the dangers that threaten our civilization of pessimism. It's true that pedagogy of disaster was born in the course of discussions concerning nuclear apocalypse, following the experience of the first atomic bombs. I think here particularly of the books of Karl Jaspers or Gunther Anders. It's also related to the thesis of collapse, a theme popularized by Jared Diamond (2005) but already developed 20 years earlier by Joseph Tainter (1988). A civilization disappears, according to Diamond, when it destroys its environment without being able to adapt to the new situation. Complex societies, for Tainter, tend to collapse because their strategies for obtaining energy are subject to the law of diminishing returns.

Disaster pedagogy falls in line with philosopher Hans Jonas' "heuristics of fear" according to which "it is better to lend an ear to the prophecy of misfortune than to that of happiness" (1990: 54). He does not masochistically hope for a taste of the apocalypse, but precisely to ward it off. His is an alternative to the suicidal optimism of "a politics of ostriches." It is this latter blissful (and passive) optimism that will lead us more certainly to disaster than an attitude of a crystalizing catastrophe.

In this, disaster pedagogy joins the more recent analyses of philosopher Jean-Pierre Dupuy. Isn't he also into a form of disaster pedagogy? Dupuy refers to Hans Jonas giving to his catastrophism a learning role. However, in his conception, it isn't the catastrophe itself that teaches, it is its anticipation. Dupuy proposed a *method* of governance for the technocrats, an experience of thought suggesting precaution in the face of major technological risk, especially nuclear risk. This disaster pedagogy aims to prevent the irreparable and in particular to prevent a collapse or final catastrophe. Neither of these two approaches expresses a wish for the worst. Both are intended to avert it. The first is based on experience and the shock experienced from warning crises, while the second wants to do without them.

It is natural to wonder whether the lessons of a tragic experience, such as Fukushima, are actually useful. Naomi Klein (2008), in her famous work, *The Shock Doctrine: The Rise of Disaster Capitalism* supports a vision radically opposed to that of a beneficial disaster. According to her, the neo-liberal and neo-conservative oligarchy takes advantage of disasters, or provokes them, to impose its solutions, which become disastrous for the lower classes but profitable, in the short term, for multinationals. Her book opens with the devastation of Louisiana by Hurricane Katrina and the calamitous management of the disaster by the Bush administration: destruction of the public school system, urban exclusion of the poor, unbridled speculation for reconstruction. Many other examples, from September 11, 2001, to the war in Iraq, are analysed in her text and reinforce a very convincing argument.

In fact, the two theses, the pedagogy of disaster and the exploitation of disasters for profit, are not mutually exclusive. The reason isn't that humanity needs to become wiser. The point is that the capitalist oligarchy has to be disarmed and neutralized. Depending on the context, in some cases, lobbies will prevail in the face of disasters. In others, people's pressure can impose life-saving solutions and changes against the wishes of these lobbies.

References

Diamond, Jared (2005) *Collapse, How Societies Chose to Fail or Succeed*, Harmondsworth: Peguin.

Dupuy, J-P. (2002) *Pour un catastrophisme éclairé. Quand l'impossible est certain*, Paris: Seuil.

Jonas, H. (1984) *The Imperative of Responsibility: In Search of Ethics for the Technological Age*, Chicago: University of Chicago Press.

Jonas, H. (1990) *Le principe responsabilité, une éthique pour la civilisation technologique*, Paris: Editions du Cerf.

Klein, N. (2007) *The Shock Doctrine: The Rise of Disaster Capitalism*, Toronto: Knopf Canada.

Partant, F. (1978) *Que la crise s'aggrave!* Paris: Parangon.

Tainter, J. (1988) *The Collapse of Complex Societies*, Cambridge: Cambridge University Press.

20

ENTROPY

Sergio Ulgiati

DEPARTMENT OF SCIENCES FOR THE ENVIRONMENT, PARTHENOPE UNIVERSITY OF NAPLES

Entropy, a measure of energy and resource degradation, is one of the basic concepts of Thermodynamics. Its definition requires a closer look at the concept of energy, usually defined as the capacity for doing mechanical work or, in a broader sense, the "ability to drive a system's transformation," which includes all kinds of physical, chemical, and biological transformations. While driving a process transformation, energy loses its ability to do it again, i.e. energy is conserved (in the form of heat) but some of the characteristics that made it capable to support the process are irreversibly lost (e.g. gradients of concentration, temperature, pressure, height, information). A similar definition and behavior also applies to material resources, not only energy, that are capable of supporting processes thanks to the dissipation of their gradients relative to the natural background. During a real process the gradient is lost, not the matter or the heat, which are, instead, conserved. The decreased ability to do work is what is broadly referred to as "entropy." The conservation of energy can be restated as "conservation of heat" (First Law of Thermodynamics), while the loss of ability to support processes pertains to the entropy concept and the impossibility of 100 percent converting heat into work, supporting the concept of "available energy," namely the amount of energy that can be actually converted.

The concept of entropy originated during the Industrial Revolution in England (beginning of the eighteenth to the second half of the nineteenth century). The development of steam-powered machines (to pump water out of coal mines and to convert coal combustion heat into work) was the starting point of huge technological and scientific research. These studies yielded a general framework for energy conversion processes, known as the Laws of Thermodynamics, describing the main principles underlying any energy transformation. Carnot in 1824 first understood and stated the constraints to the conversion of heat into work, which then received a stronger mathematical formulation by Clausius in 1850 and Thomson in 1851 (also known as Lord Kelvin). Entropy was also related to the probability of a state (Boltzmann 1872), and the natural evolution from less probable (more organized, higher concentration, higher quality) states to more probable (less organized, more diluted, lower quality) states, evolution that can only be countered by providing available energy from outside the system. Later on, the term "entropy" was also used in the economy with reference to resource degradation, namely a loss of the concentration, structure, and information content of materials and the impossibility of their full recovery (Georgescu-Roegen 1971).

The state of a system, called A, is always characterized by an entropy value, S_A, with reference to a standard state, S_0. When an energy conversion occurs, the system moves to a new state, B, characterized by a different entropy value, S_B. The new value depends on the heat exchange with the surrounding environment and the temperature of such exchange. Depending on the direction of the heat transfer, the entropy of the system may decrease or increase, while the entropy of the surrounding environment would have the opposite behavior. The variation of entropy in an irreversible transformation between two states, A and B, is always higher than for reversible ones (real processes in nature are always irreversible). If a system is isolated, i.e. it has no exchange of energy (or matter) with the surrounding environment the so-called entropy law emerges: "If an isolated system undergoes a transformation from an initial state A to a final state B, the entropy of the final state is never lower than the entropy of the initial state," which means that entropy always increases. This is the case of a dead organism, unable to use external energy to fight the entropic degradation. A building would have the same behavior and requires input energy from outside (maintenance) to prevent its entropy from increasing. Photosynthesis is a typical case: plants receive energy from the sun and use it to build polymers, i.e. decrease their entropy at the expenses of the increasing entropy of the outside environment.

What happens when entropy increases? What does it mean in practical terms? From a strictly thermodynamic point of view, the increase of a system's entropy measures the amount of energy (or material resource) no longer usable to support any further process evolution. When all the energy of a system becomes unusable, no more system transformations are possible. As a consequence, the word "entropy" is often used with less constrained and looser meanings than in the scientific community, being generally associated with disorder, lack of organization, indefiniteness, physical and social degradation, lower quality, and lower usefulness. It supports concepts of decreasing availability of high quality resources, increasing pollution due to waste, chemicals, and heat release into the environment, increasing social disorder due to degraded conditions of life in mega-cities all around the world, collapsing economies, and calls for increased attention to appropriate resource use and prevention of natural and human environment degradation (i.e. loss of stored information).

The economist Nicholas Georgescu-Roegen (1971) stressed the applicability of the entropy concept to matter degradation identified as a Fourth Principle of

Thermodynamics (see **bioeconomics**). Matter is valuable for production and consumption in that it is concentrated and organized. Use processes slowly degrade matter by decreasing these two properties: matter dilutes into the environment and loses structure. Recovering the diluted matter (e.g. metal atoms lost by metal coins) would require huge (infinite) amounts of energy, which makes recovery almost impossible. The Fourth Principle gave rise to a heated debate about its applicability and foundations (e.g. Khalil 1990) and might be rather recognized as a special case of the Second Principle (Bianciardi et al. 1993). Yet, its underlining rationale laid the foundations for a thermodynamically based culture of the limits to **growth** and the development of **bioeconomics** as opposed to neoclassical economics.

Matter and energy degradation is countered by a constant inflow of solar energy as well as other renewable sources of deep heat and tidal momentum. These powerful driving forces, at the basis of Odum's **emergy** concept, provide support to biosphere self-organization, out of disordered materials, only constrained by the available sources and sinks. During the self-organization process, entropy is generated and released towards the outer space as degraded heat. This point of view, less scaring than a perspective of total collapse, calls for adaptation to the style of Nature, by recognizing the existence of oscillations (growth and degrowth) and resource constraints (limits to **growth**), within which many options and patterns are still possible. As a consequence, we would do a disservice to the entropy concept, by limiting its significance to the concept of disorder and degradation. Provided the biosphere constraints are respected, life processes (such as photosynthesis) build organization, create new structures, assemble materials, upgrade energy, and create new information by also degrading input resources. The latter becomes again available for new life cycles, ultimately driven (and limited) by the entropic degradation of solar energy.

References

Bianciardi, C., Tiezzi, E., and Ulgiati, S. (1993) "Complete recycling of matter in the framework of physiscs, biology and ecological economics." *Ecological Economics*, 8: 1–5.

Boltzmann, L. (1872) "Further studies on the thermal equilibrium of gas molecules" ("Weitere Studien über das Wärmegleichgewicht unter Gasmolekülen") In *Sitzungsberichte der Akademie der Wissenschaften, Mathematische-Naturwissenschaftliche Klasse* (pgs. 275–370), Bd. 66, Dritte Heft, Zweite Abteilung, Vienna: Gerold.

Georgescu-Roegen, N. (1971) *The entropy law and the economic process.* Cambridge, MA : Harvard University Press.

Khalil, E. L. (1990) "Entropy Law and exhaustion of natural resources: is Georgescu-Roegen's paradigm defensible?" *Ecol. Econ.*, 2: 163–78.

Thomson, W. (1851) "On the dynamical theory of heat; with numerical results deduced from Mr. Joule's equivalent of a thermal unit and M. Regnault's observations on steam." *Math. and Phys. Papers* 1: 175–83.

21

EMERGY

Sergio Ulgiati

DEPARTMENT OF SCIENCES FOR THE ENVIRONMENT, PARTHENOPE UNIVERSITY OF NAPLES

Emergy, defined as the total amount of available energy (usually of the solar kind) that is directly and indirectly invested by the environment in a process, was suggested as a scientific measure of the biosphere's work in support of life processes on Earth (Odum 1988, 1996). Within such a "donor-side" perspective, the "value" of a resource relies on the effort that is displayed for its generation by nature and processing by society, over an evolutionary "trial and error" process that ensures the optimization of a resource cycle. Mainstream economic theories address the concept of value in monetary terms (willingness to pay, i.e. a user-side value), while emergy-based value is related to the amount of primary resources (solar energy, geothermal heat, etc) invested by nature for sustainable generation and cycling (generation of oil and uptake of carbon dioxide emissions requires the same photosynthetic activity, independently of how much are we willing to pay for an oil barrel: supply-side value). The emergy accounting method is therefore a technique of quantitative evaluation that determines the environmental value of non-marketed and marketed resources, services, commodities, and storages in common units of cumulative solar energy (seJ, solar equivalent joules) required to make a given product or service.

Solar radiation, gravitational potential and deep earth heat are the driving forces that keep the biosphere able to develop and operate, by supporting matter and information cycles. It is through cycling that systems maintain themselves far from thermodynamic equilibrium, adaptive and vital (e.g., the carbon cycle: trees generate leaves out of carbon dioxide through photosynthesis; dead leaves degrade in the ground and generate topsoil organic matter, which in turn is metabolized by microorganisms and becomes CO_2 again. Cycling applies to water, nitrogen, phosphorus, and all ecosystems components at all scales and turnover times). Emergy is not energy; it uses the driving energies as a measure of the environmental support to processes; the emergy accounting includes energy and mineral resources, time, and ecosystems services. By concentrating minerals in the earth crust, and by circulating air, water, and nutrients, the environmental flows of solar radiation, gravitational potential, and deep heat generate and keep operating the life support system within which organisms, species, populations, and entire communities interact and develop over time. Ecosystems supported by these environmental driving forces provide direct services to all species, and also contribute to build resource storages for future use: a) slow-renewable storages such as ground water, topsoil, standing biomass and biodiversity; b) non-renewable storages such as fossil fuels and minerals (the terms slow-renewable and non-renewable are relative to the lifespan of human societies).

The emergy procedure accounts for resources inflows, assigns them supply-side quality factors (named transformities or Unit Emergy Values, UEV) based on their role and cost within the environmental dynamics, and generates performance indicators that link economic performance, resource availability, environmental integrity, and the final products. A set of performance indices and ratios can be accordingly introduced in order to account for the different features of a process or system evolution: local versus outside resources, renewable versus nonrenewable, efficient versus inefficient, diffuse versus concentrated, resource-based versus monetary-based trade balance, static versus dynamic, among others. For example, the emergy method accounts for resource trade in terms of their embodied environmental cost, not in terms of their monetary value (as with economic terms of trade): even when the economic balance is approximately even, the environmental balance may not; developing countries exporting primary raw resources for money lose environmental wealth and work potential, that could have been used within in support of their economies; such loss is not generally compensated by the emergy equivalent of the money received (i.e. the emergy value of the small amounts of manufactured resources purchased in the international market using this money).

Economic activities release new flows and develop new storages. Oil is converted into electricity and transportation services; minerals are converted into infrastructures, machinery and cities; electricity, machinery, and infrastructures are in turn converted into educational, health, and recreational services. In so doing, new storages of information are created (universities, libraries, arts and museums, know how and, over longer time frames, entire cultures, religions, languages) that in turn become the basis for further development of societal system and, at the same time, feedback to the lower hierarchical levels to expand or stabilize the resource basis.

Pointing out that human societies feed on natural capital withdrawal and use different kinds of ecosystem services, Odum (1988, 1996) identified natural capital and ecosystem services as the real source of wealth, in alternative to and complement of the common belief that only labor and economic capital can be such a source. Traditional energy or economic analyses usually don't take into account inputs they cannot evaluate on a monetary or energy basis. Only monetary values are recognized by the market, but economies rely upon very large inputs from environment: if these inputs are not considered and given an appropriate value, misuse of resources can follow and future prospects for the system cannot be inferred. While it is impossible to measure most of these human-dominated flows in a way that captures their complex value, it is much easier to assess their "production cost" and generate a hierarchy of value in the biosphere processes by means of the emergy concept. Emergy advocates a different concept of value, rooted in the cost of production of resources by nature: the "effort" displayed by nature to generate resources in favor of a much larger set of users, all species on Earth, not only humans in the marketplace. Maximizing market value in the eyes of humans jeopardizes survival patterns for other species. Emergy demands optimization – not maximization – and policy choices that address the rights of all species and the quality of resources in terms of what it takes (energy, time, materials) to make them, even if this may not be recognized by market value assessments.

Natural processes have been selected over long biological timeframes and have tuned their use rate in accordance to the available flow of resources. Unfortunately, after the discovery of fossil energies, human societies have learned how to exploit resources at a higher rate than they are replaced; this raises the problem of their sustainability versus the biosphere carrying capacity and the available storages.

Economic **growth** and performance are day-by-day increasingly affected by environmental problems and constraints (climate change, energy shortage and supply, loss of biodiversity, lack of fresh water) that cannot be fully addressed in monetary terms. The total emergy driving a process becomes a measure of the self-organization activity of the planet. Such a measure provides the maximum size allowed for system's growth, i.e. represents the upper limit to the carrying capacity of the biosphere.

Environmental constraints and general systems principles force all kind of systems through cycles of growth, climax, descent, and restoration (pulsing paradigm). Accordingly Odum and Odum (2001) have designed patterns of a prosperous way down ("descent", or what in this book may be called "degrowth") for the present civilization, pointing out sustainability to be the capacity to adapt to resource oscillations rather than to reach a **steady state** to be sustained forever. Forest ecosystems with short pulsing cycles with tree blossoming and growing in spring, making fruits and seeds (stored information) in summer, losing leaves in autumn (for recycling by soil microorganisms), and recovering in winter-time, when available resources (solar energy) are reduced. Very similar resource-dependent patterns characterize all other systems and living species on Earth, including humans. As pointed out by Odum and Odum (2001), it is difficult for us to recognize societal cycles of which we are part, characterized by longer pulsing "wave-length"; instead, we easily identify the shorter pulsing cycles of ecosystems. Degrowth and resource optimization are properly addressed by the emergy method, due to its focus of embodied time and quality.

References

Brown, M. T. and Ulgiati, S. (2011) "Understanding the Global Economic crisis: A Biophysical Perspective," *Ecological Modelling*, 223(1): 4–13.

Odum, H. T. (1988) 'Self Organization, Transformity and Information," *Science*, 242: 1,132–9.

Odum, H. T. (1996) *Environmental Accounting. Emergy and Environmental Decision Making*. New York, NY: Wiley.

Odum, H. T. and Odum, E. C. (2001) *A Prosperous Way Down: Principles and Policies*, Boulder, CO: University Press of Colorado.

22

GROSS DOMESTIC PRODUCT

Dan O'Neill

SUSTAINABILITY RESEARCH INSTITUTE, UNIVERSITY OF LEEDS

Gross domestic product (GDP) is an indicator of economic activity. It measures the total value of all final goods and services that are newly produced within the borders of a country over the course of a year. Its predecessor, gross national product (GNP), was initially developed in the 1930s to help America get out of the Great Depression. At the time, the government lacked comprehensive data on the state of the economy, making it difficult to know whether policy responses were working or not. Russian-American economist Simon Kuznets prepared the first set of national GNP accounts. His basic idea was simple – to collapse economic production data into a single number that would go up in the good times, and down in the bad (Fioramonti 2013: 23–6).

The system of national accounts developed by Kuznets proved to be invaluable during the Second World War. It allowed America to locate unused capacity in the economy and exceed the production levels that many had thought possible. As Cobb et al. (1995: 63) remark, "In the United States the Manhattan Project got much more glory. But as a technical achievement the development of the GNP accounts was no less important."

Following the end of the war, the Employment Act of 1946 turned GNP into official economic policy in the US. In 1953, the United Nations published its international standards for a system of national accounts. The ideas of Simon Kuznets had gone global. Through proper fiscal management and detailed knowledge of economic performance (as measured by GNP), economists began to believe that they could finally master the dreaded "business cycle" and ensure rising prosperity (Cobb et al. 1995).

Nevertheless, GNP was not universally accepted. The Soviet Union used a different measure of economic progress – net material product – which included physical goods but excluded services. Services were not counted as primary income in the socialist approach, but were considered the result of its distribution. Throughout the Cold War, the two indicators were used as propaganda tools, with both the US and Soviet Union claiming higher rates of economic **growth** based on their respective indicators. When the Soviet Union collapsed in 1991, however, GNP became the only game in town (Fioramonti 2013: 34–40).

In the same year, gross "national" product was quietly replaced by gross "domestic" product. Although the two indicators are closely related, there is an important difference. With GNP, the earnings of a multinational company are attributed to the country where the company is owned, and where the profits end up. With GDP, on the other hand, the profits are attributed to the country where the factory is located and resource extraction occurs, even if the profits leave the country. This change in national accounting has had important consequences, in particular lending support to globalisation. As Cobb et al. (1995: 68) put it, "The nations of the North are walking off with the South's resources, and calling it a gain for the South."

As early as 1934 Simon Kuznets warned that "the welfare of a nation can scarcely be inferred from a measurement of national income" (Cobb et al. 1995: 67). By 1962, Kuznets had become an outspoken critic of the way in which his system of accounts was being used and interpreted, stating that "goals for 'more' growth should specify more growth of what and for what" (ibid).

The basic problem is that GDP does not distinguish between good and bad economic activity, but counts all activity the same. If I buy a beer or a new bicycle this contributes to GDP. If the government invests in education, this also contributes to GDP. These are both expenditures that we would probably count as positives. However, if there is an oil spill that taxpayers must pay to clean up, this also contributes to GDP. If more families go through costly divorce proceedings, the money spent contributes to GDP. War, crime, and environmental destruction all contribute to our main indicator of national progress. It is a calculator with a giant "plus" button, but no "minus" button.

At the same time, GDP does not count many beneficial activities, such as household and volunteer work, because no money changes hands. If I wash my own laundry, this does not contribute to GDP. However, if I pay you $10 to wash my laundry, and you pay me $10 to wash yours, then GDP would go up by $20, even though the number of clean shirts would not have changed.

A further problem is that GDP provides no information on income distribution. Even if GDP per capita goes up, the average person may be no better off if the additional income goes to those at the top. An unequal distribution of income and wealth implies unequal opportunities for people across society (van den Bergh 2009).

A strategy of forever increasing GDP is particularly worrisome given that a number of social indicators suggest **growth** is no longer improving people's lives in wealthy nations (see **social limits of growth**). Beyond an average income of about $20,000 a year, additional money does not appear to buy additional **happiness**. US presidential candidate Robert F. Kennedy was particularly critical of GDP, warning in 1968 that GDP "measures neither our wit not our courage, neither our wisdom nor our learning, neither our compassion nor our devotion to our country. It measures everything in short, except that which makes life worthwhile" (Fioramonti 2013: 81).

Despite these criticisms, GDP maintains its power. The economics profession has become locked in a kind of "groupthink" where the desire for conformity is stifling independent thinking and causing the profession to avoid raising controversial issues or proposing alternative solutions (Fioramonti 2013: 146–8). Policy makers fear that insufficient **growth** will lead to economic instability and rising unemployment, even though the empirical evidence for this view is weak. Fioramonti (2013: 153–6) argues that GDP is not just a number, but a way of organizing society based on the idea that markets are the only producers of wealth. To challenge GDP is therefore to challenge the market economy itself. If this is true, then replacing GDP is fundamentally a political project, not a technical one.

Nevertheless, there is a growing recognition around the world that GDP is a poor measure of progress, and a heightened desire to do something about it. The Commission on the Measurement of Economic Performance and Social Progress, established by former French President Nicolas Sarkozy and chaired by two Nobel Prize-winning economists, concluded that one of the reasons the global economic crisis took people by surprise is that we were focussing on the wrong indicators (Stiglitz et al. 2009).

So what are the right indicators, particularly if our goal as a society shifts from **growth** to degrowth? It might be tempting to use GDP as an indicator of degrowth, and just change the target (e.g. from +3 percent a year to -3 percent a year), but this would not be a good idea. Although a decline in GDP might signal a reduction in environmental pressure, it would not reveal whether the level of economic activity was environmentally sustainable. Moreover, a decline in GDP would not necessarily tell us anything about social progress. GDP is a poor indicator of progress, and changing the target on a poor indicator does not alter this fact. To paraphrase the ecological economist Herman Daly, the best thing we can do with GDP is to forget about it.

In order to measure degrowth, a different approach that includes two separate sets of indicators is required: (1) a set of *biophysical indicators* to measure how society's level of resource use is changing over time and whether this level of resource use is within ecological limits, and (2) a set of *social indicators* to measure whether people's quality of life is improving. I say "sets of indicators" (as opposed to a single indicator) to emphasize that degrowth may have many goals, and each of these may require its own indicator. This is a key difference between degrowth and neoclassical economics, which focuses on the single goal of utility maximization.

Based in part on the declaration from the first international degrowth conference (held in Paris in 2008), I have created a set of "Degrowth Accounts" to measure whether degrowth is occurring, and how socially sustainable it is (see O'Neill 2012). These accounts include seven biophysical indicators (material use, energy use, CO_2 emissions, ecological footprint, human population, livestock population, and built capital) and nine social indicators (happiness, health, equity, poverty, social capital, participatory democracy, working hours, unemployment, and infla-tion). They do not include GDP, and neither should any modern set of economic indicators.

GDP evolved in an era when the challenges facing society were very differ-ent than they are today. We are no longer facing the need to maximize wartime production; instead we are facing the need to improve the well-being of all people within the environmental constraints of a single planet. If wealthy nations decide to change their goal from the pursuit of economic **growth** to the pursuit of sustain-able degrowth, then they will also need to change the way they measure progress. They will need to abandon GDP and replace it with more relevant information.

References

Cobb, C., Halstead, T., and Rowe, J. (1995) "If the GDP is up, why is America Down?" *Atlantic Monthly*, October, 59–78.

Fioramonti, L. (2013) *Gross Domestic Problem: The Politics Behind the World's Most Powerful Number*. London: Zed Books.

O'Neill, D. W. (2012) "Measuring Progress in the Degrowth Transition to a Steady State Economy." *Ecological Economics* 84, 221–31.

Stiglitz, J. E., Sen, A., and Fitoussi, J.-P. (2009) Report by the Commission on the Measurement of Economic Performance and Social Progress. Available online at www. stiglitz-sen-fitoussi.fr (accessed May 6 2013).

van den Bergh, J. C. J. M. (2009) "The GDP Paradox." *Journal of Economic Psychology* 30(2), 117–35.

'Towards growth': the European Commission in Brussels. (Photo taken by Filka Sekulova at the Berlaymont Building, Headquarters of European Commission in Brussels, March 2014)

23

GROWTH

Peter A. Victor

FACULTY OF ENVIRONMENTAL STUDIES, YORK UNIVERSITY

Economic growth is usually defined as an increase in the goods and services produced by an economy in a given period of time, typically a year. The essence
of economic growth, as normally understood, is the increase in Gross Domestic
Product – **GDP** – in a country. This may sound simple but there are many questions that arise when it comes to measuring economic growth. For example, which
goods and services are to be included? What if their quality changes over time?
How are the many different types of goods and services, from bananas to haircuts,
to be added up to get a total that can be said to be growing, or not?

Since the 1940s, the United Nations has led an international effort to establish
procedures for measuring **GDP** that all countries are encouraged to follow. The
UN procedures have answers to these and other questions on the scope and methods for calculating **GDP** and changes in it over time. A fundamental principle
when measuring economic growth is to distinguish between increases in **GDP** that
result from increases in the quantity of goods and services produced (i.e. increases
in 'real' **GDP**), and increases in **GDP** that result simply from increases in their
prices (i.e. increases in 'nominal' **GDP**). In practice, both quantities and prices
change over time and new products and services replace old ones, all of which
complicate the measurement of real economic growth.

The history of economics is full of attempts to explain economic growth. The
classical economists, notably Adam Smith and David Ricardo, emphasized the
contribution of specialization, the division of labour and the extent of markets and
foreign trade based on comparative advantage, as key sources of economic growth.
Later in the nineteenthcentury and into the twentieth century, there were various
attempts to classify growth according to 'stages' through which, presumably, every
economy had to pass as it expanded, though with very different outcomes. Where

Karl Marx (1887) saw economic growth in its capitalist phase as containing the seeds of its own destruction, at the other end of the ideological spectrum W.W. Rostow (1960) saw 'take-off', 'maturity' and 'high mass-consumption' as stages in a process of self-sustaining economic growth. Somewhere between these two perspectives are the insights of Joseph Schumpeter. He popularized the term 'creative destruction' to describe the process by which new innovations destroy older technologies and the businesses which depend on them, to be replaced by new, more profitable ones.

In his *General Theory of Employment, Interest and Money* (1936) John Maynard Keynes explained that unemployment was caused by insufficient spending. He emphasized the role of investment in new buildings, equipment and infrastructure, which fluctuates more than other components of a nation's expenditures (e.g. consumption and government), but he paid little attention to the role that investment plays in expanding the productive capacity of the economy over time. In the 1950s and 1960s, this aspect of investment became the focus of attention of neo-classical economists, who produced mathematical models of economic growth in which the accumulation of capital and technological change play a pivotal role by increasing labour productivity. Increased labour productivity (i.e. GDP/employed labour), combined with a rising labour force, yields economic growth. However, while these economists, Robert Solow being the most famous example, recognized the importance of technological change in economic growth, their models did not explain how it came about. This was subsequently addressed under the heading of 'endogenous' growth theory in the 1980s, which, with the right assumptions about investment and innovation, suggested that the process of economic growth could go on forever.

An alternative to endogenous growth theory came from those who saw economic growth as a physical process as well as an economic one. Explanations of economic growth they said must be based on principles from the natural sciences as much as on economic ones. Robert Ayres (2008) made the case that exergy (i.e. useful work obtained from energy), and not technological change, is the omitted variable in the neo-classical growth theory of Robert Solow. By analyzing the hundred-year history of economic growth in Japan and the USA, he found that it is no longer necessary to call upon technological change to account for that part of economic growth not attributable to increases in capital and labour. Ayres concluded that

> we can be quite certain that exergy . . . is indeed a third factor of production . . . and that future economic growth depends essentially on continued declines in the cost of primary exergy and/or on continued increase in the output of useful work from a decreasing exergy input.
>
> *(Ayres 2008: 307)*

Critiques of economic growth have a history almost as long as economic growth itself. Malthus, a contemporary of Smith and Ricardo, argued that increases in population would inevitably outpace increases in food production, making a sustained increase in living standards unachievable. Most economists repudiated Malthus, but the attention he paid to the capacity of natural systems to support ever expanding economies remains a primary line of critique of economic growth to this day. Most recently, these limits have been expressed as 'planetary boundaries', such as climate change, biodiversity loss, ocean acidification and interference with biophysical cycles, plus concern about diminishing sources of low cost fossil fuels on which economic growth has depended for two centuries. So even if economic growth remains desirable it may not be possible. The downward trend in the rate of economic growth in many advanced countries since the 1960s suggests that its demise may be nearer than most expect.

But is economic growth still so important in rich countries? As early as 1848, John Stewart Mill bemoaned 'the trampling, crushing, elbowing, and treading in each other's heels, which form the existing type of social life' (Mill 1848: 113) and went on to describe many of the negative aspects of economic growth so familiar today. Ezra Mishan's book *The Costs of Economic Growth* (1967) sparked a lively debate punctuated by the celebrated *Limits to Growth* (Meadows et al. 1972), which contained scenarios of expansion and collapse bearing an unnerving correspondence to the data of the past 40 years (Turner 2012).

Others have challenged the usually implicit assumption that economic growth in advanced economies improves well-being. Rather than assume that higher incomes make people happier, researchers have investigated this supposed connection and found it difficult to demonstrate (Layard 2005). It seems that beyond income levels surpassed by many in advanced economies, further increases in income add little to self-declared levels of **happiness**.

And then there's the line of critique that says that increases in **GDP**, taken to be synonymous with economic growth, are a deeply flawed measure of anything of real significance. **GDP** can increase for all sorts of reasons unrelated to well-being. If activities normally conducted without a financial transaction become a matter of commerce, **GDP** will rise. This may partly explain unusually high rates of economic growth in developing countries. Rather than real increases in production, **GDP** rises because commercialization and **commodification** replace more traditional practices. Similarly, increases in **GDP** may be at the expense of resource depletion and environmental contamination, neither aspect being captured in the conventional measure of economic growth. Neither are increases in inequality. Although by some measures overall global inequality has decreased in the past two decades, the majority of the world's population lives in countries which have experienced increasing income inequality. And feminist scholars have drawn attention to disparities between the economic circumstances of men and women to which **GDP** is blind, as further evidence of the inadequacy of its validity as a measure of well-being (see **feminist economics**).

There are two main reasons why these critiques of economic growth matter. First, by pursuing economic growth as a primary policy objective, economies may well be failing to meet other objectives that would contribute more directly to well-being and prosperity such as full employment, more leisure, richer social lives, greater democratic participation and a resilient environment. Second, in an ecologically and resource constrained world, the pursuit of economic growth in rich countries is likely to be at the expense of economic growth in developing countries where its benefits are more apparent.

For all these reasons it's time for those living in advanced economies to think about managing without growth, or even, with degrowth.

References

Ayres, R. U. (2008) 'Sustainability Economics: Where do we Stand?' *Ecological Economics*, 67(2) 281–310.

Keynes, J. M. (1936) *General Theory of Employment, Interest and Money*. London: Palgrave Macmillan.

Layard, R. (2005) *Happiness: Lessons from a New Science*. London: Penguin.

Mill, J. S. (1848) *Principles of Political Economy*, Book IV, Chapter VI. London, UK: J. W. Parker. Page reference is to the 1970 Penguin Books edition.

Rostow, W. W. (1960) *The Stages of Economic Growth: A Non-Communist Manifesto*. Cambridge: Cambridge University Press.

Schumpeter, J. (1942) *Capitalism, Socialism, and Democracy*. New York: Harper & Row.

Turner, G. (2012) 'On the Cusp of Global Collapse? Updated Comparison of The Limits to Growth with Historical Data', *GAIA – Ecological Perspectives for Science and Society*, 2: 116–23.

Victor, P. A. (2008) *Managing without Growth*, Cheltenham, UK Edward Elgar.

24

HAPPINESS

Filka Sekulova

RESEARCH & DEGROWTH AND ICTA (INSTITUTE OF ENVIRONMENTAL SCIENCE AND TECHNOLOGY),
AUTONOMOUS UNIVERSITY OF BARCELONA

Happiness is a component of subjective well-being and a construct which somewhat overlaps with life-satisfaction, given high correlation levels between reports on life-satisfaction and happiness. Notions of happiness differ through the philosophical currents. Hedonic happiness stands for the positive effects associated with obtaining material objects or pleasurable experiences. It is located empirically closer to life-satisfaction, and is operationalized through numerical scales where the lowest digit corresponds to complete dissatisfaction with life, and the highest to complete satisfaction with life. Eudemonic happiness, on the other hand, implies living in coherence with one's best potentials and life-purpose. It is formalized using questionnaires assessing positive psychological functioning. While some activities give rise to both eudemonic and hedonic happiness, not all forms of hedonic enjoyment give rise to eudemonic happiness.

The first relevant aspect of the happiness literature is the treatment of subjective well-being as a composite construct including both tangible and intangible components. It has been shown that non-monetary domains (such as health, social capital, relational goods, marital status and temperament) tend to carry a heavier weight in happiness than pecuniary ones (such as the material conditions, or the level of disposable income) (Easterlin 2003). Disruptions in the non-monetary domains of happiness tend to cause deeper and more permanent ruptures in well-being than losses in the pecuniary ones. These findings are in line with degrowth theory and the idea of reshuffling the importance of economic components of life towards the ones based on human relations, social connectedness and **conviviality**.

The second relevant insight concerns utility theory in economics. If life-satisfaction could be taken as an imperfect proxy of utility, happiness studies indicate that the satisfaction a consumer receives from augmenting a particular consumption bundle would cease to positively contribute to utility over time. Thus, happiness studies indicate that even in a pure utilitarian economist framework, **growth** would fail to comply with its initially set objective.

The third finding is related to the Easterlin paradox. This refers to the lack of association between income growth and reported subjective well-being over time within countries over time. This disassociation mostly happens for two reasons. One is the influence of social comparison on affective moods, or the process of drawing inferences on what consists a good, or 'happy', life from a particular reference group, or environment (see also **social limits of growth**). The other is the adaptation of material expectations, or the so-called continuously rising aspirations, which offsets the positive impact of income increase on well-being over time.

How do these three insights relate to specific degrowth ideas? An intuitive first-hand answer is that if degrowth translates into a widespread and equitable decline in consumption, this will not necessarily have a negative effect on subjective well-being. Firstly, because of adaptation. People tend to grow accustomed to improvements in their material conditions. Lottery winners, for example, are not happier than people in a control group with similar characteristics over time. In the same way, adaptation to lower material consumption might not create permanent dents in happiness, if social status is taken into account. This relates to the second reason, namely: social comparison. A decrease in consumption, which affects everyone will bring downwards reference income standards, and therefore off-set the associated adverse social and psychological effects. However, if degrowth translates into a consumption decrease for a small fraction of the population, surrounded by a society characterized by abundant material wealth, as in times of economic crisis, well-being would decline.

Beyond the general understanding of degrowth as a multidimensional transformation involving complementary actions, policies and strategies, one could try to explore the repercussion of certain emblematic degrowth proposals on happiness. One of these can be generally defined as a reduction of formal working hours and an introduction of **work sharing**. There is some evidence in the happiness literature that part-time work is associated with higher levels of life-satisfaction. Again, if raising the incomes of all does not increase the happiness of all, a decline in the incomes of all (resulting from the reduction of formal working hours), is not likely to reduce the happiness of all. Along the lines of prospect theory, one might argue that monetary losses are more hurtful than monetary gains of the same size. Yet, the empirical verdict on the existence and persistence of such an asymmetry in the long term is mixed.

The proposal for **work sharing** within degrowth is accompanied by an increase of free time and the life-space dedicated to non-monetary, reciprocal, communal activities, many of which can be defined as reproductive. Given that the quality of social and family interactions (see **care**) has been found to be a major positive determinant of well-being, increasing the share of community-based work might not decrease happiness. Furthermore, freedom, understood as having the locus of control over your time and life, has been found to predict changes in life satisfaction better than health, employment, income, marriage or religion, across countries and within countries. Thus, the increased share of the time dedicated to the activities that one considers meaningful could boost satisfaction with life. Volunteering, for example, has been found to positively contribute to happiness for increasing empathic emotions and creating shifts in aspirations.

Furthermore, in degrowth we often talk about a democratically established and fixed ratio between the minimum and maximum levels of pay (see **basic and maximum income**). Income inequality has been shown to have a highly negative effect on life satisfaction. Individuals living in areas of high inequality tend to score low in both health and happiness terms. Thus, if the income gap between individuals and countries narrows down as a result of degrowth, subjective well-being could improve due to the associated decline in rivalry.

Another emblematic idea in degrowth has to do with downscaling car-dependence, as well as fast transport modes and polluting infrastructure in general. As long as such a transformation allows for an increased space for (wild) nature in urban and rural landscapes without creating social deprivation, it is likely to have a positive effect on well-being. Studies on commuting indicate that spending many hours in a motorized vehicle bears a permanent negative effect on happiness. Moreover, there is a growing literature indicating that environmental degradation upsets well-being. Various studies indicate that poor air quality, for example, is associated with lower scores on happiness. This is found for both London and big cities in China, where traffic congestion emerges as a menace to well-being. In terms of car use, if most of the people in a given city switch from car to public transport, or select working placements based on the proximity principle, it is unlikely that they are going to suffer a decrease in life-satisfaction. On the contrary, abandoning your car is likely to be disturbing in a society which functions on the basis of cars.

One proposal which often emerges in public talks on degrowth is the introduction of bans on advertising in public spaces. The literature indicates that individuals with high scores on materialism and who place greater emphasis on financial security, tend to be less satisfied with their lives (Kasser, 2002). Thus if such a measure dampens material aspirations, it could enhance well-being. Moreover, there is a small literature demonstrating that watching television depresses relational activities, which are an important component of happiness.

A more abstract, but classic, degrowth proposal concerns challenging the dominant imaginary of **growth** and the extraction of social prestige from material possession and accumulation. The few studies exploring the relation between non-materialistic values and well-being report that the former are often associated with higher levels of life-satisfaction. Intrinsic values (such as altruism, for example) are generally associated with higher level of well-being and little material resources requirements for the fulfilment of basic needs. Moreover, considering the negative impact of rivalry-based, consumption on happiness, one could expect that cultivating a social imaginary that is not colonized by material domains, on either individual or societal level, would positively affect happiness.

The foregoing review of the implications of some references proposals in degrowth for happiness is far from exhaustive. It is naïve to believe that degrowth is and will be 'happy' by default, nor should happiness be the only objective of society. It is rather suggested here that satisfaction with life is unlikely to decrease with degrowth, especially if the following hold: any reductions in income or paid work are equally experienced by all, as well as an increase of personal free time and autonomy; increasing the time dedicated to reciprocity/community work is compensated by improvements in relational goods; downscaling fast modes of transportation – by the increase in the time available for travelling; reduction in luxury goods consumption/comfort levels by adaptation to goods sharing and **conviviality**. In other words, if degrowth involves a trajectory of multiple actions and policies which compensate for each other's (possible) negative effects, it might not endanger personal happiness. If degrowth stirs an improvement in the determinants of happiness to which adaptation is limited, such as allocation of free time, state of the urban and natural environment, health status, personal freedom and the quality of social relations, the associated effect on subjective well-being is likely to be lasting and positive.

References

Diener, E. and Biswas-Diener, R. (2002) 'Will Money Increase Subjective Well-Being? A Literature Review and Guide to Needed Research', *Social Indicators Research Vol.* 57(2): 119–69.

Di Tella, R., Haisken-De New, J. and MacCulloch, R. (2010) 'Happiness Adaptation to Income and to Status in an Individual Panel', *Journal of Economic Behavior and Organization*, 76(3): 834–52.

Easterlin, R. A. (2003) *Building a Better Theory of Well-Being*, IZA Discussion Paper No. 742.

Kasser, T. (2002) *The High Price of Materialism*, Cambridge, MA: MIT Press.

Porta, P. L. and Bruni, L. (eds) (2005) *Economics and Happiness*, Oxford: Oxford University Press.

25

IMAGINARY, DECOLONIZATION OF

Serge Latouche

FACULTÉ DE DROIT, ÉCONOMIE ET GESTION JEAN MONNET, UNIVERSITÉ PARIS-SUD

The idea and the project to decolonize the imaginary has two main sources: the philosophy of Cornélius Castoriadis, on the one hand, and the anthropological critique of imperialism, on the other. Alongside the ecological critique, these two sources, are the intellectual origins of degrowth. In Castoriadis, the focus is on the imaginary, while among the anthropologists of imperialism the focus is on decolonization. Going back to these two sources illustrates the exact meaning of the term.

In Castoriadis' work the performative phrase, "to decolonize the imaginary," is obvious, though, to my knowledge, he has never used it as such. For Castoriadis, author of *The Imaginary Institution of Society*, social reality is the implementation of "imaginary significations," that is to say representations that mobilize feelings. If **growth** and **development** are beliefs, and therefore imaginary significations like "progress" and all founding categories of the economy, then to get out, to abolish and go beyond them (the famous Hegelian Aufhebung), means that the imaginary must be changed. The achievement of a degrowth society therefore in part, means to decolonize our imaginary; to really change the world before the change of the world condemns us. This is the strict application of Castoriadis' lesson. Castoriadis argues:

> [W]hat is required is a new imaginary creation of a size unparalleled in the past, a creation that would put at the center of human life other significations than the expansion of production and consumption, that would lay down different objectives for life, ones that might be recognized by human beings as worth pursuing. . . . Such is the immense difficulty to which we have to face up. We ought to want a society in which economic values have ceased to be central (or unique), in which the economy is put back in its

place as a mere means for human life and not as its ultimate end, in which one therefore renounces this mad race toward ever increasing consumption. That is necessary not only in order to avoid the definitive destruction of the terrestrial environment but also and especially in order to escape from the psychical and moral poverty of contemporary human beings.

(Castoriadis 1996: 143–4)

In other words, the required exit from the hyper-modern society of consumption and spectacle is also eminently desirable. However, Castoriadis adds:

[B]ut that sort of revolution would require profound changes in the psychosocial structure of people in the Western world, in their attitude toward life, in short, in their imaginary. The idea that the only goal in life is to produce and consume more is an absurd, humiliating idea that must be abandoned. The capitalist imaginary of pseudo-rational pseudo-mastery, and of unlimited expansion, must be abandoned. Only men and women can do that. A single individual, or an organization, can only prepare, criticize, encourage, and sketch out possible orientations, at best.

(Castoriaadis 2010: 199)

However, to attempt to think of an exit out of the dominant imaginary, we must first of all go back to the way we entered into it, that is to say, to the process of economization of minds concomitant to the **commodification** of the world. For Castoriadis, the economy is an invention. The last pages of *The Imaginary Institution of Society* are precisely on this subject. They are the seeds which I have tried to develop in my book *The Invention of the Economy*, meaning an analysis of how the economy is instituted in the Western modern imaginary (Latouche 2005).

In Castoriadis, **development** and **growth** are not subjects of extensive analysis. His account of both is settled in a few sharp sentences, either at the turn of a discussion, or during reflections devoted to other subjects. Speaking of the crisis of **development**, he analyses it as a crisis of the correspondent imaginary significations and, in particular, of progress. The incredible ideological resilience of **development** is based on the no less astonishing resilience of progress. As he admirably puts it:

[N]obody really believes in progress any more. Everyone wants to have a bit more next year, but no-one thinks that happiness resides in a 3 per cent annual rise in consumption. The imaginary of growth definitely still exists: it's even the only imaginary that subsists in the Western world. Western man doesn't believe in anything, except in the fact that he'll soon be able to buy a high-definition television set.

(Castoriadis 2010: 181)

One form of uprooting a belief is readily formulated through the metaphor of decolonization in the analysis of North/South relations. The term "colonization," as commonly used by anti-imperialist anthropologies in relation to mentalities, can be found in the title of several books. The oeuvre by Octave Manonni on the psychology of the colonized, is one of the first. More explicitly, Gérard Althabe, a disciple of Balandier, titled his 1969 study of Madagascar, *Oppression and Liberation within the Imaginary*. In 1988, Serge Gruzinski published *The Colonization of the Imaginary*, whose subtitle refers to the process of Westernization. However, when Gruzinski talks of the colonization of the imaginary, this is still a continuation of the colonial process in its strict sense and the conversion of the natives by the missionaries. That change of religion was both a de-culturation of minds and an acculturation to Christianity and Western civilization by the imperialist project. This is a real oppression in the imaginary, conducted by means that are not just symbolic: think of the pyres widely used in the New World by the Spanish conquerors during the Inquisition.

With **growth** and **development**, we are dealing with a process of conversion of mentalities, a process of an ideological and quasi-religious nature, aiming at establishing the imaginary of progress and economy. However "The rape of the imaginary," to use the beautiful expression of Aminata Traoré (2002), remains still symbolic. In the West, when we speak of the colonization of the imaginary we are dealing with a mental invasion in which we are the victims and the agents. It is largely self-colonization, a partly voluntary servitude.

Hence the term "decolonization of the imaginary" marks a semantic shift. The originality lies in the emphasis on the particular form of the inverse process to the one analyzed by the anthropologists. It is a change of "software" or paradigm, a "veritable revolution of the imaginary," as Edouard Glissant calls it. It is first and foremost a cultural revolution. But that is not all. It is also about exiting the economy, changing values, and thus de-Westernizing. This is precisely the program developed within the post-development project of the "partisans" of degrowth.

The question of exiting the dominant or colonial imaginary, for Castoriadis as for the anti-imperialist anthropologists, is a central issue but very difficult because we can not decide to change our imaginary and even less that of others, especially if they are "addicted" to **growth**. One cannot but think first of education, paideïa, which for Castoriadis has an essential role.

> [W]hat does it mean, for example, freedom or the opportunity for citizens to participate, he asks, if in the society of which we are talking about there is not something – which disappears in contemporary discussions . . . - and that is the paideïa, the education of the citizen? It does not mean teaching arithmetics, it means to teach him to be a citizen. Nobody is born a citizen. And how to become one? Learning to be. We learn it, first, looking at the city in which we live. And certainly not watching today's TV.
>
> *(Castoriadis 2010)*

This detoxification, however, is not fully possible if a degrowth society has not been already established. We should first have exited the consumer society and its system of "civic stupidification," which locks us into a circle that needs to be broken. Denouncing the aggression of advertising, a vehicle of today's ideology, is certainly the starting point of the counter-offensive out of what Castoriadis called the "consumerist and TV onanism." The fact that the newspaper *La décroissance* is derived from the association "Casseurs de pub" (ad-busters) is not a coincidence. Advertising is the key driver of the **growth** society. The movement of degrowthers and growth objectors is widely and naturally linked to a resistance against advertising's aggression.

References

Castoriadis, C. (1987) *The Imaginary Institution of Society*, Cambridge: Polity Press.

Castoriadis, C. (1996) *La montée de l'insignifiance*, Paris, Les carrefours du labyrinthe IV, Paris. English translation, *The rising tide of insignificancy (The big sleep)*. Translated from the French and edited anonymously. Electronic publication date: 2003. Available at http://www.costis.org/x/castoriadis/Castoriadis-rising_tide.pdf (accessed 19 May 2013).

Castoriadis, C. (2010) Démocratie et relativisme, Débat avec le MAUSS, Paris, Mille et une nuits. p. 96.

Castoriadis, C., Escobar, E. , and Gondicas, M. (eds) (2005) *Une société à la dérive*, Paris, Seuil. English translation (by Helen Arnold) (2010), *A Society Adrift*, New York: Fordham University Press.

Latouche, S. (2005) *L'invention de l'économie*, Paris: Albin Michel.

Traoré, A. (2002) *Le viol de l'imaginaire*, Paris: Actes Sud/Fayard.

26

JEVONS' PARADOX (REBOUND EFFECT)

Blake Alcott

RETIRED ECOLOGICAL ECONOMIST

In the heyday of the Industrial Revolution, as Britain worried about running out of coal, William Stanley Jevons (Jevons 1865; Alcott 2005) pondered two simultaneous phenomena: (1) required coal input per unit of smelted iron or work done by steam engines had long been falling; and (2) total coal consumption had been rising. Likewise, demand for labour input had been rising alongside rising labour productivity. From these observations, he derived the general claim that technological change which increases the efficiency with which a resource is used increases rather than decreases the rate of consumption of that resource.

This claim was later exemplified by electric lighting, where a hundred-fold decrease in the amount of electricity needed for a lumen spawned a thousand-fold increase in the amount of electricity used for lumens to light buildings and streets. Jevons called this a 'paradox', because for psychological reasons we expect a *per unit* decrease in an input/output ratio to cause a decrease in the *overall* consumption of the input. The input could, of course, also be water, phosphorus, arable soil or work-hours as well as energy.

First, a few definitions. Suppose the average kettle becomes 10 per cent more energy-efficient at boiling water. Suppose also that the number of kettles and the amount of water boiled per kettle doesn't change. Then the amount of energy used to boil water would fall by 10 per cent. This 10 per cent of the total amount of energy previously used to boil water would be an absolute amount of saved energy, known by the technical term engineering savings. But this amount is theoretical only. In reality, less than this gets saved because, aided by lower prices both of outputs and of the energy inputs, the energy momentarily saved gets used by consumers to do other things. Unless suppliers lower supply, thus counteracting the price falls, latent consumer demand snaps up this temporarily fallow-lying energy. This new demand is called rebound consumption.

Jevons held that rebound consumption is higher than engineering savings. That is, *even more* energy gets consumed than if efficiency were to stay the same; had steam-engine efficiency remained at James Watt's level around the year 1800, we would be consuming much less coal. A second possible outcome is rebound equals 100 per cent of engineering savings. This happens when the technological efficiency increases do not affect input consumption, which simply continues its rising trend. A third outcome would be when some of the fallow-lying energy remains permanently undemanded, rebound then being between 1 per cent and 99 per cent. As rebound nears 100 per cent, policies to induce increased efficiency become *cost*-ineffective. At 100 per cent, they are simply ineffective; at over 100 per cent – Jevons' paradox – they backfire, and they are counterproductive.

Is it then a reasonable degrowth strategy to encourage or legislate greater efficiency? Not if latent demand and population growth pounce on all the resources temporarily freed up by the efficiency increases, and certainly not if Jevons is right. Historians, anthropologists and psychologists usually find it completely plausible that we don't leave any theoretically conservable energy lying in the ground unused. More consumers, new discoveries of energy, new uses for it and more efficient technology in mining it – all these affect the level of overall combustion. But efficiency increases also contribute. They expand society's production possibilities, amounting to a rise in society's total purchasing power; they encourage discovery of new uses for energy; and they aid population increase by increasing food yield and by providing healthy, heated buildings.

There is evidence that world-wide, over perhaps 20 decades, output per unit of input has gone up: one hour of work, one joule of fossil fuel, one hectare of farmland produces more goods and services than before. We can measure this as an increase in the ratio of the sum of the world's gross domestic product (GDP) to physically-measured inputs like worked hours, energy, fresh water or metals like copper, iron or rare earths. But has the increase in this efficiency ratio been accompanied, globally, by a decrease in amounts of energy used, people working or minerals mined? No. In fact, the big empirical picture shows that rebounds are at least 100 per cent. Interestingly, for labour-hours, no historian or economist claims anything but that rebound is greater than per cent: higher productivity has meant economic **growth** and more jobs.

Those who believe that rebound is less than 100 per cent do not of course deny that efficiency increases to date have not saved a drop of oil. However, they claim counterfactually that without them, even more oil would have been burnt. This points to the fact that today's rebound discussion is basically theoretical. To be sure, we can use micro-economic methods to measure so-called *direct* rebound: if a given consumer drives a more fuel-efficient car, thereby saving money previously spent on fuel, some of this income gets spent on driving more. The output – driven kilometres – increases, so rebound is greater than 0 per cent (Khazzoom 1980). Further indirect rebounds are however also certain, namely a so-called *income effect* enabling this consumer to use his or her saved purchasing power to buy a gadget, clothes or a plane ticket. These two types of rebound give us the environmentally relevant number we want – *total* rebound. Indirect rebounds, however, are notoriously difficult to measure, and there is moreover no methodology to derive indirect and total rebound from the direct rebounds for the various economic sectors, however precisely these may have been measured.

Studies of rebound in single countries or groups of countries, rather than at world level, face a further problem: if they count only the amount of energy consumed within the countries, ignoring the amounts 'embodied' in the countries' net imports such as cars or computers, the result is distorted. A final difficulty in judging average rebound for all countries is that studies of total rebound in poorer societies yield higher estimates (often backfire) than studies of Organisation for Economic Co-operation and Development countries, perhaps because consumers there are less satiated. Given these problems of method, it is no wonder that even after 30 years of micro-economic study, total-rebound estimates vary by more than an order of magnitude (Sorrell 2009).

Thus, to say the least, it is only with high uncertainty that one can claim real savings through technological efficiency, and it is tempting to turn to the alternative strategy of living more 'sufficiently' – working, producing and consuming less. Here too, though, there is rebound: if I unilaterally decide to buy less energy, my evaporated demand lowers energy's price by an increment in the world-wide energy market. This in turn enables the world's billions of 'marginal consumers', who wish to work as much as usual and consume more output, to demand what I no longer demand. This might contribute to equitable consumption, but not to energy conservation. Unless the entire world population starts living more sufficiently, which is immoral since billions live in involuntary poverty, other people take up the slack in demand left by those who voluntarily 'do without' some energy.

Rebound is relevant to degrowth because what must degrow down to sustainable size is not utility, happiness or even necessarily GDP, but rather the amount of bio-physical *throughput* caused by humans – the total amount of natural resources consumed plus the emissions and waste caused by this consumption. And there is in fact a well-known policy option that reduces throughput directly and with certainty: legal caps on the amount of a resource mined and consumed. Communities have, for instance, for centuries capped what can legally be pumped from aquifers, and the Kyoto process is now trying to cap air emissions.

As in Jevons' time, instead of degrowing resource consumption by means of physically defined caps, many people bank on the uncertain strategy of more efficient use of the resource. But what happens to the energy that could thus be saved? Is it saved? If some of us live with lower throughput, perhaps working less through **work sharing**, won't the rest of humanity demand the freed resources, which after all continue to be supplied at a profit? Input consumption rebounds, and the tail, moreover, cannot wag the dog: If society first caps its resource consumption, people will automatically live more efficiently and sufficiently – and perhaps not less happily.

The hope of our 'inner engineer' is that technological, per-unit efficiency gains will somehow lower overall levels of depletion and pollution, and this is what gives birth to the environmental strategy of increased efficiency. The environment, however, doesn't 'care about' ratios such as our human efficiency, or – which comes to the same thing – the economy's **dematerialisation**. Only real amounts matter, regardless of how much utility we squeeze from our budgeted amounts of resources.

If there is something to Jevons' claim that humans will ecologically expand through a combination of population increase and greater material affluence, we should move away from technical or purely personal changes to political solutions based on the insight that natural resources are collectively-owned **commons** (Sanne 2000).

References

Alcott, B. (2005) 'Jevons' paradox'. *Ecological Economics* 54(1): 9–21.

Jevons, W. S. (1865) *The coal question*, 3rd ed. 1965. New York: Augustus M. Kelley.

Khazzoom, D. (1980) 'Economic implications of mandated efficiency in standards for household appliances'. *Energy Journal* 1(4): 21–40.

Sanne, C. (2000) 'Dealing with environmental savings in a dynamical economy – how to stop chasing your tail in the pursuit of sustainability'. *Energy Policy* 28 (6/7): 487–95.

Sorrell, S. (2009) 'Jevons' paradox revisited: the evidence for backfire from improved energy efficiency'. *Energy Policy* 37(4): 1456–69.

27

NEO-MALTHUSIANS

Joan Martinez-Alier

RESEARCH & DEGROWTH AND ICTA (INSTITUTE OF ENVIRONMENTAL SCIENCE
AND TECHNOLOGY), AUTONOMOUS UNIVERSITY OF BARCELONA

Authors known as "Neo-Malthusians," and among them Stanford ecology professor Paul Ehrlich, raised in the 1960s and 1970s a strident alarm on population growth. In fact, the alarm was justified because human population increased in the twentieth century from 1.5 billion to 6 billion. In the 2010s, world population reached 7 billion, but fertility (the number of children per woman) is now decreasing fast in many countries, and it is persistently below two in many other countries. World population will probably reach a maximum at about 8.5 or 9 billion by 2050 and will then decline slightly. Not only rural depopulation will take place, there will also be urban depopulation in some countries.

Ehrlich, who published *The Population Bomb* in 1968, acknowledged that overpopulation was only one of the factors in environmental degradation. He introduced a well-known equation, $I = f(P, A, T)$, meaning that environmental impact (for instance, increased production of greenhouse gases changing the composition of the atmosphere) depended on the size of the population, of its income per capita ("affluence") and on the technologies used. Population indeed remained one important factor.

The degrowth movement has rarely discussed population growth. On the whole, while it adopts a position contrary to population growth, it puts more emphasis on social inequality in consumption per capita. This is common to other currents on the Left.

The degrowthers dislike, in general, the top-down population policies and the restriction to migration that Neo-Malthusians such as Paul Ehrlich and even more Garrett Hardin preached in the 1960s and 1970s. They dislike forced sterilizations and also the Chinese policy of one child per family imposed by the state. But the degrowthers, as opposed to Marxists, worry or should worry about population.

True, Malthus in his *Essay on the Principle of Population* of 1798 took a pessimistic view on the growth of agricultural production. He believed in the existence of decreasing returns to the labour input. Population growth would make more people available to work in agriculture but the production would increase less than proportionally. Hence, the final outcome would be a crisis of lack of food. The Marxists disliked Malthus because Malthus believed in decreasing returns and even more because he implied that improving the economic situation of the poor was useless because any improvement would result in increased fertility. He was truly a reactionary. Marxists also disliked Malthus' emphasis on crises of subsistence when Marx explained crises as due to excessive investment compared to the purchasing power of the exploited proletariat. Population growth for Marxists is driven by the need of **capitalism** for cheap labor, and as Engels noted, in a non-capitalist social formation, population could be much better controlled.

The degrowthers know all such arguments and although they also dislike Malthus' reactionary politics, they think nevertheless that Malthus had a point and that population cannot grow without checks. Degrowthers take issue with optimistic economists who assume that human population growth is no major threat to the natural environment. Such economists are in favor of population growth pointing out that productivity per hectare and even more per hour of work could increase with technical progress. Indeed, Ester Boserup in her 1965 book *The Conditions of Agricultural Growth* explained that population growth led to increased production (turning the tables on Malthus) because it allows more intensive systems of production with shorter rotations (from itinerant agriculture to irrigated double cropping). However, this might apply to remote periods of human economic history but since the mid-nineteenth century in Europe agriculture has increasingly relied on imported fertilizers like guano and, later, factory-made fertilizers. The modern food system is very intensive in fossil fuel energy. It can be argued that there is no increase in productivity of agriculture from an ecological-economic point of view.

The degrowthers are the inheritors not of Malthus himself but of the radical, feminist Neo-Malthusians of 1900 (in Europe and the United States) who were in favor of "conscious procreation." Poor women and men were deemed capable of voluntary, "conscious procreation" (Masjuan 2000; Ronsin 1980). This was a feminist and proto-environmental movement. Instead, today's Neo-Malthusianism of the rich considers the larger reproductive rate among the world's poor as a threat to their own environment through migration. In Hardin's case this developed into a so-called "lifeboat ethics." Hence, the need for top-down population policies. Instead, the Neo-Malthusianism of 1900 was not a doctrine imposing population policies from above.

The degrowthers feel close to the "bottom up" feminist Neo-Malthusians and do not share the views of the optimistic economists regarding population growth. They make fun of the argument that in order to pay pensions to old people there is a need for more and more employed young people, who will in due course become pensioners in a kind of demographic Ponzi pyramid.

The Neo-Malthusian anarcho-feminists preached women's freedom to choose the number of children they wanted to have. Many of them were explicitly concerned about environmental issues, and they asked themselves how many people the Earth could feed sustainably. This successful international social movement (with leaders such as Emma Goldman and Margaret Sanger in the United States and Paul Robin in France) called itself deliberately Neo-Malthusian but in contrast to Malthus, it believed that population growth could be stopped among the poor classes by voluntary decisions. Birth control, including voluntary vasectomies, was recommended. This Neo-Malthusian movement did not appeal to the State to impose restrictions on population growth. On the contrary, it was based on "bottom up" activism based on women's freedom, the avoidance of the downward pressure of excessive population on wages, and the threat to the environment and human subsistence. An excess of population was foreseen, and this led to anticipatory ideas and behavior. In France and elsewhere, Neo-Malthusians challenged the political and religious authorities of the time through the idea of a "womb strike" (*la grève des ventres*), and also through anti-militarism and anti-capitalism. Controlling population voluntary was a refusal to provide **capitalism** with the cheap labor of the "reserve army of workers."

Outside Europe and the United States, the movement was active in Argentina, Uruguay, and Cuba. In Brazil, in 1932, Maria Lacerda de Moura wrote a book entitled *Love One Another, And Do Not Multiply*. In South India, E.K. Ramaswami (Periyar) formed the Self-Respect Movement in 1926. He developed a political philosophy against caste and in favor of freedom for women. He preached birth control, arguing against Hindu religious notions of purity of blood and consequent control over women's sexuality (Guha, 2010). Sixty years later, when attempting to explain the low birth rate in Tamil Nadu, demographers notice that education levels for women have been low (compared to Kerala), and poverty is high, so that perhaps the political will and the social reform movements initiated by Periyar played a role in the demographic transition.

When Françoise d'Eaubonne (1974) introduced the word "ecofeminism" she was active as a late-day militant of this radical Neo-Malthusian current, still fighting at the time for the right to abortion and also for sexual freedom not only for women (which had advanced very much already) but also for homosexuals who were still criminalized in Europe at the time.

To conclude, there have been different varieties of Malthusianism and Neo-Malthusianism in the last 200 years:

- According to Malthus, human populations would grow exponentially unless checked by war and pestilence, or by the unlikely restraint of chastity and late marriages. Food would grow less than proportionately to the growth of the labor input, because of decreasing returns. Hence, subsistence crises.
- The Neo-Malthusians of 1900 believed that human populations could regulate their own growth through contraception. Women's freedom was required for this, and it was desirable for its own sake. Poverty was explained by social inequality. "Conscious procreation" was required in order to prevent low wages, and pressure on natural resources. This was a successful bottom-up

movement in Europe and America against States (which wanted more soldiers) and against the Catholic Church.

* The Neo-Malthusians of the 1960s and 1970s appeared because of delayed demographic transitions and the lack of success in the world at large of the Neo-Malthusians of 1900. They preached a top-down doctrine and practice sponsored by international organizations and some governments. Population growth was seen as one main cause of poverty and environmental degradation. Therefore States must introduce contraceptive methods, even sometimes without the populations' (particularly women's) prior consent.

For degrowthers, the first and third points are abhorrent but the second point is very close in spirit. The idea of a voluntary restriction of procreation, a collective act of self-limitation against the engine of **growth,** continues to inspire degrowth. Yves Cochet (a long serving member of the European Parliament and partisan of degrowth) has proposed a *grève du troisième enfant* (a strike of the third child) (Guichard 2009).

References

Boserup, E. (1965) *The Conditions of Agricultural Growth: The Economics of Agrarian Change under Population Pressure*. London: G. Allen and Unwin.

D'Eaubonne, F. (1974) *Le féminisme ou la mort*. Paris, France: Pierre Horay Editeur.

Erlich, P. R. (1968) *The Population Bomb*. San Francisco: Sierra Club/Ballantine Books.

Guichard, M. (2009) *Yves Cochet pour la «grève du troisième ventre»*. *Libération*. Available online at www.liberation.fr/societe/2009/04/06/yves-cochet-pour-la-greve-du-troisieme-ventre_551067 (accessed January 28 2014).

Lacerda de Moura, M. (1932) *Amai e não vos multipliqueis*. Rio de Janeiro: Civilizacao Brasileira Editora.

Malthus, T. R. (1798) *Essay on the Principle of Population*. London: J. Johnson, in St. Paul's Church-yard.

Masjuan, E. (2000) *La ecología humana en el anarquismo ibérico. (Urbanismo "orgánico" o ecológico, neomalthusianismo y naturismo social)*. Barcelona/Madrid: Editorial Icaria y Fundación Anselmo Lorenzo.

Ronsin, F. (1980) *La grève des ventres. Propagande neo-malthusienne et baisse de la natalité en France 19-20 siècles*. Paris: Aubier-Montaigne.

Ramaswami, E. V. "The Case for Contraception," In R. Guha (ed.) *The Makers of Modern India*, Penguin: New Delhi, pp. 258–9.

28

PEAK-OIL

Christian Kerschner

IRI THESYS, HUMBOLDT-UNIVERSITÄT ZU BERLIN AND DEPARTMENT
OF ENVIRONMENTAL STUIDES, MASARYK UNIVERSITY

Collin Campbell and Aleklett Kjell developed the concept of 'Pea-Oil' when they founded ASPO (the Association for the Study of Peak Oil) in 2002. All too often observers misinterpret Peak-Oil as the depletion or 'running out' of oil and therefore often equate the term to the biophysical (resource) limits debates of the 1970s and 1980s. That debate missed the fact that non-renewable resources are not only limited in stock (the economically extractable physical quantity of deposits) but, like renewables, also in flow (rate). Hence the concept can be equally applied to renewable resources, which has already happened in the literature e.g. Peak-Water, Peak-Fertile-Land, etc.

A 'resource flow' is the physical amount that can be extracted per unit of time (usually days) given external constraints, which may be geologic, economic, environmental or social. The peak can therefore be defined as 'the maximum possible flow rate of a resource (i.e. production and consumption) given external constraints'. According to Peak-Oil literature, this rate is about 85 million barrels per day (mb/d), in the case of oil. Peaks are the crucial moment in terms of resource scarcities and their resulting impact on society. In contrast, the often-quoted time left until resource depletion (calculated by dividing the estimated remaining resource by current yearly consumption flows) is highly misleading. British Petroleum, for example, estimates these numbers to be about 40 years for oil, 60 for gas and 120 for coal. Such numbers create the wrong impression that the remaining time for action to respond to resource limitations is still far off.

Hence the first key message of Peak-Oil is that supply constraints are much closer in time than is commonly assumed. When this will happen is the subject of the 'below ground' Peak-Oil literature dominated by geologists whose main concern is with the quantity dimension of the phenomenon, i.e. possible flow rates and recoverable stocks. Petroleum geologist King Hubbert developed a curve fitting methodology that mirrors production and discovery trends in order to show ultimate crude-oil production. He almost exactly predicted Peak-Oil for the US (Hubbert predicted a 1971 peak, the real peak happened in fall 1970) and estimated a world peak of oil production for the year 2000. Campbell and Laherrere (1998) updated Hubbert's work. They placed the peak at 2006. This prediction was further refined for ASPO's first press release in 2002, which predicted 2010 for the peak at a flow rate of 85 mb/d. For now this estimate appears to hold, as production has currently plateaued at about that level. The most extensive meta-analysis of "below ground" Peak-Oil studies so far concluded that a production peak of conventional oil for geological reasons was likely before 2030, with a significant risk for this to occur before 2020 (Sorrell *et al.* 2010).

The URR (ultimately recoverable resource) focuses debate regarding the timing of Peak-Oil. This is the estimated total amount (historic and future) of a given resource ever to be produced. ASPO uses 1900 Gigabarrels (Gb) of conventional and 525 Gb of unconventional oil (i.e. deep sea, heavy oils e.g. tar sands, shale oil and gas, oil shale and polar oil) for its calculations. Given total historic consumption of oil to date of around 1160 Gb, this means we are about half way through the resource. URR estimates of those denying an imminent peak of world oil production are much higher. The IEA (International Energy Agency) produces its forecasts on the basis of 1,300 Gb for conventional and 2,700 Gb for unconventional oil. Recent advances in fracking technology for extracting shale oil and gas has given new 'fuel' to such optimistic outlooks. However a significant part of the IEA figures relies on 'yet to be found' oil, without stating where this oil could possibly be located and according to many analysts the 'shale hype' is a bubble that is to burst at any moment.

When URR numbers are discussed, Peak-Oil deniers often omit reference to the possible flow rate of the deposit in question, which is the determining variable for this matter. Sorrell, Miller et al. (2010) found that, given the current trend in decline rates of existing oil fields (4 per cent annually), the world would have to discover daily production capacities equal to that of Saudi Arabia every three years in order to keep up with current demand. Saudi Arabia holds approximately 264.2 Gb, which is why Canadian tar sands with 170.4 Gb are often seen as a possible successor. However, Saudi oil fields release about 10.85 mb/d onto world markets while Albertan tar sands struggle to increase its current production level of 1.32 mb/d.

Apart from geology, the possible oil flow rate is determined by many other constraints. For example, many oil-producing countries have substantially decreased exports due to increases in (often subsidised) domestic demand. Geopolitics could be another such constraint. Most importantly, however, the quality dimension of Peak-Oil, which belongs to the 'above ground' Peak-Oil literature, may determine flow rates.

The second key Peak-Oil message is that the phenomenon will prove significantly harmful to the present socio-economic system. This is mainly due to the fact that higher quality oil has been extracted first (best first principle). Lower quality oil not only translates directly into greater economic costs per unit of resource obtained, but into social and environmental costs, as well. We can distinguish the quality of the resource itself and the quality of the location. In resource terms, we are now more and more dependent on heavy oils (e.g. tar sands) or oil with high levels of contaminants (mostly sulphur). In location terms, we are increasingly faced with difficult geological (e.g. deep sea, impregnated rocks, liquid salt layers, scattered pockets/shale), geopolitical (e.g. hostile regimes, political instability) and geographic (e.g. polar oil, extreme weather, open sea, etc.) conditions. What we face is an expansion of oil's **commodity frontiers**.

These increasing exploration, extraction and production costs inevitably reduce our energy return on investment (EROI), which has already been decreasing for most energy resources over the years. The EROI is the net energy remaining after subtracting the amount necessary to explore, extract and refine an energy resource. In the 1970s, this used to be about 30:1 for domestic oil in the US. In 2005 it was already down to about half that. In comparison, tar sands are situated between 2 and 4:1 (Murphy and Hall 2010). It's still too early to know exactly the EROI for shale oil and gas produced with hydraulic fracturing (fracking). Experts already point to the fact that shale wells are very expensive and tend to peak fast (not to mentions its seismic and environmental impacts). Most renewable forms of energy (except hydropower) also have very low EROIs.

According to energy analysts, the change in the quality of our main energy resource is bound to have significant consequences for economies. Adherents of the 'Olduvai theory' even predict an imminent societal collapse. Some argue that the economic crisis of 2008 was due mainly to high oil prices caused by scarcities and that Peak-Oil is in fact behind the current global economic crisis. Orthodox economists on the other hand continue to deny any such relation, as they believe that with the help of technological innovation any resource can be substituted. One problem with this belief is that, apart from the lower EROIs of most substitutes, the same dynamics described previously for oil are evident in other resources. Ever-lower ore grades drive up the prices of minerals (e.g. Peak-Phosphorous) and metals (e.g. Peak-Copper), some of which are desperately needed for renewable energy technology, in particular the so-called rare earth minerals (e.g. terbium, yttrium and neodymium).

In other words, resource peaks highlight the fact that human society has reached important biophysical limitations. Economic degrowth from this perspective is no longer an option, but a reality. The challenge for the degrowth movement is to help develop a path towards a post-carbon society that is socially sustainable. Some energy analysts argue that such a managed or prosperous descent is not possible because the economic system is too complex and specialized and thus very hard to change smoothly. To them, tweaking the wheels is likely to cause more harm than good. For this reason it is important to study economic vulnerabilities to Peak-Oil in order to design adaptation policies carefully (e.g. Kerschner et al. 2013). A first starting point would be the voluntary advancement of biophysical limits via resource caps in order to reduce the decline curve and give more time for adaptation. However, the goal of the degrowth movement should not only be to 'survive' Peak-Oil with the least social cost, but to use this crisis to stimulate the creation of a more equitable and sustainable world that questions the current modes of socio-economic organization and a civilization based on the careless over-exploitation of non-renewable resources.

References

Campbell, C. and Laherrere, J. (1998) 'The end of cheap oil'. *Scientific American*, 278(3): 78–84.

Kerschner, C., Prell, C., Feng, K. and Hubacek, K. (2013) 'Economic vulnerability to Peak Oil.' *Global Environmental Change*, 23: 6, 1, 424–1, 423.

Murphy, D. J. and Hall, C. A. S. (2010) 'Year in review: EROI or energy return on (energy) invested'. *Annals of the New York Academy of Sciences*, 1185 (Ecological Economics Reviews), 102–18.

Sorrell, S., Miller, R. Bentley, R. and Speirs, J. (2010) 'Oil futures: A comparison of global supply forecasts'. *Energy Policy*, 38(9): 4,990–5,003.

29

SIMPLICITY

Samuel Alexander

MELBOURNE SUSTAINABLE SOCIETY INSTITUTE, UNIVERSITY OF MELBOURNE & SIMPLICITY INSTITUTE

In broad terms, voluntary simplicity can be understood to imply a way of life that involves consciously minimizing wasteful and resource-intensive consumption. But it is also about reimagining 'the good life' by directing progressively more time and energy toward pursuing non-materialistic sources of satisfaction and meaning. In other words, voluntary simplicity involves embracing a minimally 'sufficient' material standard of living, in exchange for more time and freedom to pursue other life goals, such as community or social engagements, more time with family, artistic or intellectual projects, home-based production, more fulfilling employment, political participation, spiritual exploration, relaxation, pleasure-seeking, and so on – none of which need to rely on money, or much money. Variously defended by its advocates on personal, social, political, humanitarian, and ecological grounds, voluntary simplicity is based on the assumption that human beings can live meaningful, free, happy, and infinitely diverse lives, while consuming no more than an equitable share of nature (see generally, Alexander and Ussher 2012).

A social philosopher named Richard Gregg coined the term 'voluntary simplicity' in 1936, although obviously the way of life to which he referred is as old as civilization itself. Throughout history there have always been individuals and communities who have expressed doubts about the merits of living a materialistic life focused on material wealth and possessions. A history of simplicity could begin with Siddhartha Gautama – the Buddha – who at the age of twenty-nine gave up what he considered to be the superficial luxuries of a royal existence and sought spiritual truth in a life of extreme asceticism. After nearly starving himself to death through his practice of self-deprivation, Siddhartha reconsidered his path and after years of inner struggle he is said to have found Enlightenment in what Buddhists call 'the Middle Way' – a path of meditative self-discipline that lies between the paths of worldly indulgence and asceticism. A similar message about the spiritual value of living a materially simple life can be found in almost all of the world's religious and spiritual texts (if not always in their practices!), as well as many of the world's indigenous wisdom traditions.

Simplicity of living also found many advocates among the great philosophers of ancient Greece and Rome, the Cynics and the Stoics, in particular. In one of the most radical expressions of simplicity, Diogenes the Cynic voluntarily embraced a life of poverty to show by example that a free and meaningful life could not be measured by conventional accounts of wealth. Less extreme were the Stoics, such as Epictetus, Marcus Aurelius, and Seneca, who advocated disciplined and thoughtful moderation rather than poverty. In various ways the Stoics argued that people cannot always be in control of how much worldly wealth and fame they attain, but they are or can be in control of the attitudes they adopt in relation to such things. Similarly, the Chinese philosopher Lao-Tzu once said, 'He who knows he has enough is rich,' suggesting also that they who have enough, but who do not know it, are poor.

Leaping forward to the Victorian era in England, one finds passionate support for simple living in the works of the great 'moralists,' John Ruskin and William Morris. Ruskin refused to treat **money** as a neutral meeting place of mere exchange and instead highlighted the ways in which the obscuring distances of a money economy pushed the social and environmental consequences of consumption out of sight. Ruskin urged people to recognize that material things are worthwhile only to the extent that they further some worthwhile end, a perspective encapsulated in his maxim, 'There is no wealth but life.' William Morris developed this line of thought in important ways, drawing particular attention to how consumption is always dependent upon labour. Morris suggested that huge reductions in 'useless toil' could be achieved if people would reduce their consumption of 'those articles of folly and luxury.' The Bohemians in Europe, on the other hand, tended to live simple lives for the sake of their art and for pleasure. Quite different again are the Amish, the Trappist monks, and the Quakers, who exemplify varieties of the simple life grounded upon religious belief. In the twentieth century, towering figures such as Gandhi, Lenin, Tolstoy, and Mother Teresa all lived lives of great material simplicity.

Given that the US is the birthplace of hyper-consumerism, it might surprise some people to discover that in fact the US has always had an undercurrent of 'plain living and high thinking' (Shi 2007). In the mid-nineteenth century there were the fascinating versions of the simple life articulated by the New England Transcendentalists. This was a colourful group of poets, mystics, social reformers, and philosophers – including Henry Thoreau (see Bode 1983) – who lived on modest means in order to afford the luxury of creativity and contemplation. As leading Transcendentalist, Ralph Waldo Emerson, once asserted: 'It is better to go without than to have possessions at too great a cost'. Other early Americans highlighted the tension between profiteering and civic virtue, and insisted on the close connection between simple living and a flourishing democracy. There were also the warnings of Benjamin Franklin, who railed against consumers thoughtlessly going into **debt**:

[W]hat Madness must it be to run into debt for these Superfluities! . . . think what you do when you turn in Debt; you give another power over your liberty . . . Preserve your Freedom; and maintain your Independency:. . . .be frugal and free.

Franklin 1817: 94

In more recent decades, US President Carter advocated material restraint on the grounds that 'owning things and consuming things does not satisfy our longing for meaning.' Referring to 'a crisis of spirit', he felt that the worship of 'self-indulgence and consumption' was based on 'a mistaken idea of freedom' (see generally, Shi 2007).

What could be called the 'modern' simplicity movement is typically traced back to the North American and European counter-cultures of the 1960s and 1970s, for these movements had deep anti-consumerist and environmentalist sentiments that generally supported simple living. This was especially so with respect to the so-called '**back-to-the-landers**' movement of that era, exemplified by the inspired lives of Helen and Scott Nearing and echoed in contemporary neo-rurals. More recently the Transition Town, Permaculture, and Eco-village movements also advocate moving away from consumerist lifestyles toward less consumptive, less energy-intensive ways of living (see **eco-communities**). These movements are trying to build the alternative society by living the solution, even if presently their impact is modest. There have also been more focused theories of simplicity, advocating a 'sufficiency economy' (Alexander, 2012) or 'The Simpler Way' (Trainer 2010). These theories variously argue for a restructuring of society with the aim of creating low-energy, highly localized, **steady state** economies, based on a politicized culture of simple living (see **de-politicization**). It is certainly the case that a simple living movement without a politics would be insufficient to change political and macro-economic structures. Simple living movements must not seek to 'escape' the system, but radically 'transform' it.

The purely macro-economic perspective on degrowth, as a process of planned contraction, fails to highlight the cultural values and practices that must accompany, and perhaps precede, a degrowth transition. After all, if a culture is generally comprised of individuals seeking ever-higher levels of income and consumption, it follows that such a culture would desire and indeed require a **growth** economy. In order for an economics and politics of degrowth to emerge, therefore, it would seem that people at the cultural level must be prepared to give up or resist high-consumption 'affluent' lifestyles and instead embrace 'simpler' lifestyles of reduced or restrained consumption. Ideally this would be a voluntary transition – a 'planned economic contraction' – but it may end up being a transition imposed on people by way of recession or even collapse. There is some ground for optimism in that throughout history, from East to West, people have simplified their lives to engage in a variety of enriching pursuits, including philosophy, religious devotion, artistic creation, hedonism, revolutionary or democratic politics, humanitarian service, and ecological activism. At the same time, the values of voluntary simplicity have generally been dominated by more materialistic values. In the present age of gross ecological overshoot and economic instability, however, perhaps simplicity of living is at last a way of life whose time has come. Degrowth surely depends on it.

References

Alexander, S. (2012) 'The Sufficiency Economy: Envisioning a Prosperous Way Down' *Simplicity Institute Report, 12s*. Available online available at: www.simplicityinstitute.org/publications (accessed 7 July 2013).

Alexander, S. and Ussher, S. (2012) 'The Voluntary Simplicity Movement: A Multi-National Survey Analysis in Theoretical Context', *Journal of Consumer Culture*, 12(1): 66–86.

Bode, C. (ed.) (1983) *The Portable Thoreau*, New York: Penguin.

Trainer, T. (2010) *The Transition to a Sustainable and Just World*, Sydney: Envirobook.

Shi, D. (2007, revised edition) *The Simple Life: Plain Living and High Thinking in American Culture*, Georgia: University of Georgia Press.

Weems, M. L. (1817) *The Life of Benjamin Franklin*, Philadelphia: M Carey.

30

SOCIAL LIMITS OF GROWTH

Giorgos Kallis

RESEARCH & DEGROWTH, ICREA AND ICTA (INSTITUTE OF ENVIRONMENTAL SCIENCE AND
TECHNOLOGY), AUTONOMOUS UNIVERSITY OF BARCELONA

Above a certain level of economic **growth**, which satisfies basic material needs, a rising proportion of income goes to so-called 'positional goods' (Hirsch 1976). Exclusive real estate, an expensive car, a rare painting, a degree from a top private university; these are all positional goods. Access to such goods signifies one's position in society and depends on relative income. Unlike normal goods, the more of a positional good our peers have, the less satisfaction we derive from it. Positional goods are inherently scarce since scarcity is their essence; by definition, not everyone can have high status, own a *rare* painting or *the most* expensive car. Economic **growth** can never satisfy the desire for positional goods. Worse, **growth** makes positional goods less accessible. As the material component of the economy becomes more productive, positional consumption, inherently limited as it is, gets more expensive. Witness the rising price of a house with a vista or the life-costs of a degree from a top university. Positional goods signal therefore the social limit *of* growth, i.e. a limit on what growth can deliver, as compared to limits *to* growth, i.e. limits to the continuation of growth.

Nevertheless, what sustains the desire for **growth** in wealthy economies is precisely the dream of access to positional goods. Consider pundit Daniel Ben-Ami who in a book against degrowth defends the dream of 'Ferraris for All'. Let us for a moment follow his argument, and assume away **peak oil** or climate change since *in theory* technological progress could supersede such limits. Let us assume away also the congestion if everyone had a Ferrari, a congestion that would make Ferraris slower than bicycles. *In theory*, cities and highways could be rebuilt to accommodate 7 billion Ferraris running at full speed. Even so, the fundamental limit of Ben-Ami's dream is still that if everyone had a Ferrari, then a Ferrari would no longer be a 'Ferrari'. It would be the equivalent of a Fiat Cinquecento, a car of the masses. Aspirations would have shifted to another, faster car, which would signify wealth and position. Those without access to the new model would remain as frustrated as those who do not have a Ferrari today. The pursuit of positional goods is a zero-sum game (Frank 2000).

Yet this is a zero-sum game with a substantial social cost (imagine the resources wasted in reconfiguring territories or cleaning up the air for 7 billion Ferraris). The personal and public resources wasted in such zero-sum positional games could be used beneficially elsewhere (Frank 2000). In fact, in affluent societies a rising proportion of social income is wasted on private, positional consumption, while public goods that would improve the quality of life for all are left to deteriorate (Galbraith 1958). Positional consumption increases also the cost of free time, making leisure less attractive, undermining sociability and reducing the time devoted to family, friends, community, or politics (Hirsch 1976). Time is budgeted and increasingly valued in money; as a result, social relations get increasingly commodified. **Commodification** is also the result of enclosures that are enforced to maintain privileged access to positional goods (e.g. a private beach or a college fee; Hirsch 1976). In a vicious cycle, as more and more goods and services come under the sway of money and positional competition, the love of money is further inflated, undermining even more social relations and social mores (Hirsch 1976; Skidelsky and Skidelsky 2012).

The social limits thesis is central for degrowth. It is not only that **growth** will not last forever or that it is becoming uneconomical because of its social and environmental costs. It is that growth is 'senseless', a goal without reason, the pursuit of an elusive dream (Skidelsky and Skidelsky 2012: 7). In affluent countries there is enough to satisfy the basic material needs of everyone; positional inequalities are a matter of distribution not aggregate growth (Hirsch 1976). If rising productivity and growth make positional goods more expensive, then degrowth will make them less expensive, increasing wellbeing and releasing collective resources from unnecessary positional consumption. A degrowth trajectory could lead in this way to an improvement, and not a deterioration as is often alleged, of basic goods such as education, health, or public infrastructure.

There remain however some unexplored issues in this account. First, in much of the degrowth literature, especially that related to voluntary **simplicity**, abstinence from positional and conspicuous consumption is presented as a moral and individual matter. This is wrong: positional consumption is not a personal vice. It is a structural social phenomenon to which individuals conform to remain part of the mainstream. Exiting the 'rat race' and downshifting has first-mover risks, such as reduced respectability, fewer job opportunities and loss of income (Frank 2000). People from less privileged backgrounds facing economic insecurity are understandably less confident with taking such risks. There is also a healthy dose of civic ethic in the desire to conform to the average lifestyle and not to differ too much. In fact, under late **capitalism**, it is the desire to differ that constantly creates new positional goods and fuels accumulation. Paradoxically, frugal, 'simple' life-styles have become signifiers of distinction and position, since they are first adopted by members of the educated or artistic elites who can appreciate and afford them (Heeth and Potter 2004). Think of the jeans, first used by **back-to-the-landers** in the 1960s, or of the rise of property values in the remote parts of the countryside 'discovered' by counter-culturals and settled by **eco-communities**. Somewhat tragically, those wishing to escape from positional consumption become the pioneers of new positional goods.

If the problem is structural, then the solution should also be structural. Some economists want governments to make positional goods more expensive. Proposals include taxing luxury goods or shifting taxation from income to consumption, basically by subtracting savings from taxable income (with steeply progressive rates to account for the fact that the rich save more [Frank 2000]). Others go further. One proposal is for a radical redistribution, since if everyone had similar levels of wealth no one could bid up for positional goods. Another proposal is the removal of positional goods from the commercial sector (decommodification) making them available through public access or public, non-market allocation (Hirsch 1976).

A second, related, issue is whether positional competition can be tamed with taxes and regulation within capitalism, or whether overcoming it marks a transition out of **capitalism**. Inequalities are central, rather than incidental, to capitalism's dynamism, as noted by Joseph Schumpeter. Unequal access to positional goods sustains a generalized insatiability that is essential if **capitalism** is to constantly extract social energy from everyone, even after material needs have been satisfied. Vice versa, while positional goods and money competition have existed in all human societies, it is only capitalism that has 'released them from the bounds of custom and religion within which they were formerly confined' (Skidelsky and Skidelsky 2012: 40). Insatiability may have psychological roots, but it is capitalism that made it the psychological basis of a civilization. A society that would consider itself satisfied to have 'enough' would have no reason to accumulate and would no longer be capitalist (Skidelsky and Skidelsky 2012).

Socialist economies suppressed positional goods by decree, redistribution and forced collectivization. But positional competition resurfaced into competition for positions in the bureaucracy and for scarce goods from the West. Some ancient societies channelled competition to symbolic sports events, potlatches and gift-giving. Anthropologists have documented also how in primitive egalitarian societies positions existed, yet they were not that important, either because they rotated, or because they were socially controlled and reprimanded, making sure that no individual or group accumulated too much power. Assuming that any given collective (nation, community or other) decides today to move in such an egalitarian direction in the contemporary world of globalized communications and states of reference, one question is why wouldn't its members compare themselves to those of wealthier individuals in less egalitarian neighbours and find themselves wanting. This may be part of what happened in socialist countries. Although the competition for positional goods is a structural problem, its solution can never be imposed solely from above. It has to be part and parcel of an ethico-political project of self-limitation, **simplicity** and equality to which the members of a collective autonomously subscribe to.

References

Frank, R. (2000). *Luxury fever: Weighing the cost of excess*. New York: The Free Press.

Galbraith, J. K. (1958). *The affluent society*. Boston: Houghton Mifflin.

Heeth, J. and A. Potter (2004). *Nation of rebels. How counter-culture became consumer culture*. New York: Harper Collins.

Hirsch, F. (1976). *Social limits to growth*. Cambridge: Harvard University Press.

Skidelsky, R. and Skidelsky, E. (2012). *How much is enough? Money and the good life*. London: Penguin.

PART 3
The action

31

BACK-TO-THE-LANDERS

Rita Calvário[1] and Iago Otero[2]

[1]ICTA (INSTITUTE OF ENVIRONMENTAL SCIENCE AND TECHNOLOGY), AUTONOMOUS
UNIVERSITY OF BARCELONA
[2] RESEARCH & DEGROWTH AND IRI THESYS, HUMBOLDT-UNIVERSITÄT ZU BERLIN

Back-to-the-landers (or neorurals) are people with no agrarian background who migrate from the city to the countryside to adopt a radically new agrarian or artisan lifestyle. Their motivations are linked to the search for a simpler, self-sufficient, autonomous (free from wage labor and market), close-to-nature, and ecological way of life. They do this by following a critique of materialist mainstream culture, modern farming practices, and the globalization of the agri-food systems. Back-to-the-landers perceive their choice as a lifestyle project and a way for social transition towards ecological sustainability. This explains why they may be considered actors of a diversified strategy of socio-ecological change towards a degrowth future.

Organic small-scale farming, re-localization of production and consumption, alternative economies and networks are some of the qualities associated with the "rural" by back-to-the-landers. These qualities conflict with other representations of rurality (e.g. agribusiness views). Even if "radical ruralities" often adopt a rural–urban divide for their discursive frame, connections with the "city", through alternative economies and networks, are common.

Back-to-the-land is not new in Western history. Since the advent of **capitalism**, the "countryside" has played a role of critique to rationalist abstraction, **commodification** of land and labor, modern state and politics, individual alienation, and the dissolution of social bonds. These critiques – which feature strongly in the degrowth discourse – have been expressed in different ways by different actors across time. For instance, the countryside has been a place for the elite's mourning of a lost past and also a place for utopian socialist or libertarian quests for a new social order. Alternately, the countryside has been a place of refuge from the degrading conditions of industrial labor and urban life. States have also been promoters of urban-to-rural migration, small-scale agrarian capitalism, or an undifferentiated "peasantry" as a way of shifting the cost of social reproduction through self-provision, reducing relief payments, and tackling urban unrest during crisis periods.

The 1960s and 1970s are of considerable significance for back-to-the-land ideals, the restructuring of **capitalism**, and rural change. Hippie and May 1968 social movements led to a rise of back-to-the-landers, which paralleled the broader process of counter-urbanization, i.e. the outmigration of urbanites to rural areas attracted mainly by a better quality of life, but without any counter-cultural motivation. Back-to-the-land echoed the growing environmental consciousness, the reaction to consumerism, and the discourses on the limits to growth after the energetic crisis of the 1970s. It was inspired by a return to both "nature" and to an idealized rural society as a way of rejecting commodity fetishism, alienation of wage labor, and the modern values of progress and technological improvement. Several of these back-to-the-land experiences and communes ended due to internal conflicts, disillusionment, debts, and poverty, while others thrived and still exist today.

The persistence of the back-to-the-land movement can be partly explained by the people's engagement in a countryside increasingly turned into a place of leisure for an increasingly urban population. Rural areas changed as a result of a growing service economy and consumerist lifestyles, identities, and culture. Paradoxically, back-to-the-landers may have acted as pioneers of rural gentrification and **commodification**, facilitating the (re)production of "nature" and "rurality" valued for new consumption demands. Integration of the activities of initially radical back-to-the-landers into new markets and access to State funding to recreate a nostalgic rural environment were some of the forms of co-optation. This co-optation signals more broadly the way the critique of the alienation of everyday life of the 1960s was recuperated into a "new spirit of **capitalism**" arising from the mid-1970s onwards. Ideas such as autonomy, network, creativity, flexibility, individual initiative, and liberty were integrated into the dominant (neoliberal) discourse. The removal of its initial anti-capitalist ethos undermined the power of back-to-the-land social critique.

Back-to-the-landers sustained in other ways: the rise of alternative economies and networks worked as modes of contesting the increasingly globalized agri-industrial systems. Some authors argue that alternative economies and networks create spaces outside **capitalism**, building networks of local counter-powers that resist and subvert capitalism's ideological hegemony. This view allows us to look at back-to-the-landers' experiences and projects as ways of building imaginaries of a degrowth (post-capitalist) society. Others, however, argue that alternatives that reinforce the notions of consumer sovereignty, State incapacity, and self-reliant, ordered communities are reproducing neoliberal subjectivities and practices. Or, that living in a highly competitive capitalist market makes it very difficult for alternative projects to maintain their intended differences. Yet another criticism is that by remaining small, local, and marginal, such initiatives are not capable of challenging the conventional farming and distribution channels and the root causes of the unequal social access to high-end quality food. Self-provisioning at a micro-level may also facilitate the ongoing accumulation of capital at a more macro-level.

Back-to-the-landers have the potential to transform the dominant agri-food model and an increasingly commodified countryside, which makes them actors of a degrowth transition. The challenge is to transcend being only a residual fraction of the agri-food system and the rural space. For this, and against the risk of being co-opted, political action involving strategic alliances with other actors towards emancipation from capitalist social relations seems crucial. More than the shape of local experiences, it is their direction that counts. Opening small windows of emancipation may be important for feeding imaginaries of degrowth and to empower individuals. But to formulate emancipation in a capitalist global market as a concrete possibility involves a broader and articulated collective struggle for social change, in which networks of local experiences can play an important role. Networked action has been important in struggles against land speculation, privatization of resources, rural gentrification and **commodification**, and agribusiness expansion. This networking has been made possible by empowering localities and their inhabitants with resistance capacity and by amplifying their capacity. Reclaiming the **commons** is a key point for such land-based social movements. More than defending their own interests, this should be seen as a vision of transcending capitalist relations of private property and of reconnecting inhabitants with their territories.

References

Boyle, P. and Halfacree, K. (eds) (1998) *Migration into Rural Areas: Theories and Issues*, Chichester, UK: John Wiley & Sons.

Brown, D. (2011) *Back-to-the-Land: The Enduring Dream of Self-Sufficiency in Modern America*, Madison: University of Wisconsin Press.

Halfacree, K. (ed.) (2007) "Back-to-the-Land in the Twenty-first Century – Making Connections with Rurality", *Tijdschrift voor economische en sociale geografie*, 98(1): 3–67.

Jacob, J. (1997) *New Pioneers: The Back-to-the-Land Movement and the Search for a Sustainable Future*, Philadelphia: The Pennsylvania State University Press.

Wilbur, A. (2013) "Growing a Radical Ruralism: Back-to-the-Land as Practice and Ideal", *Geography Compass*, 7:149–60.

32

BASIC AND MAXIMUM INCOME

Samuel Alexander

MELBOURNE SUSTAINABLE SOCIETY INSTITUTE, UNIVERSITY OF MELBOURNE AND SIMPLICITY INSTITUTE

To eliminate poverty, capitalist societies generally rely on growing the economic pie, not slicing it differently. If the pursuit of **growth** were given up, however, and a degrowth process of planned economic contraction were embraced, poverty would have to be confronted more directly. Among other things, this would require a restructuring of the property and tax systems for the purpose of redistributing wealth and ensuring everyone had 'enough' (Alexander 2011). The Basic Income and the Maximum Income are two policies that could help achieve these important egalitarian goals, without relying on **growth**.

Although there is considerable variety in forms of Basic Income, the core idea is relatively straightforward. In its idealised and most radical form, every person living permanently in a nation would receive from the state a periodic (e.g. fortnightly) payment, and this payment would be sufficient for an individual to live at a minimal though dignified standard of economic security. Advocates typically argue that a Basic Income payment should be *guaranteed* by the state, *unconditional* on the performance of any labour, and *universal*.

Within a fully developed Basic Income system, some advocates argue that other state transfers could be abolished – such as unemployment benefits, family allowances, pensions, etc. – since the Basic Income grant would be sufficient to provide everyone with a decent, though minimal, subsistence. Existing 'social welfare' has proven unable to eliminate poverty, even in the richest nations, so the powerful moral attraction of a Basic Income lies in how directly it confronts poverty. It is a policy based on the idea that the distribution of an economy's wealth must begin by ensuring that everyone has 'enough' to live with dignity. The Basic Income could also include non-monetary benefits, such as free health care, or direct provision of food, clothes, and accommodation to those in need.

The feasibility of a Basic Income System is typically questioned on two main grounds (Fitzpatrick 1999). The first objection is that making the Basic Income unconditional on the performance of any labour would give rise to a society of 'free-loaders' and ultimately lead to economic collapse. This objection, however, arises out of a debatable conception of human beings. While it may be the case that the 'free-loader' problem would exist to some extent, a case can be made that human beings, by and large, are social creatures, who find being engaged in their community's work more meaningful and fulfilling than being isolated, idle, and parasitic on their community. Furthermore, even if there were a minority that chose not to contribute productively in any way, this could well be a tolerable social burden – more tolerable, one might argue, than the levels of poverty that exist today. Alternatively, the Basic Income could mandate some form of social contribution, even if that contribution were outside the 'formal economy'.

The second objection typically levelled at the Basic Income concerns its financial feasibility, a pragmatic issue that is obviously of great importance. However, this is arguably more a matter of political commitment than a financing challenge, especially since the state has the power to issue **money** for worthwhile or necessary purposes. To ease the burden on the public purse and soften the transition, one policy option is to begin the Basic Income payments at some very low level and increase them gradually over time to a level of dignified subsistence. Another option would be to establish a Negative Income Tax system, which differs from a Basic Income in that it provides a tax-credit to people, not universally, but only to those with incomes below the subsistence level. This would provide low-income earners with a guaranteed minimum income but via an alternative route. Over time, the Negative Income Tax system could evolve into a Basic Income system.

The social benefits of a successful Basic Income system would be profound and far-reaching. Beyond eliminating poverty and economic insecurity, its institution would also strengthen the bargaining position of employees, since it would give people a property right that was independent of their paid employment, and thus more power to demand decent working conditions. It would also mean that people did not have to accept alienating, exploitative, or degrading jobs just to survive; nor would there be any real pressure to sacrifice social and political autonomy in order to achieve economic security. Furthermore, a Basic Income would also effectively acknowledge the worth of unpaid work and other forms of social contribution, thereby extending economic citizenship beyond participants in the traditional labour market or 'formal economy' (see **care,** the **New Economy**). For these reasons, among others, a Basic Income would produce far more democratic and egalitarian societies than any capitalist society ever could, which is why it receives support from many advocates of degrowth.

As well as a Basic Income – or income 'floor' – some degrowth advocates also insist that there should be an income 'ceiling' – that is, an upper limit to the size of any individual's income. This is sometimes called a 'maximum income,' and like the Basic Income it could be achieved in various ways. For example, a tax rate could increase progressively as the taxable income increases, culminating in a 100 per cent tax on all income over a specified level. This would avoid the creation of a stratified society of Basic Income recipients, on the one hand, and the super-rich, on the other. Such a policy also finds support in the voluminous evidence showing that great inequalities of wealth are socially corrosive and that more equal societies do better on a whole host of social and economic indicators (Pickett and Wilkinson 2010). The 'maximum income' idea finds further justification in the sociological research indicating that once basic material needs are met, further increases in income contribute little if anything to subjective wellbeing or **happiness** (Alexander 2012). What this research suggests is that high incomes are essentially wasted so far as wellbeing is concerned, making a maximum income an extremely important means of avoiding wasteful consumption and creating more egalitarian societies. The tax procured from the maximum income could be used to fund a basic income.

References

Alexander, S. (2011) 'Property beyond Growth: Toward a Politics of Voluntary Simplicity', (doctoral thesis, University of Melbourne).

Alexander, S. (2012) 'The Optimal Material Threshold: Toward an Economics of Sufficiency', *Real-World Economics Review* 61: 2–21.

Fitzpatrick, T. (1999) *Freedom and Security: An Introduction to the Basic Income Debate*, New York: Palgrave.

Pickett, K. and Wilkinson, R. (2010) *The Spirit Level: Why Greater Equality Makes Societies Stronger*, London: Penguin.

Raventós, D. (2007) *Basic Income: The Material Conditions of Freedom*, London: Pluto Press.

33

COMMUNITY CURRENCIES

Kristofer Dittmer

RESEARCH & DEGROWTH AND ICTA (INSTITUTE OF ENVIRONMENTAL SCIENCE
AND TECHNOLOGY), AUTONOMOUS UNIVERSITY OF BARCELONA

Money is conventionally defined through its three main functions: a unit of account, a medium of exchange, and a store of value. Currencies refer to the medium of exchange function. Community currencies (CCs) are unconventional monies, i.e. monies not being declared by any national government to be a legal tender. CCs are created for a range of different purposes. With varying connotations, they are also often referred to as alternative, complementary, or local currencies. An attempt at a strict definition appears inadvisable; however, the terms refer to currencies that are mostly created by civil society and sometimes by public authorities, circulating at subnational levels.

Since the early 1980s, there has been worldwide experimentation with community currencies at a scale unparalleled since the Great Depression. The five most significant contemporary types are LETS (usually Local Exchange Trading System or Scheme), time banks, HOURS, barter market currencies, and convertible local currencies (see North 2010 for a book-length introduction). Many of these have spread through the international green movement, for which they embody green principles like "small is beautiful" and grassroots economics. However, the ideological legacy of community currencies goes back at least to nineteenth century utopian socialists Owen and Proudhon's attempts to construct more progressive markets by means of monetary innovations. Contemporary experimentation with community currencies within the Left can be understood as part of its reappraisal of market-based approaches in view of the failure of central planning in socialist countries. Community currencies are also favoured by right wing libertarians in the tradition of E. C. Riegel, though more likely by other names such as "mutual credit systems."

The relevance of community currencies to degrowth depends on what is meant by the latter. In one sense, degrowth can be thought of as an intentional departure from **growth**-based society, meant to pre-empt further environmental destruction and human suffering. Alternatively, in the context of a long-term crisis of global **capitalism** manifested as chronically deficient growth levels (a scenario that many degrowth advocates consider likely for the not-too-distant future), degrowth can be imagined as a socially equitable adaptation to a society without **growth**. Since contemporary experimentation with community currencies has taken place within the ordinary ups and downs of **capitalism**, their existing track record is of larger relevance to the former scenario than the latter. According to this track record, community currencies have not significantly facilitated any voluntary departure from the **growth** path. Their potential for purposive degrowth can be assessed with respect to four criteria which are among the most common motivations for setting up and participating in community currency systems: *community-building*, i.e. the resurrection and improvement of local social networks; advancing *alternative values* mediated through economic exchange (i.e. challenging mainstream values regarding race, class, gender, and nature); facilitation of *alternative livelihoods*, where larger self-determination over productive activity weakens the imperative to seek employment irrespective of its environmental consequences; and *eco-localization*, i.e. the ecologically and politically motivated localization of networks of production and consumption. A recent review of the academic literature on LETS, time banks, HOURS, and convertible local currencies found that the basis for advocating them as tools for purposive degrowth was very weak judging by their performance with respect to these four criteria (Dittmer 2013).

The relevance of community currencies to degrowth in the second sense is more speculative, as there is no precedent for a long-term crisis of **capitalism**. Existing experience does suggest that community currencies may have a role to play in situations where increased restrictions on popular access to conventional money generate widespread unmet needs together with idle productive capacities. The usefulness of barter currency networks to millions of Argentineans during the crisis of 2001–2 is the outstanding case in point (see e.g. Gómez 2009; North 2007). However, these networks were largely based on the second-hand exchange of domestic possessions of the middle class, accumulated in previous years of relative wealth, and the networks were overwhelmed and collapsed partly because this spare capacity had become exhausted. Fortunately, important welfare policies were introduced by the government at this stage of the crisis. The mitigation of a more long-term crisis, in which weaker welfare policies may be expected, would require a much larger positive impact on broader productive sectors than achieved by the Argentinean barter currencies.

A major challenge to the adoption of community currencies by formal productive sectors is the problem of overcoming the contradiction between the increased access to resources that comes with large-scale circulation, and the difficulties of currency management. Worldwide, community currencies have only escaped this contradiction, to a limited extent, through backing the money supply with conventional money; an unworkable solution in a situation of monetary drought. In Argentina, the large-scale currencies that had served the overwhelming majority of participants collapsed in hyperinflation from bad monetary management combined with widespread forgery. As this illustrates, large-scale monetary systems require vast amounts of financial and organizational resources, and it may be generalized that stable ones have historically been the work of states (see also **money, public**). This leaves little scope for the maintenance of materially significant currency systems in a position of resistance against the state. However, in Argentina, some smaller networks were able to continue despite the collapse of the larger ones. But by then the worst phase of the crisis was over, so these networks were useful only to a few people, often for social rather than economic reasons. Perhaps in a long-term crisis, such smaller networks could play a more lasting role. Their potential for democratic management, in contrast to unaccountable large-scale networks, will sustain their attraction to many degrowth advocates. In a scenario of long-term crisis of **capitalism** in which large populations were left to fend for themselves, superfluous to the interests of governments and capitalists, community currencies could become especially useful.

References

Dittmer, K. (2013) 'Local Currencies for Purposive Degrowth? A Quality Check of some Proposals for Changing Money-as-Usual', *Journal of Cleaner Production*, 54: 3–13.

Gómez, G. M. (2009) *Argentina's Parallel Currency: The Economy of the Poor*, London: Pickering & Chatto.

North, P. (2007) *Money and Liberation: The Micropolitics of Alternative Currency Movements*, Minneapolis: University of Minnesota Press.

North, P. (2010) *Local Money: How to Make it Happen in Your Community*, Totnes: Transition Books.

34

CO-OPERATIVES

Nadia Johanisova[1], Ruben Suriñach Padilla[2] and Philippa Parry[3]

[1]MASARYK UNIVERSITY, [2]CENTRE FOR RESEARCH AND
INFORMATION ON CONSUMPTION; [3]FORUM FOR THE FUTURE SCHOLAR

The term co-operative (or co-op) refers to a type of organisational structure applicable to various types of enterprises in many sectors. Many co-operatives also see themselves as part of a worldwide movement which was born in Europe in the mid-nineteenth century. The International Co-operative Alliance (ICA – a federation of co-operative networks representing one billion individuals) defines a co-operative as an 'autonomous association of persons united voluntarily to meet their common economic, social, and cultural needs and aspirations through a jointly-owned and democratically-controlled enterprise.' In 1995, the ICA accepted the following seven co-operative principles: voluntary and open membership; democratic member control (the one-member-one-vote principle: members participate in co-operative governance and elected representatives are accountable to them); members' economic participation; autonomy and independence; commitment to education about the ethos and practice of co-operation; co-operation among co-operatives; concern for the sustainable development of their communities (Birchall 1997: 64–71).

Co-operatives operate in a number of sectors and consist of three main types: producer or worker co-ops (first developed in France and Italy), consumer co-ops (first developed in the United Kingdom by the Rochdale Pioneers) and credit co-ops or credit unions (first developed in Germany). Another important group are farmers' buying and selling co-ops (especially successful in Scandinavia).

Co-operatives have gone through a difficult history, co-opted by dictatorships (e.g. Spain under Franco, Czechoslovakia under communism), promoted indiscriminately by many governments in the 1950s and 1960s, then reviled in Central and Eastern Europe and many Global South countries under neoliberalism (Birchall 1997: 143, 169). Some modern co-ops that began with a strong ethos have since lost it and are predominantly motivated by profit. The reasons why so many successful co-operatives have lost their ethos and drifted close to the mainstream are varied.

One cause is linked to economic pressures in a competitive environment. To survive economically, a co-operative may decide to reduce its staff, out-source production, or limit local and fair-trade ingredients in its products. Another root cause involves scale. Growing co-operatives may find they cannot access enough capital from their members under the strict co-operative rules. They may then discard the co-op structure. In addition, as the turnover and membership of a co-op grows and its management gets more complex, members may cease to identify with it and become passive, while managers may usurp ever-more power. In some large British building societies variants of this have led to a process of demutualisation ('carpet-bagging'), where members voted to transform themselves into shared companies. Within the Austrian credit union movement, there have been allegations of federations (umbrella-groups) usurping the decision-making power of their member co-ops.

Ways of making sure that co-operatives stick to their ethos are varied. An important factor is an emphasis on education about co-op principles and explicit policies to strengthen member participation in management. Another is building links between co-operatives to bypass the mainstream economy. This can involve ethical and community investment institutions. Co-operatives that have what Richard Douthwaite called a 'community market', such as the reader-members of a co-operatively-owned newspaper or the client-members of community-supported-agriculture schemes do not have to depend on price as the only motivation for clients. Finally, opting for a strategy of replication (more smaller co-ops) rather than growth (one large co-op) may help in retaining member empowerment and loyalty.

Compared to the mainstream for-profit enterprise model based on external shareholder ownership, the co-operative enterprise model is more suited to a degrowth economy due to the following (Johanisova and Wolf 2012: 565):

- Share ownership rules: shares which members have invested in their co-operative are usually not transferable to others and can normally only be redeemed at their original value ('par value shares'). This discourages a growth-for-growth's sake approach since the value of a member's share does not increase with the growth of the co-op. As shares cannot be speculated with, it also makes for a more-long term and place-based membership, more likely to consider long-term community and environmental values.
- Governance structure: the democratic governance structure opens the decision-making arena to a wider spectrum of stakeholders. The co-operative structure at its best collapses the distance between owners, shareholders, workers and consumers and operates within a mutual-aid needs-satisfying logic.
- Money as 'servant not master': a co-operative is free from the requirements of fiduciary duty (the legal obligation to maximise return to shareholders). Again, this allows for objectives such as the prioritisation of the long-term existence

of the organisation, job protection and environmental concerns. Also, a co-operative prioritising service to its members tends to satisfy real rather than spurious needs. As the third co-operative principle emphasises that members who work for the co-operative or otherwise actively engage with it have the same right to a share in the profit as those who have invested money rather than labour, financial assets are more equitably distributed within the co-op.

Few of the large mainstream co-ops and their federations have had any interaction with degrowth and environmental movements and debates. At the same time, there are two emerging areas that offer examples of newer co-operative structures intertwined with degrowth ideas and practices.

First, the Solidarity Economy (or Social and Solidarity Economy) movement, which is relatively young – only a few decades old – and has been boosted by the anti-globalisation movement, integrates different approaches to social change, linking social justice to environmental issues. The International Network for the Promotion of the Social and Solidarity Economy (RIPESS) declared after the Rio+20 summit held in June 2012:

> many economic and social initiatives . . . exist on all continents . . . They cover many sectors . . . and are the living proof of the concrete, vibrant possibility to build different development models, forms of organisation and society where life, plurality, self-management, environmental and social justice define solidarity economy, an economy that is different from that of capital.
>
> *(RIPESS 2012)*

The dominant structure of the organisations represented by RIPESS is that of a co-operative.

An example would be Som Energia, a Catalan renewable energy co-operative, whose members source renewable energy via the co-op and can also invest in new renewable energy projects (http://www.somenergia.coop, accessed 12 January 2014).

Second, there are many initiatives under what has been called 'Grassroots Innovations in Sustainability' (GI). This concept describes a range of initiatives of community self-organisation and has so far been applied mainly to Global North countries. Grassroots Innovations develop production and consumption structures based upon the values of community empowerment and sustainability (Seyfang 2009). They include local organic food networks and consumer groups, barter markets and time banks, local currencies, community gardens, community housing, etc. GIs are often informal co-operative structures, which merge the values of **environmentalism** and social justice (Suriñach-Padilla 2012). In European countries, degrowth-related movements have identified GI as one of the main political means by which to achieve their goals (e.g. Decrece Madrid in Spain, or the Transition Towns Movement worldwide).

References

Birchall, J. (1997) *The International Co-operative Movement*. Manchester: Manchester University Press.

Johanisova, N. and Wolf, S. (2012) 'Economic Democracy: A Path for the Future?', *Futures*, 44(6): 562–70.

Réseau Intercontinental de Promotion de l'Economie Social Solidaire (2012) *The economy we need: Declaration of the social and solidarity economy movement at Rio +20*. Available online at www.ripess.org/ripess-rio20-declaration/?lang=en (accessed 10 July, 2013).

Seyfang, G. (2009) *The New Economics of Sustainable Consumption: Seeds of Change*, Basingstoke: Palgrave MacMillan.

Suriñach-Padilla, R. (2012) 'Innovaciones Comunitarias en Sostenibilidad, ¿Cómo lidera la sociedad civil?', p. 124–38 in CRIC (ed.) *Cambio Global España 2020/50. Consumo y estilos de vida*, Barcelona, CCEIM.

35

DEBT AUDIT

Sergi Cutillas[1][2], David Llistar[1] and Gemma Tarafa[1][2]

[1]OBSERVATORI DEL DEUTE EN LA GLOBALITZACIÓ (ODG)
[2]PLATAFORMA AUDITORIA CIUTADANA DEL DEUTE (PACD)

Debt is a moral obligation between persons. When indebted, a party must fulfil its obligations to the other party. These obligations are often monetary in nature. At times, they originate in circumstances that are unjust due to violence and the exercise of undue power; such debts are illegitimate and should not be paid. The anti-debt movement has raised awareness regarding the importance of citizen audits. In these audits, citizens decide which debts are legitimate, who is responsible for these debts and which debts should be abolished.

Powerful social classes use debt to maintain hierarchical order. This is accomplished by social customs and laws that prioritise debt repayment. There are records since the Bronze age of protest movements aimed at reversing this unjust use of debt. In Mesopotamia, peasants revolted often against a system whereby the non-payment of obligations could lead to the enslavement of debtors and their family members (Toussaint 2012). To preserve social order, the dominant classes periodically annulled outstanding debts and restored peasants' rights. There are many other instances of debt cancellation in ancient Greece and Rome as well as medieval times, in all cases result of social struggles that were exacerbated by crises and increasing inequality. With the discovery of Americas and then the advent of **capitalism**, there was a mobilization of massive manpower utilising debt, taxes and inflation to coerce individuals to work as wage-labour. Debt kept the masses obedient to those in power and mobilised them to work in order to pay off debts and taxes. In this environment, practices such as debt cancellation became a taboo, and the non-payment of debts was associated with humiliation and the loss of social rights.

Dominance in our times is secured by international institutions such as the International Monetary Fund (IMF) and the World Bank, founded in 1944 to promote global **development**. The neoliberal period of deregulation, not least of financial flows and products, which began in the 1970s, has led to Financialization, a new phase of **capitalism** in which the financial sphere has become superior to and controls the productive sphere. Financialization is associated with a marked increase in the generation of debt and the formation of complex financial relationships that reproduce imperialism by providing a pretext for applying pressure or resorting to violent measures if an indebted or financially dependent state does not adhere to the conditions imposed by the dominant powers.

Debt has fuelled material and energetic growth and the payment of debts has legitimated this growth. But this might be coming to an end as debt is growing much more rapidly than material wealth. Kallis *et al.* (2009) hypothesize that limits in the 'real-real economy' (*Oikonomía*) of energy, materials and reproduction are limiting the growth of the 'real' economy of production. Growth has been maintained, but only for a while, by producing paper wealth in the financial sphere of capital circulation. This framework links debt and degrowth. First, while growth is considered necessary to pay debts, in reality debt is created in the first place to sustain an unsustainable growth. Second, distributing debts equitably and cancelling illegitimate debts is necessary for a sustainable 'way down', i.e. a prosperous and not a forced degrowth based on austerity. This is the goal of Citizen Audits.

The origins of contemporary debt audit movements are traceable to global coalitions of civic campaigns, such as *Jubilee 2000, CADTM (Committee for the Abolition of Third World Debt)* and *Jubilee South,* created in the early 1990s to lobby for the cancellation of large portions of the debt accumulated by the world's most impoverished countries in the Global South. Over time, and since 2007 when the crisis hit the 'North', the movement has adopted an increasingly global and multidimensional outlook that recognizes also the ecological limits of the planet. Citizen debt audits, which have arisen in this context, have identified as illegitimate those debts which are produced by an order based on the abuse of power and which contribute to the continued function of this unjust order (Ramos 2006). Norway and Ecuador are two emblematic precedents to consider. In 2006, after considering its responsibilities as a co-creditor, the Norwegian government cancelled the debts owed to Norway by seven countries. In 2007, Ecuador's Public Credit Audit Commission (CAIC) conducted an audit of Ecuador's debt and declared this debt to be illegitimate.

These examples are instances of mixed audits, which are conducted by elements of civic society and by the government. Brazil and the Philippines, among other countries, have conducted debt audits driven solely by civic movements. In Egypt, Tunisia, Greece, Portugal and Ireland, social movements have begun the process of conducting civic audits or have pressured governments to institute public debt audits. Each of these cases features a common protest: a desire to determine how debts were generated, which individuals are responsible for the generation of the relevant debts and what effects these debts produce. Movements demand accountability from the responsible parties and propose alternative economic models to turbo-**capitalism**. Civic audits usually include the following stages: accessing information, data analysis, advocacy, networking, dissemination, public education and the prosecution of responsible parties.

In Spain, a civic audit process is being conducted with the support of the Citizen Debt Audit Platform (PACD). PACD performs general analyses of Spanish national debt, at different administrative levels and concurrently conducts sector specific debt assessments (with respect to healthcare, education, environment or electricity). These efforts aim to promote audits as a way of understanding the causes and consequences of the debt crisis. An integral part of this process is the demand to have permanent access to debt-related information and, most importantly, the promotion of civic empowerment with respect to political, social and economic questions. PACD regards its audit as a citizen's audit involving an open, collective, permanent and decentralized process in which different organically created working groups reach decisions based on consensus. This type of audit is not limited to expert analysis but allows all parties to request information, demand governmental explanations, share relevant information, analyse data from their particular perspectives, denounce irregularities and propose alternatives.

References

Graeber, D. (2011) *Debt: The First 5000 Years*. New York: Melvillehouse.

Kallis, G., Martinez-Alier, J. and Norgaard, R. B. (2009) 'Paper Assets, Real Debts: An Ecological-Economic Exploration of the Global Economic Crisis'. *Critical Perspectives on International Business*, 5(1/2): 14–25.

Plataforma Auditoría Ciudadana de la Deuda (2013) '*¿Por qué no debemos pagar la deuda?*'. *Razones y alternativas*. Barcelona: Icaria Editorial.

Ramos, L. (2006) *Los crímenes de la deuda: deuda ilegítima*. Barcelona: ODG & Icaria Editorial.

Toussaint, E. (2012) *The Long Tradition of Debt Cancellation in Mesopotamia and Egypt from 3000 to 1000 BC*. CADTM. Available online at http://cadtm.org/The-Long-Tradition-of-Debt (accessed 10 October 2013).

36

DIGITAL COMMONS

Mayo Fuster Morell

INSTITUTE OF GOVERNMENT AND PUBLIC POLICIES, AUTONOMOUS
UNIVERSITY OF BARCELONA AND BERKMAN CENTER FOR INTERNET AND SOCIETY,
HARVARD UNIVERSITY

With the adoption of information and communication technologies (ICTs), communities of individuals are following common goals and are collaboratively building resources through technologically mediated communication (Benkler 2006). We define as digital commons (DC) those "online creation communities" (OCCs) which share non-exclusive digital information and knowledge resources that are collectively created. Generally these resources are owned and/or used freely between or among the community, and are also available for use by third parties. They are used and reused but not exchanged as commodities. The people who are part of an online community that is building and sharing digital commons can intervene in the governance of their interaction processes and shared resources (Fuster Morell 2010).

A first root of the digital commons community is the hacking culture. The hacker ethic is characterized by a passion for creating and sharing knowledge. In the 1950s most software circulated freely between developers. However, in the 1970s a proprietary sense towards software started to grow. In order to preserve the free character of the software Richard Stallman (founder of Free Software movement) established the "General Public License," a legal frame for free software. Another root of the DC and cyber-culture more generally, is the counter-cultural movement of the 1960s (Turner 2006). **Back-to-the-landers** communities were among the first to see a social use for the Internet and created "virtual" communities such as The Well, which influenced digital culture. **Environmentalism** and ecology were important inspirations – present in the language, terminology, and ecosystemic thinking of Internet communities.

The spread of the Internet and personal computers lowered barriers, and expressions of a new "free culture" emerged, with the aim of collaboratively creating cultural content and generating universal access to knowledge. The most well-known example is Wikipedia.

Another prominent case of file-sharing and peer-to-peer architecture that facilitates access and exchange of cultural products is the Swedish Pirate Bay.

DC ideals have also reached the scientific world, with struggles over access to anti-retroviral drugs to treat HIV/AIDS in South Africa during the 1990s and the movement to reclaim the public character of research through open access, such as the Public Library of Science, an open access set of scientific journals.

Finally, social movements against "software patents" have been able to stop the creation of such patents in Europe. A huge range of legislative efforts to put the Internet under the control of corporate interests has been stopped in Europe and elsewhere.

After the "dot-com" crash in 2001, a new commercial model – ex-post known as the information economy, Web 2.0, or Wikinomics – emerged, which was based on providing services and infrastructures for online collaboration (Tapscott and Williams 2007). Examples include YouTube, provided by Google, and Flickr (a photo sharing platform), provided by Yahoo. Such sites popularized online collaborative infrastructure but changed the conditions of their use from a logic of commons to one where corporations are the main providers. In digital commons such as Wikipedia, the community is involved in infrastructure provision and has more control over the design of the process. Under corporate logic, most sources of control are in the hands of the infrastructure provider, and the community of users is mostly disempowered. For example, with Flickr the community does not have control over the design of the platform, does not participate to the decision-making mechanism of the site, and cannot define the rules that govern community interaction.

There are several commonalities between degrowth and the digital commons movement. Both question the mainstream paradigm of consumption. The digital commons promote the figure of "prosumer" (producer-consumer), an individual who partakes in the online community and "consumes" value, but also produces value. Products and value are not a commodity, but accessible as public services. Indeed, the digital commons realize degrowth's call for de-commodification. Moreover, in digital commons, there is open access to the value created, which is universally accessible (without establishing discrimination mechanism others than internet connectivity and "visibility"). Finally, the production or creation of the common resource is not driven by commercial motivations and labor contracts, but by voluntary engagement. The access to the value produced is separated from its production. Some sectors of the digital commons movement have also called for a **basic income** or they promote social online currencies (see **community currencies**) to reduce dependency on monetary exchange. Digital commoners, like degrowthers are critical of and resist advertising (see for example Wikipedia, where the commitment to zero advertising is one of the online community's strongest principles).

Additionally, in DC the means of production are under the control of the communities aiming to cover its social necessities and its common mission, in contrast to **capitalism** where they are privately-held and serve the aim of profit. In DC, information and knowledge are conceived of as part of our human heritage and access to knowledge is a human right. DC therefore contest neoliberal visions that try to restrict access to knowledge (through its privatization or **commodification**).

Unlike traditional **commons**, the new technologies of information and communication provide accessibility to information and knowledge that is not rivaled nor exhaustible. On the other hand, DC depends on an infrastructure that consumes and contributes to the exhaustion of environmental resources (scarce materials for mobile phones, electricity for the computers, cables in oceans, electromagnetic camps). Although some in the digital commons movement are sensitive to questions of environmental impact, this is not a predominant issue in the movement's agenda and is something it has much to learn from degrowthers. Energetics and energy limitations also do not feature in DC communities, which generally have an optimistic view of the capacities of cooperation and communication-based productivity improvements to maintain economic development. However, beyond such differences concerning environmental questions, or the degrowthers' imaginary of "less" that the DC movement does not share, DC and degrowth meet one another in their call for a paradigmatic shift in value production and consumption and the reclaim and re-politicization of the **commons**.

References

Benkler, Y. (2006) *The Wealth of Networks*, New Haven, CT: Yale University Press.

Fuster Morell, M. (2010) *Governance of Online Creation Communities*, (Ph.D. thesis ed.), European University Institute.

Tapscott, D. and Williams, A. (2007) *Wikinomics. Portfolio*, New York, NY: Penguin.

Turner, F. (2006) *From Counterculture to Cyberculture*, Chicago, IL: University of Chicago Press.

37

DISOBEDIENCE

Xavier Renou

LES DÉSOBÉISSANTS COLLECTIVE

Civil disobedience is a political method of resistance which consists in a collective action of disobedience to a law considered unjust. To be "civil," as US intellectual Henry David Thoreau (2008) in the nineteenth century called his first actions of resistance to the war against Mexico, one must be willing to break the law in the name of conscience. To Thoreau, this would never be an act of delinquency done secretly for individual interests, but must be perpetuated openly. In the twentieth century, the Indian activist and leading figure of civil disobedience, Gandhi (2012), added a crucial dimension: an exclusive stance of non-violence which entailed the will (the result being always beyond will) to harm the adversary, his or her human person and psychology, as well as his or her family and goods, as little as possible. He rejected the old, ends justify the means view. To Gandhi, the ends were in the means; it was not possible to achieve just goals with unjust means. He considered non-violent means the only way to convince the public that his ends were just and that the struggle should therefore be supported.

Quite near to civil disobedience are the concepts of direct action and conscientious objection, also called non-cooperation, a possible first step towards civil disobedience and the collective organization of one's refusal. The French La Boetie (2012), in the sixteenth century, expressed the idea that in order to keep oppressing the people, tyrants need their cooperation: the tyrant never has enough police to force every single subject to constantly obey orders. In other words, the tyrant needs our cowardly acceptance and daily obedience to maintain power. Stopping to cooperate with what offends our consciousness is therefore a moral obligation and a principle of coherence. Direct action is the twofold idea that we should act directly when offended, without waiting for others (such as elected people) to act in our name. The concept holds that we should act directly on problems and their origin. Non-violent direct action is a version of this political strategy. It strictly prohibits the use of violence and therefore greatly resembles the concept of civil disobedience but without the necessity to break any law. When one disobeys an unjust law this is indeed a non-violent direct action: building dry toilets in one's home as a form of resistance to water contamination is also a non-violent direct action, although perfectly legal.

In the past, civil disobedience proved to be a powerful tool to fight for equal rights (women's, gay and lesbian's and Blacks' emancipation), labor rights, independence (such as India and Zambia), peace (such as opposition to nuclear bomb testing, to the Vietnam war), and political liberation (the fall of numerous Western, Eastern, and recently Arabic dictatorships).

Civil disobedience shares a lot with the degrowth idea and movement. Thanks to a growing awareness, an increasing number of struggles involving civil disobedience and non-violent direct actions have been influenced by, if not conducted in the name of, degrowth-related values, visions, or claims. These have included actions to stop mining projects, to introduce radical changes in energy and water policies (anti-privatization of water movements in Italy, France, Greece), to oppose major infrastructural projects of airports, highways and fast train railways (Spain, Italy, France), etc. As it is sometimes necessary to disobey to live according to degrowth principles, some struggles involving civil disobedience have been directly initiated by degrowth activists. For example, in France in 2011, squatter camps were installed in several cities and successfully opposed a law targeting free housing (tents, caravans, squats) and the right to self-build one's home. The mass mobilization against the introduction of genetically modified crops in France by the end of the 1990, which saw hundreds of people taking part in the uprooting of GM fields, was largely motivated by degrowth (and the same in Spain and Belgium), as was the battle for the right to grow and trade traditional seeds (following an international campaign of civil disobedience called "Act for Seeds," initiated by Indian activist Vandana Shiva). Civil disobedience has been used against advertising (with activists provoking trials by painting billboards) or new intrusive technologies (neo-luddite mobilizations such as those against nanotechnologies in the UK and France). In the emblematic case of Catalan degrowth activist Enric Duran, acts of "financial civil disobedience" were directly aimed at sponsoring degrowth. Duran openly "expropriated" (in his own words) 492,000 euros from 39 banks, drawing attention to the unsustainable Spanish credit and banking system, just before the crisis imploded in 2008. Duran, who used the money to fund alternative movements and projects, including many related to degrowth, declared that he had no intention to repay the debt and was prepared to face the consequences and go to jail.

These political struggles remind degrowth activists that fighting the law through civil disobedience might be necessary. They will not save themselves by changing their way of life while the world around them is collapsing, and they will not defeat **capitalism** and productivism only by the virtue of their example, as the "utopian socialists" of the nineteenthcentury or the hippies of the 1970s thought they could do.

On the other hand, civil disobedience and non-violent direct actions are primarily methods and tactics and are sometimes chosen by activists who have nothing to do with environmental and progressive values, such as anti-abortion activists. Nonetheless, tactics are not neutral and can't be successful if not supported by strong values. These values are often very close to those of degrowth supporters. First, the value of direct action, including the rule of direct democracy, often refers to consensus-based decision-making processes and leaderless movements. Second, the value of a pragmatic approach relates to keeping an open mind to differences and the choice of realistic and reachable objectives, with trial-and-errors-based processes as opposed to dogmatic postures and too abstract and unrealistic objectives. Third, because activists know they can be wrong just like anybody and they know they can be misled by their conscience, they choose not to cause damages that would be irreversible – as damages provoked by the use of violence are – by practicing non-violence against humans. This non-violence includes, increasingly, life and goods in general.

Last, it is the search for coherence between values and actions which has driven some of the main figures in the history of civil disobedience to live according to principles strongly resembling those of degrowth: Thoreau practiced and advocated self-sustainability, Tolstoï and Gandhi distributed their goods and embraced sobriety. The three of them shared a strong concern for the environment and all living creatures. Gandhi also insisted on the need for campaigns of civil disobedience driven by a pragmatic, alternative/constructive program. Obstructive programs of civil disobedience get more momentum and strength if stimulated by a constructive program and positive alternatives to oppression that show what a victory could lead to.

Many civil disobedience activists consider degrowth to be a constructive program of that sort, a possible response to what they're struggling against, which is often **capitalism**. Degrowth-related solutions were articulated with civil disobedience in most of the recent campaigns mentioned previously, with encampments involving collective kitchens based on vegan, organic, or recycled free food, alternative moneys or bartering, dry toilets and solar powered low technology showers, etc. These acts of disobedience prove that it is possible to create strong resistance and build up degrowth-compatible alternatives, both at the same time.

References

de la Boetie, E. (2012) *Discourse on Voluntary Servitude*, Indianapolis, Indiana: Hackett Publishing Co.
Gandhi, M. K. (2012) *Autobiography. The Story of my Experiments with Truth*, CreateSpace Independent Publishing Platform. Available online at www.createspace.com (accessed April 3 2013).
Thoreau, H. D. (2008) *On the Duty of Civil Disobedience*, Radford, Virginia: Wilder Publications.

38

ECO-COMMUNITIES

Claudio Cattaneo

RESEARCH & DEGROWTH AND ICTA (INSTITUTE OF ENVIRONMENTAL SCIENCE AND TECHNOLOGY), AUTONOMOUS UNIVERSITY OF BARCELONA

Eco-communities are specifically planned and set up for people to come and live together with the goal of living and working according to ecological principles by promoting a degree of sharing (see also **work-sharing**) and pursuing well-being through more sustainable life-styles, direct democracy and a degree of **autonomy**.

Eco-communities include eco-villages, which according to Gilman (1991: 10) are characterized by 'human-scale, full-featured settlement, in which human activities are harmlessly integrated into the natural world in a way that is supportive of healthy human development and can be successfully continued into the indefinite future'. Although eco-villages represent the most common form, eco-communities can also be established in isolated buildings or within cities (some of them in forms of co-housing).

Eco-communities are generally characterized by their relatively small size – below or around one hundred people. There are both urban and 'rurban' projects, yet the majority of eco-communities are located in rural areas where access to natural means of production is easier and rent and property cheaper. Participants practice small-scale organic agriculture and permaculture, craft and workshop production, self-construction or DIY practices and favour renewable energies or energy-conserving means of production and transport, such as bicycles (c.f. **Nowtopias**). Materials and production processes tend to be low-impact and often items are recycled from waste or re-used or repaired. The conjunct of these types of agricultural, material and service provisioning expresses the idea of convivial places where the means of production are held in common (Illich 1973, see **conviviality**).

Eco-communities can be considered as both material and immaterial **commons** because they manage land and physical resources communally while, at the same time, set norms, beliefs, institutions and processes that empower a common identity which in turn contributes to the preservation and reproduction of the community.

Willing to set-up places where tthey can live and cultivate their own utopian ideals, their participants form part often of a **back-to-the-landers** wave inspired in magazines such as *In Context* or *Integral* (in Spanish). The movement originated in the 1960s, and in 1994 the Global Ecovillage Network was constituted.

Some remarkable examples, which also constitute different typologies of eco-communities, are: The Farm, in Tennessee, on a property communally bought by vegan Californian hippies; Twin Oaks, an egalitarian rural community in Virginia based on a structured labour-credit system (Kinkaid, 1994); Lakabe, a squatted village in the Basque Region with a communally-managed commercial bakery; and Longomai, a pragmatic out-spring of the May 1968 movement, with a main property in South France and several satellite communities bought elsewhere in France, Switzerland and Germany.

Utopian values are manifest in the creation of a group identity, in the sharing of certain cultural and political ideals (also spiritual ideals sometimes), and in the establishment of organizational practices that might include anything from simple residential living to developing a common life project.

An eco-community constitutes a particular entity that exists between the individual and the larger society. They are characterized by their environmental (eco-) and social dimensions (community), which, in combination, are considered by eco-commoners to be largely missing from living arrangements in (post-) industrial societies.

There is a lot of variation among communities with respect to the relevance of the individual sphere within the community and degrees of autonomy from the rest of society. These constitute challenging issues in the development of every eco-community project.

Bridging the individual/family scale and the large societal scale, eco-communities are internally constituted by self-organized decision-making processes which, among other things, determine the nature and ecological dimension of the project and the integration between individual and communal economies. Normally, horizontal decision-making and deliberative non-representative processes characterize eco-communities, while some adopt consensus rather than majority decision rules.

Eco-communities are in a sense Aristotelian *oikonomies* (referring to the art of the good life and, literally, to "managing the house"). Money does not play a primary role; it is simply a means to satisfy necessities. Eco-communities prevent accumulation because the community guarantees the maintenance of a certain level of welfare to all its members. The type of economic model varies a lot among communities. Some share all money among members, others maintain a strong individual economic sphere. A study of rural squats, which can be considered a particular case of an eco-community, postulates the existence of a correlation between a community's degree of isolation and its degree of communalism. Eco-communities closer to large cities are more likely to maintain a higher degree of personal (monetary) economies (Cattaneo 2013).

The sources of monetary income vary a lot. In general, principles of co-operative self-management prevail and the eco-community collectively produces commodities that can be sold in place or off-site, for instance at market-fairs. Larger communities, such as Logomai in France, depend on fundraising and, increasingly, crowd-funding. Eco-communities with a high degree of financial integration among their members function as 'integral **co-operatives**', where workers, producers and consumers are embedded within the same organization.

Eco-communities provide insights as to how a degrowth society might look. Any realization of utopian intentions depends on a strong willingness and a pragmatism that might clash with original ideals. In the start-up phases (relevant for the beginning of a societal transition) getting things done is the priority: in such difficult circumstances self-imposed austerity and self-exploitation of members often occur. Through self-organized processes, an eco-community chooses to live independent from society at large. As Marcuse has observed in *One-Dimensional Man*, a society freed from external control and manipulation will be able to self-determine its need satisfiers; participants choose to become protagonists of their lives and foment a degrowth imaginary by conferring to the community the source of economic and socio-political authority normally found in capitalist markets and in the state apparatus.

If the community survives this initial phase, then a degrowth practice made of sound ecological performance and social **conviviality** is likely to emerge. There is no empirical data for eco-communities on the trends in material and energy consumption over time. A plausible hypothesis is that most eco-communities start with a drastic fall in personal material and energy consumption but as they enter into a mature phase more comfortable, though not more sustainable, living conditions replace more precarious ones (although the former still conserve more resources when compared to society on average).

Eco-communities develop practices of voluntary **simplicity**. Although this forms part of the degrowth imaginary, some simplifiers can be criticized because they avoid engagement with societal problems and political actions. Generally, eco-communities cannot be characterized as political or a-political. At one extreme, some can be considered as 'lifeboats', with a clear limit and 'closed borders', while in others, particularly those characterized by radical left-wing political ideals, members are more aware of the need to cooperate beyond boundaries and promote universal societal change. Most eco-communities are aware of their limited power and endorse a philosophy similar to that of Holloway about 'changing the world without taking power'. This can occur through the constitution and consolidation of bottom-bottom networks – rather than bottom-up processes – that contribute to strategically leaving the system (Carlsson and Manning 2010) in increasingly larger numbers and to the consequent shrinkage in the role, size and power played by the establishment. The enlargement of these practices to larger sectors of society other than those inhabited by ecologically attentive persons has not occurred yet. The enduring economic and ecological crisis might be an opportunity to foment more eco-communities and create a social phenomenon that will go beyond the counter-cultural movement that preceded it.

References

Carlsson, C. and Manning, F. (2010) 'Nowtopia: Strategic Exodus?' *Antipode*, 42(4), 924–53

Cattaneo, C. (2013) 'Urban squatting, rural squatting and the ecological-economic perspective', In: Squatting Europe Kollective (ed) *Squatting in Europe, Radical Spaces, Urban Struggles*. London, New York: Minor compositions – Autonomedia. Available online at: www.minorcompositions,info/wp-content/uploads/2013/03/squattingeurope-web.pdf (accessed 11 December 2013).

Gilman, R. (1991) 'The eco-village challenge'. Context Institute. Available online at www.context.org/iclib/ic29/gilman1/ (accessed 14 May 2014).

Illich, I. (1973) *Tools for Conviviality*. Available online at http://clevercycles.com/tools_for_conviviality/ (accessed 12 October 2013).

Kinkaid, K. (1994) *Is It Utopia Yet? An Insider's View of Twin Oaks Community in Its Twenty-Sixth Year, 2nd edition*. Louisa, Virginia: Twin Oaks Publishing.

39

INDIGNADOS (OCCUPY)

Viviana Asara[1] and Barbara Muraca[2]

[1]RESEARCH & DEGROWTH AND ICTA (INSTITUTE OF ENVIRONMENTAL SCIENCE
AND TECHNOLOGY), AUTONOMOUS UNIVERSITY OF BARCELONA
[2]SOCIOLOGY INSTITUTE, UNIVERSITY OF JENA

The Indignados or Occupy movement is an ongoing social movement that began
in 2011 in many different countries to protest against austerity policies, high rates
of unemployment, worsening trends of social inequalities, and the collusion of
government politics with the interests of corporate and financial **capitalism**, while
campaigning for "real" democracy and social justice. Although the two movements refer to two separate dynamics that originated respectively in Spain and in
the United States and then spread to other countries, they share similar claims, the
methodology of occupations of urban space, and the use of assemblearian direct
democracy.

At the beginning of 2011, in Spain, a new platform of different collectives and
networks, named "Real Democracy Now", published a manifesto on Facebook
and called for a demonstration on May 15th with the slogan "we are not mer-
chandize in the hands of politicians and bankers." In the manifesto, the activists
declared themselves to be outraged (the Spanish term for indignados) at the "dic-
tates of big economic powers," party dictatorship, the dominance of economism,
social injustices, and the corruption of politicians, bankers, and businessmen. Their
call successfully brought to the streets tens of thousands of people in 50 cities
throughout Spain, and, following the demonstration, occupations spread out in
a few days to more than 800 cities around the world. In Spain, many encampments continued until June or July, producing a rich debate and proliferation of
working groups, commissions, and, in many cities, a long and difficult process of
elaboration of a consensus concerning the minimal demands of the mobilization.
The Barcelona-manifesto included the following demands: no more privileges for
politicians, bankers, and big incomes, decent salary and quality of life for all, the
right to a home, quality of public services, liberties (connected to freedom of information and expression in internet), direct democracy, and environment. After the
(not always) voluntary removal of the camps, some working groups, commissions,

and assemblies continued to be operative, and neighborhood assemblies gained in importance, periodically gathering in spaces of coordination. The movement entered into a more latent phase, gaining visibility in general strikes and demonstrations, such as the symbolic "surrounding" of the Parliament in September 2012. The manifesto for the first anniversary of the movement included claims such as the refusal of bail-out for banks, a citizens' **audit of the debt**, public education, economic redistribution and **basic income**, work redistribution, the refusal of precarious work, and the valuation of reproductive, domestic, i.e. **care** work.

The Occupy Wall Street movement initiated on September 17, 2011 with the occupation by roughly one hundred people of the Zuccotti Park, in Manhattan's financial district. Massive occupations surged after the Adbusters magazine published a call in July to occupy Wall Street, and occupations mushroomed in many American cities, continuing until November. Some of the main issues Occupy Wall Street raised included an equal distribution of wealth, a reform of the banking system, a reduction of the political influence of corporations, and the need to change the system to address issues of injustice and inequality.

Both movements share similar structure and organization of the internal decision processes: the General Assembly (GA) is the (open) apparatus that owns decision-making power. Specific issues are dealt with by commissions and working groups, which periodically report to the GA. Decisions are most of the times taken by consensus, which can also be visualized with a system of hand signals. The "medium of assemblearian occupations" mirrors the core claim for a "real" democracy and embodies in a prefigurative way the implementation of consensus-oriented basis-democratic forms of decision-making and self-management. The current representational system of democracy is critiqued as a corrupted "plutocracy" or "corporate-party system" subdued to the interests of financial capitalism and denounced as unable to represent the will of the people.

Like other social movements before them, Occupy and Indignados constitute a significant arena where different conceptions of democracy can meet and be experimented, with an explicit challenge to the minimalist, individualistic, and liberal vision of liberal democracy (Della Porta 2013). While some activists call for the generalization of direct democratic-assemblearian system and self-organization to replace parliamentarian systems, others seek to strengthen actual participation within institutional politics and to improve representation mechanisms by a reform of the electoral laws with injections of direct democracy at the local level.

The implementation of a 'real' democracy, however, implies more than the transformation of forms of representation and of political decision making: social rights and redistribution of wealth are necessary conditions for people to really and effectively participate in democratic processes. While current democracies are hijacked by economic powers, real democracy requires economic democracy, i.e. the democratic (self) management of neighborhoods, work, and production. Real democracy, accordingly, is "to imagine a democracy in all the realms of life" (see Asara, 2014).

Far from being merely a reaction to austerity policies and to the undemocratic character of (liberal) representative democracies, the Indignados movement embodies a more radical, cultural critique of contemporary societies with respect to their values of productivism, economism, individualism, and consumerism. There is quite evidently common ground between Indignados/Occupy and the degrowth movement: the claim for a systemic change is, as in most degrowth perspectives, compounded with the perception of an undergoing systemic multi-dimensional crisis, which includes not only political and economic, but also ecological and cultural (value) dimensions. Instead of protesting for a resumed growth, both plead for different socio-economic models in which degrowth claims are intertwined with redistributive and social justice appeals (Asara 2014). The prefigurative politics of the movement and its imaginary significations, such as the occupations, encampments, and reclaims of public squares, the urban orchards, the collective kitchens and cleanings of the occupied spaces, or the free and barter exchange markets, are also primary significations of degrowth.

The current crisis marks a turning point in the fragile alliance between democracy and **capitalism** as we know it: indeed, such an alliance seems to have been rather conjunctural to the virtuous relationship between economic growth and the welfare state and to the mediation of political mass parties and party competition (Offe 1984; Macpherson 1977). In the meantime, while the former promise of prosperity and freedom attached to economic **growth** no longer holds, policies aiming at austerity as a means to **growth** as the sole remedy to the crisis are jeopardizing democracy itself.

The hegemonic neoliberal program, however, seems to be undergoing a legitimation crisis with respect to its ability to consolidate a large consensus. How far social movements like Indignados or Occupy might start building the core for a counter-hegemonic block is too early to say. Yet, they could become the springboard for a long-term transformation due to their original recipe: the successful merging of contentious forms of opposition with creative practices, in which feasible alternatives are collectively experimented and improved; the pluralistic openness of decision making processes that can become a platform for a larger consensus; the shared and on-going articulation of an alternative value system; and the ability to global networking and communication. Their "prefigurative politics" that try to build "here and now" societal alternative visions, have a strong, attractive potential.

References

Asara, V. 2014. 'The Indignados movement. Framing the crisis and democracy'. Forthcoming in *Sociology*.

Della Porta, D. (2013) *Can democracy be saved?* Cambridge: Polity Press.

Macpherson, C. B. (1977) *The life and times of liberal democracy*. Oxford: Oxford University Press.

Offe, C. (1984). *Contradictions of the welfare state*. London: Hutchinson & Co.

40

JOB GUARANTEE

B. J. Unti

DEPARTMENT OF ECONOMICS, UNIVERSITY OF MISSOURI

A job guarantee (JG) is a policy proposal calling on government to promise a job to any qualifying person seeking employment. The proposal stems from the recognition that capitalist economies are characterized by chronic involuntary unemployment. While several versions of the program have been proposed, the most general approach calls for a *universal* guarantee, with the national government providing the funds necessary to offer a uniform wage and benefit package to anyone willing and able to work (Mitchell 1998; Wray 1998, 2012). Most proposals also call for a decentralized administration of the program, relying on local governments, non-profits, and community organizations to propose and oversee JG projects. The wage and benefit package is set by the national government and serves as a floor for wages throughout the economy. With the floor price of labor set, the quantity of labor that the government promises to purchase is allowed to float over the business cycle. Consequently, the government's deficit automatically moves counter-cyclically in just the right amount to maintain full employment.

The idea of a JG appeared as early as the 1930s. Just as the central bank acted as a lender of last resort, it was argued that the treasury should act as an employer of last resort (Wray 2012: 222). Building on the works of Keynes, Lerner, and Minsky over the last two decades, economists associated with the Center for Full Employment and Price Stability (CFEPS) at the University of Missouri – Kansas City, the Center of Full Employment and Equality (CofFEE) at the University of New Castle, and the Levy Economics Institute in New York, have refined proposals for a JG.

Advocates of the JG argue that its benefits extend beyond simply creating jobs. Eliminating unemployment will help to address related social and economic problems such as poverty, inequality, crime, divorce, domestic violence, discrimination, mental illness, and drug abuse (Wray and Forstater 2004). While existing welfare programs (as well as proposals for a **basic income**) aim to address similar issues, proponents of the JG point out that such programs carry the stigma of dependence without ensuring that those who are willing to work can find work. A JG will not only offer jobs to the unemployed, but also training, skills, and work experience. Most importantly, by making employment and not merely income a right, a JG will provide those who want to work with an opportunity to participate productively in their communities. The benefits of the program are not limited to its participants. A JG will also improve working conditions in the private sector: since private sector workers always have the option of entering the JG, private employers will be forced to provide pay, benefits, and conditions at least on par with those of the program (Wray 2012: 223–4). In this regard, a JG can serve as a tool for achieving a variety of policy goals. With respect to degrowth for example, the JG might initiate a four-day workweek, pressuring private employers to follow suit. Last, JG work can be directed toward provisioning society with needed public goods and services not produced by the private sector.

The two most common objections to the JG relate to inflation and affordability. Conventional wisdom holds that full employment and price stability are incompatible goals because tight labor markets place upward pressure on wages and prices. Thus, unemployment is viewed as the necessary cost of fighting inflation. However, JG advocates argue that the program will *increase* price stability by creating a buffer stock of workers employed in the program, allowing for loose labor markets at full employment (Mitchell 1998; Wray 1998). Under a JG, government promises to buy all labor offered at a floor price and to "sell" labor to the private sector at any price above the floor. The buffer stock of workers in the JG acts like a reserve army of the *employed*, providing the flexibility required by a dynamic economy (Forstater 1998). During an expansion wage pressures are held in check as the government "sells" labor. If the pool of JG workers becomes too small to restrain inflationary wage demands, the government can cut discretionary spending or raise taxes, replenishing the buffer stock. On the downside of the cycle, the buffer stock places a floor under incomes and aggregate demand, counteracting deflationary pressures. Finally, because labor is a key input into the production of all goods, stabilizing its price will help to stabilize prices throughout the economy (Wray 2012: 224).

Several estimates of the monetary cost of a JG program (calculated prior to the financial crisis) put total expenses at less than 1 percent of GDP for the US. Much of the monetary cost will be offset by reductions in spending on other programs such as unemployment insurance and welfare (Wray 1998). More importantly, proponents of the JG argue following modern money theory (MMT) that a sovereign currency government can always finance a JG. The perceived problem of affordability arises from a false analogy in neoclassical theory between government and household finances. This analogy overlooks the fact that while households are *users* of the currency, the government is the *issuer* of the currency (see **public money**). Because the government is the monopoly issuer of the currency, it must as a matter of logic, issue money (i.e. spend) first in order to collect it back through taxes or bond sales. This stands conventional wisdom on its head – the government does not need the public's money in order to spend, rather the public needs the government's money in order to pay taxes or purchase bonds. And because a sovereign government spends by issuing money, it can always afford to buy anything for sale denominated in its own currency, including all unemployed labor (Wray 1998; 2012).

A JG is consistent with degrowth on multiple fronts. Most obviously its potential relates to issues of social and economic justice. Indeed, the program was originally conceived with a narrow focus on the problem of unemployment. However, reconsidered in light of environmental decline, the JG presents unique possibilities for simultaneously addressing socioeconomic and environmental issues.

In the near term, a JG offers a means for reconciling the apparent contradiction between employment and the environment faced by capitalist societies. Unlike traditional policies that rely on increasing aggregate demand and accelerated growth to stimulate employment, a JG guarantees full employment regardless of the level of aggregate demand. Decoupling employment from aggregate demand allows for full employment even as growth ceases or becomes negative.

In the longer term, a JG may offer a transitional path away from existing, environmentally and socially destructive forms of production based on money profits, and toward a system organized around meeting fundamental social and ecological needs. The most promising feature of the JG is that it is not constrained by profits. It thus creates the possibility for people to earn a living outside the sphere of accumulation. And because JG work involves production for use rather than exchange, it can be channeled toward environmentally sustainable projects and methods of production that will not and cannot be undertaken by the private sector (Forstater 1998; Mitchell 1998). Workers under a JG can be employed doing anything democratically deemed to be of social value, potentially broadening our conception of work to include things like: raising children, caring for the elderly and infirm (see **care**), education, habitat restoration, community gardening, the arts etc. As such, a JG is an open-ended policy tool that might serve to complement, support, or incorporate any number of other proposed measures for degrowth.

References

Forstater, M. (1998) "Flexible Full Employment: Structural Implications of Discretionary Public Sector Employment." *Journal of Economic Issues*, 32(2): 557–64

Mitchell, W. F. (1998) "The Buffer Stock Employment Model and the Path to Full Employment." *Journal of Economic Issues*, 32(2): 547–55.

Wray, R. L. (1998) *Understanding Modern Money: The Key to Full Employment and Price Stability*. Northhampton, MA: Edward Elgar.

Wray, R. L. (2012) *Modern Money Theory: A Primer on Macroeconomics and Sovereign Monetary Systems*. New York: Palgrave Macmillan.

Wray, R. L. and Forstater, M. (2004) "Full Employment and Economic Justice." In C. Dell and J. Knoedler (eds.) *The Institutionalist Tradition in Labor Economics*. Armonk, NY: M.E. Sharpe.

41

MONEY, PUBLIC

Mary Mellor

DEPARTMENT OF SOCIAL SCIENCE, NORTHUMBRIA UNIVERSITY

The case for action around public money sees money as a public resource (Mellor 2010). It is argued that public creation and circulation of money, free of debt, under democratic control could enable the provisioning of large-scale societies on the basis of social justice and ecological sustainability (Robertson 2012). To support this notion of public money it is important to explore how new money is created in modern economies (Ryan-Collins *et al.* 2011). In modern economies there are two sources of new money: money created by monetary authorities such as central banks (usually referred to as High Powered Money or Base Money) and money created through the banking system as loans (usually referred to as Credit Money). The production of national currencies (notes and coin) is a monopoly of public monetary authorities, but public money can also be issued in electronic form, as when central banks issued large amounts of new money in response to the 2007/2008 financial crisis (quantitative easing).

The main difference between the two sources of new money (monetary authorities or bank credit) is that publicly authorised money *may* be issued as debt, but bank credit can *only* be issued as debt (Ingham 2004). Banks are not allowed to mint coins or print notes (they must buy these from the central bank), but they can set up loan accounts, that is new money issued to a borrower (personal, business or government) through adding figures to a bank account (as in a mortgage loan). Conventional banking theory claims that monetary authorities have the ability to control the amount of new money created by banks as loans, but the financial crisis indicates that bank lending can spiral out of control. Most money in modern economies is created and circulated by the banking sector as debt, over 97 per cent in the case of the UK (Jackson and Dyson 2013). Effectively, the money supply in modern economies has been privatised and is issued on a commercial basis. Several factors have led to this 'privatisation' of money supply as debt: neo-liberal ideology and deregulation; increased public and private debt; less use of notes and coin and more reliance on transfers between bank accounts; public backing for bank accounts as in deposit insurance; and the role of central banks as a seemingly unlimited lender of last resort.

The link to degrowth lies in the role of debt in the issuing of new money. Whereas new public money could be issued without debt, by being spent into circulation, (for example, as quantitative easing for the people, rather than the banking system), money issued through the banking system is always issued as debt; that is, the money must be returned, with interest, to the issuing bank. This creates a huge **growth** dynamic. If nearly all money is issued as loans that have to be repaid with interest, the money supply has to be constantly expanded through the issue of new debt. If the willingness of the banks to lend, or people to borrow, ceases then the money supply breaks down. Debts to the banks default, or if they are repaid, shrink the money supply even further. During such crises the only source of new money is the state/central bank. However, although the emergency issue of public money could be spent directly into the economy, current monetary policy demands that it is issued to the banking system or to governments as debt. There is a logic to providing public money as debt to the banking system (which will lend it on with interest) but not to the public to whom the money should belong. Instead, the public is deemed to have borrowed the money used to rescue the banks, pushing state budgets into deficit and resulting in the imposition of severe austerity measures.

The simplest way to remove bank created debt and its **growth** dynamic is to remove from the banking system the right to create new money, or to severely limit it. Banks would be restricted to doing what most people think they do: lending savers' existing money to borrowers. Instead of money created through bank-issued debt, new public money could be issued free of debt directly into the economy to meet public needs. At present, public expenditure has to wait for the commercial circulation of money to produce a profit which can be taxed. That is, public expenditure relies on growth in the commercial sector. Equally, most people cannot produce directly the goods and services they need, they first have to work in private profit-driven, or public profit-dependent, activities to obtain access to money.

Proposals to create new public money as a public resource would aim to create all new money either under democratic control through a national monetary budget or through an independent monetary authority (Jackson and Dyson 2013). Public money would be issued free of debt and would be spent directly into the economy. Enough money could be circulated to enable sufficiency provisioning and needs-led economic activity (Mellor 2010). Public money could be issued in various ways at national, regional, local or even international level. New money could be used to finance key public provisioning such as the health and **care** services or low carbon energy systems. Flexibility within the economy could be achieved by issuing money as a **basic income** or as a fund for social investment or community based economic development. Newly issued public money could be made available to commercial banks to lend, as long as the money was used in the wider public interest. There would still be a role for taxation, which would be used to remove money from the economy if there was a threat of inflation. Tax could also be used to encourage the most efficient use of natural resources and to redistribute wealth. The case for public money is the need to rescue money from profit and **growth**-oriented control and return it to where it belongs – to the public, but this time under democratic control and according to principles of ecological sustainability and social justice.

References

Ingham, G. (2004) *The Nature of Money*. Cambridge: Polity.

Jackson, A. and Dyson, B. (2013) *Modernising Money: Why our Monetary System Is Broken and How it Can Be Fixed*. London: Positivemoney.

Mellor, M. (2010) *The Future of Money: From Financial Crisis to Public Resource*. London: Pluto Press.

Robertson, J. (2012) *Future Money: Breakdown or Break through?* Totnes: Green Books.

Ryan-Collins, J. Greenham, T., Werner, T. and Jackson, A. (2011) *Where Does Money Come From? A Guide to the UK Monetary and Banking System*. London: New Economic Foundation.

42

NEW ECONOMY

Tim Jackson

CENTRE FOR ENVIRONMENTAL STRATEGY, UNIVERSITY OF SURREY

Society is faced with a profound dilemma: to resist growth is to risk economic and social collapse, but to pursue it relentlessly is to endanger the ecosystems on which we depend for long-term survival. The response to the recession was a ubiquitous call to re-invigorate consumer spending and kick start **growth**. Those inclined to question the consensus were swiftly denounced as cynical revolutionaries or modern day luddites.

With that confusingly-attired bogey-man looming over us, kick starting **growth** looked like a no-brainer. And the closest we got to doing anything other than business as usual was the possibility that somehow out of the crisis we might create a 'different engine of **growth**' as Achim Steiner from the UN Environment Programme called it. Green growth became the holy grail of economic recovery.

This idea is still essentially an appeal to decoupling (see **dematerialization**). **Growth** continues, while resource intensity (and hopefully throughput) declines. But at least in the idea of a green economy, unlike technological dreams of decoupling – that somehow expect miraculously in a world of 9 billion people all aspiring to Western lifestyles, we will manage to reduce the carbon intensity of every dollar of output 130 times lower in 2050 than it is today – there is something in the way of a blueprint for what an alternative economy might look like. It gives us more of a sense of what people are buying and what businesses are selling in this new economy. Its founding concept is the production and sale of de-materialised 'services', rather than material 'products'.

Clearly it can't just be the 'service-based economies' that have characterised certain Western development over the last few decades. For the most part those have been achieved by reducing heavy manufacturing, continuing to import consumption goods from abroad and expanding financial services to pay for them.

So what exactly constitutes productive economic activity in this new economy? Selling 'energy services', certainly, rather than energy supplies. Selling mobility rather than cars. Recycling, re-using, leasing, maybe yoga lessons, perhaps, hair-dressing, **urban gardening**: so long as these aren't carried out using buildings, don't involve the latest fashion and you don't need a car to get to them. The humble broom would need to be preferred to the diabolical 'leaf-blower', for instance.

The fundamental question is this: can you really make enough money from these activities to keep an economy growing? And the truth is we just don't know. We have never at any point in history lived in such an economy. It sounds at the moment suspiciously like something the *Independent on Sunday* would instantly dismiss as a yurt-based economy – with increasingly expensive yurts.

But this doesn't mean we should throw away the underlying vision completely. Whatever the new economy looks like, low-carbon economic activities that employ people in ways that contribute meaningfully to human flourishing have to be the basis for it. That much is clear.

So rather than starting from the assumption of **growth**, perhaps we should start by identifying what we want a sustainable economy to look and behave like. Clearly, some form of stability – or resilience – matters. Economies that collapse threaten human flourishing immediately. We know that equality matters. Unequal societies drive unproductive status competition (see **social limits of growth**) and undermine wellbeing not only directly but also by eroding our sense of shared citizenship.

Work – and not just paid employment – still matters in this new economy. It's vital for all sorts of reasons. Apart from the obvious contribution of paid employment to people's livelihoods, work is a part of our participation in the life of society. Through work we create and recreate the social world and find a credible place in it.

Perhaps most vital of all, economic activity must remain ecologically-bounded. The limits of a finite planet need to be coded directly into its working principles. The valuation of ecosystem services, the greening of the national accounts, the identification of an ecologically bounded production function: all of these are likely to be essential to the development of a sustainable economic framework.

And at the local level, it's possible to identify some simple operational principles that these new economic activities need to fulfil. Let's call these activities ecological enterprises if they satisfy three simple criteria:

- They contribute positively to human flourishing.
- they support community and provide decent livelihoods.
- They use as little as possible in the way of materials and energy.

Notice that it isn't just the outputs from economic activity that must make a positive contribution to flourishing. It's the form and organisation of our systems of provision as well. Ecological enterprise needs to work with the grain of community and the long-term social good, rather than against it.

Interestingly, ecological enterprise has a kind of forerunner. The seeds for the new economy already exist in local, community-based social enterprise: community energy projects, local farmers' markets, slow food **co-operatives**, sports clubs, libraries, community health and fitness centres, local repair and maintenance services, craft workshops, writing centres, water sports, community music and drama and local training and skills. And yes, maybe even yoga (or martial arts or meditation), hairdressing and gardening.

People often achieve a greater sense of wellbeing and fulfilment, both as producers and as consumers of these activities, than they ever do from the time-poor, materialistic, supermarket economy in which most of our lives are spent. So it's ironic that these community-based social enterprises barely count in today's economy. They represent a kind of Cinderella economy that sits neglected at the margins of consumer society.

Some of them scarcely even register as economic activities in a formal sense at all. They sometimes employ people on a part-time or even voluntary basis. Their activities are often labour intensive. So if they contribute anything at all to **GDP**, their labour productivity growth is of course 'dismal' – in the language of the dismal science. If we start shifting wholesale to patterns of de-materialised services, we wouldn't immediately bring the economy to a standstill, but we'd certainly slow down growth considerably.

We're getting perilously close here to the lunacy at the heart of the growth-obsessed, resource-intensive, consumer economy. Here is a sector that could provide meaningful work, offer people capabilities for flourishing, contribute positively to community and have a decent chance of being materially light. And yet it's denigrated as worthless because it's actually employing people.

This response shows up the fetish with labour productivity for what it is: a recipe for undermining work, community and environment. Of course, labour productivity improvements aren't always bad. There are clearly places where it makes sense to substitute away from human labour, especially where the working experience itself is poor. But the idea that labour input is always and necessarily something to be minimised goes against common sense.

In fact, there's a very good reason why de-materialised services don't lead to productivity growth. It's because for many of them it's the human input to them that constitutes the value in them. The pursuit of labour productivity in activities whose integrity depends on human interaction systematically undermines the quality of the output.

Besides all that, work itself is one of the ways in which humans participate meaningfully in society. Reducing our ability to do that – or reducing the quality of our experience in doing so – is a direct hit on flourishing. Relentless pursuit of labour productivity in these circumstances makes absolutely no sense.

So in summary, it seems that those calling for a new engine of growth based around dematerialised services are really onto something. But they may perhaps have missed a vital point. The idea that an increasingly serviced-based economy can (or should) provide for ever-increasing economic output doesn't quite stack up.

On the other hand, we've made some clear progress here. This new 'Cinderella' economy really does offer a kind of blueprint for a different kind of society. New, ecological enterprises provide capabilities for flourishing. They offer the means to a livelihood and to participation in the life of society. They provide security, a sense of belonging and the ability to share in a common endeavour and yet to pursue our potential as individual human beings. And at the same time they offer a decent chance of remaining within ecological scale. The next economy really does mean inviting Cinderella to the ball.

Reference

Jackson, T. (2009) *Prosperity without Growth: Economics for a Finite Planet*. London: Earthscan.

43

NOWTOPIANS

Chris Carlsson

Tinkerers, inventors, and improvisational spirits who bring an artistic approach to important tasks that are ignored or undervalued by market society are what I call Nowtopians. Rooted in practices that have been emerging over the past few decades, Nowtopians' relationship with work highlights an important thread of self-emancipatory class politics beyond the traditional arena of wage-labor. These practices include such activities as **urban gardening**/farming, do-it-yourself bicycle repair co-operatives often called "bike kitchens," hacker collectives engaged in developing free software tools and expanding and improving social communications, recycled clothing makers, biofuels co-ops, and more. Characteristic of many of these activities is that people are taking their time and technological know-how out of the market and — working for free — reappropriating the waste stream of modern **capitalism** while using technologies in unanticipated ways. Taken at a broad level, they are inventing the social and technological foundation for a post-capitalist form of life. More and more people, recognizing the degradation inherent in business relations, are creating networks of activity that refuse the measurement of money. Nowtopian activities cross paths with the degrowth movement in practice, even if not explicitly declared. When people take their time and technological know-how out of the market and decide for themselves how to dedicate their efforts, they are short-circuiting the logic of the market society that depends on incessant **growth**. They are "exiting the economy," which is the slogan of degrowth. Their common use of discarded and recycled materials from **capitalism**'s waste stream also demonstrates a shift to productive activity that is by definition not "**growth**."

The self-directed work carried on outside of wage-labor can be best understood in terms of class and ultimately, a classless society. The two crucial components are *time* and the *technosphere*. People are engaged in activities that go on outside of their jobs, in their so-called "free" time. These practices, often very time-consuming and strenuous, require sharing and mutual aid and constitute the beginnings of new kinds of communities. This represents a "re-composition" of the working class, even though most of the participants wouldn't embrace such a framework. Because these people are engaged in creative appropriation of technologies to purposes of their own design and choice, these activities embody the (partial) transcendence of the wage-labor prison by "workers" who have better things to do than their jobs. When freed from the coercive constraints of wage-labor and arbitrary hierarchy, people *work hard*. They are tinkerers and smiths working in the waste streams and open spaces of late **capitalism**, conjuring new practices while redefining life's purpose.

In a society that perpetually celebrates itself as democratic, public discussion about our greatest public secret, work, is rarely heard. There isn't any public control over the fundamental decisions that shape our lives, whether it be *what* work is done, *how* work is done, who we will work with, or more broadly, the nature of scientific research, the types of technologies we might choose or refuse (depending on a public airing of the consequences of various choices), and so on. It is in this deep separation that class arises, the separation of most of us from the world we (re)produce with our shared labor.

Engaging with technology in creative and experimental ways, Nowtopians are involved in a guerrilla war over the direction of society. In myriad behaviors and in small, "invisible" ways, Nowtopians are making life better right now – but also setting the foundation, technically and socially, for a genuine movement of liberation from market life.

As **capitalism** continues its inexorable push to corral every square inch of the globe into its logic of money and markets, while simultaneously seeking to colonize our very thoughts and control our desires and behaviors, new practices are emerging that are redefining politics and opening spaces of unpredictability. Instead of traditional political forms like **unions** or parties, people are coming together in practical projects.

The same inventiveness and creative genius that gets wrongly attributed to capital and business is being applied to planetary ecology. Acting locally in the face of unfolding global catastrophes (many avoidable were we to really try), friends and neighbors are redesigning many of the crucial technological foundations of modern life. These redesigns are worked out through garage and backyard "research and development" programs among friends using the detritus of modern life. Our contemporary **commons** takes the shape of discarded bicycles and leftover deep fryer vegetable oil, of vacant lots and open bandwidth. "Really really free markets," anti-commodities, festivals, and free services are imaginative *products* of an anti-economy, provisionally under construction by freely co-operative and inventive people. They aren't waiting for an institutional change from on-high but are getting on with building the new world in the shell of the old.

What we see in the Nowtopian movement is not a fight for workers' emancipation within the capitalist division of labor (which is the best that could be hoped for from the **unions'** strategy, *if* we give it the benefit of the doubt). Instead we see people responding to the overwork and emptiness of a bifurcated life that is imposed in the precarious growth-driven marketplace. They seek emancipation from being merely workers. To a growing minority of people, the endless tread-mill of consumerism and overwork is something they are *working* to escape. Thus, for many people, time is more important than money. Access to goods has been the major incentive for compliance with the dictatorship of the economy. But in pockets here and there, the allure of hollow material wealth, and with it the disci-pline imposed by economic life, is breaking down.

This is the grassroots essence of a politics of degrowth, too. The incessant logic imposed by the faceless economy finds its rebuke in the everyday assertion of sub-jectivity and creative productivity that takes place outside of the money economy. Degrowth in this context doesn't mean a crash in material well-being, but a self-designed reorganization of human activity so that we can work less, waste less, have everything we need and want, and enjoy life to the fullest. The only people who can reorganize life in this way are the people who today get up and produce a global capitalist society – in other words, we can only do this together. Reclaiming control over what we do and how we do it is the first step off the treadmill of incessant **growth**, the first crucial step towards a society that embraces degrowth.

References

Carlsson, C. (2008) *Nowtopia: How Pirate Programmers, Outlaw Bicyclists, and Vacant-Lot Gardeners Are Inventing the Future Today*, London: AK Press.

Gorz, A. (1982) *Farewell to the Working Class: An Essay on Post-Industrial Socialism*, Boston: South End Press.

Gorz, A. (1999) *Reclaiming Work: Beyond the Wage-Based Society*, Malden, MA: Blackwell Publishers Inc.

Holloway, J. (2002) *Change the World without Taking Power: The Meaning of Revolution Today*, New York: Pluto Press.

Holloway, J. (2010) *Crack Capitalism*, New York: Pluto Press.

44

POST-NORMAL SCIENCE

Giacomo D'Alisa and Giorgos Kallis

RESEARCH & DEGROWTH AND ICTA (INSTITUTE OF ENVIRONMENTAL
SCIENCE AND TECHNOLOGY), AUTONOMOUS UNIVERSITY OF BARCELONA

Post-normal science (PNS) is a problem-solving strategy to be used "when facts are uncertain, values are in dispute, stakes are high, and decision urgent" (Funtowicz and Ravetz 1994: 1,882). Such contexts characterize environmental problems from climate change, hazardous waste dumping, and contamination, to the siting of nuclear plants. Just as in cases with ethical complexities (as in biomedical science), so in environmental, development and equity policy debates there must be an "extended peer community," consisting not only of scientists but also other legitimate participants, i.e. all those people with a stake in the issue, who will participate in assuring the quality of the scientific input (Funtowicz and Ravetz 1994).

The notion of PNS is better grasped by comparing it to "pure" (basic, core, or normal) science on the one hand, and on the other, to the other two, currently dominant, modes of problem-solving science: "applied," mission-oriented science and "professional consultancy". In the pure science of laboratory research, decision stakes are negligible, as there are no external participants, and research is (mostly) investigator-driven. Uncertainty is also very low: research is undertaken when a research problem is (reasonably) expected to be solved. Applied science extends pure science to respond to clear-cut needs to implement or improve a certain product or process. But stakes and uncertainty tend to be low, and manageable typically by standard statistical processes. Professional consulting in turn is broader than applied science, and it involves the application of judgement and creativity by an "expert." Compare, for example, the applied science of a surgeon operating on a broken leg, to the professional consultancy of a pathologist or a psychiatrist. Uncertainty in professional consultancy is higher, and so are decision stakes, as the consulting is conducted for a client whose needs must also be served.

For illustrative purposes consider dams (Funtowiz and Ravetz, 1994). For a long time the design and location of dams has been in the realm of applied science. Given flood control, water storage, and irrigation purposes, uncertainties were managed scientifically with statistical techniques. With the emergence of disputes over dams, professional consulting came into the picture, with experts judging on costs and benefits, suitable locations, environmental impacts, etc. The decision entered the political process and each group with a stake mobilized its own experts/consultants. By now, the whole rationale of dams and water-fuelled growth is under question, with different values at stake and uncertainties and criticisms on all fronts, from the hydrological to the social and religious. This is the realm of PNS.

The epistemic postulates of PNS first appeared in Jerome Ravetz' (1971) *Scientific Knowledge and its Social Problems*. Like Jacques Ellul, an influential thinker for many degrowthers, Ravetz (2011) criticized an "industrialized science" that is "entrepreneurial" and which produces a "runaway technology." The transition from craft to industrial science, Ravetz argued, has had the same consequences on scientists as it had on industrial workers, i.e. a loss of control and direction over their creation. In the case of scientists this marked a loss of **autonomy** over their research. Ravetz criticized the dominance of profit and financing criteria in industrial science, which have reduced science to a factor of production, and pointed to a shift away from traditional forms of quality assurance based on the (moral) traits and skills of scientists and towards a concern with the profitability and technological applicability of results.

In the 1980s, Ravetz and Funtowicz began collaborating and published *Uncertainty and Quality in Science for Policy*, a book whose main contribution was the design of a notational system called NUSAP – Numeral Unit Spread Assessment Pedigree, with the aim to assess (and assure) the quality of processes that deal with uncertainty in policy settings. The authors were motivated by the growing (global) environmental problems of the time, themselves outcome of the runway technology that Ravetz had criticized in his past work, and the proliferation of new technologies, such as nuclear or GMOs, and new technology-produced problems, such as climate change. There was a great deal of uncertainty over the causes and impacts of these phenomena, high stakes (including the survival and wellbeing of whole human populations) and irreducible value conflicts, such as weighing the worth of one generation over another, one community over another, or one species over another. In such conditions, Funtowicz and Ravetz argued, we can no longer talk about simple "puzzles" of the normal science type. The search for a single "truth" cannot be the organizing principle of scientific activity, given that irreducible (incommensurate and only weakly-comparable) values are involved. For example, the uncertainty of a sea level rise cannot be reduced to uncertainty of the methodological or technological sort, addressable in principle with more computational power; the assessment of the impacts from sea level rise involves also an epistemological uncertainty. PNS indicates that the normal (in the Kunhian sense) science developed in the laboratory and extended through applied science to the conquest of nature is no longer adequate for the solution of global environmental problems.

"Quality assurance" is a core concept in PNS. Quality is not simply the proper management of uncertainty, but an integrated social process that is able to respond to the different concerns emerging from the multiple narratives of the issue at stake. PNS marks a shift from a substantive rationality, a science-informed decision process of looking for optimal solutions, to procedural rationality, which involves a process aimed at finding shared and "satisfying" solutions (Giampietro 2003). The peer review process of normal science is necessary but not sufficient in PNS. An extended peer community has to assure quality. This involves not only the certified experts of a certain discipline but an enlarged group of laypersons with the desire to participate in the resolution of the issue. Instead of a community of experts, this shift entrusts sustainability-related decisions to an "expert community," an extended group of peers that emerges in the process of assessment. This expert community should be able to articulate a configuration of "extended facts," including a diversity of knowledge (scientific, indigenous, local, traditional), a plurality of values (social, economic, environmental, ethical), and beliefs (material, spiritual), which all together, and together with conventional "scientific facts," inform the analysis of the problem at stake. Applied science and professional consulting can be part of the overall activity, but can no longer dominate the decision-making process. And make no mistake: there are still many other contexts, where normal, applied, or professional science alone may be adequate; but not for the most pressing environmental, social, or economic problems.

Until now, degrowthers have challenged scientists as truth-holders, mainly "economists", whose expertise and claims to truth have tended to colonize and depoliticize the social sphere (see **depoliticization**). Still, there is limited reflection concerning the role of science and of the ways problems will be solved in a hypothetical degrowth society. Problem-solving science will remain an important part of a degrowth transition, in choosing for example among a range of socio-environmental courses of action, and it will remain essential even in a hypothetical degrowth society, since even a downscaled and qualitatively different society, will have to manage the legacies of our generation, i.e. dams, nuclear plants, hazardous dumps and an altered climate. For several reasons, the starting point for such reflection of "science for a degrowth society" cannot be other than PNS.

First, because there is a strong bond between the community of degrowthers and ecological economists, the community within which PNS evolved. A new generation of degrowthers, many educated in ecological economics, are already imbued with the epistemic reasoning of PNS. The very praxis of the degrowth international conferences is inspired by the PNS ideal, attempting to do away with ex-cathedra experts and create an "extended peer review community" for degrowth research (Cattaneo et al. 2012).

Second, the denunciation of runaway technology by Ravetz resonates with fundamental degrowth theories. The epistemological roots of PNS meet degrowth's criticism about technology such as Illich's critique of radical monopoly, exercised by large scale technology (see **conviviality**), and Ellul's claims of the need to escape from an autonomizd "technological system," a self-referential system that discovers what can be discovered for the sake of itself.

Third, the democratization of science promoted by PNS advocates is in line with degrowthers' call for reshaping (supposedly) democratic institutions in western societies, including scientific institutions, reclaiming them from the rule of experts (Cattaneo et al., 2012).

Last but not least, dialogue, value commitment, plurality of legitimate perspectives, recognition of uncertainty, and the eradication of the monopoly of experts from collective decision-making are fundamental tenets of both PNS and degrowth.

References

Cattaneo C., D'Alisa G., Kallis G., and Zografos C. (2012). "Degrowth Futures and Democracy," *Futures*, 44(6): 515–23.

Funtowicz, S. O. and Ravetz, J. R. (1990) *Uncertainty and Quality in Science for Policy*, Netherlands: Kluwer Academic Publishers.

Funtowicz S. O. and Ravetz J. R., 1994. "Uncertainty, Complexity and Post Normal Science," *Environmental Toxicology and Chemistry*, 12(12): 1,881–5.

Giampietro, M. (2003). *Multi-Scale Integrated Analysis of Agroecosystems*, London: CRC Press.

Ravetz, J. R. (1971) *Scientific Knowledge and its Social Problems*, Oxford: Clarendon Press.

Ravetz, J. R. (2011). "Postnormal Science and the Maturing of the Structural Contradictions of Modern European Science," *Futures*, 43(2): 142–8.

45

UNIONS

Denis Bayon

RESEARCH & DEGROWTH

In Western countries – and most of the world – the principal worker unions are opposed to the idea of economic degrowth for historical and pragmatic reasons. Since it became obvious that no proletarian revolution would happen, labor unions have been acting as reformist organizations committed to full employment and increasing the workers' share from economic **growth**. In industrialized countries, this strategy proved quite successful between 1950 and 1980. As a consequence, social inequality and poverty decreased greatly. Even though some "class struggle unions" kept on fighting for the development of non-capitalist institutions (social security, public services in health, education, culture, etc.), they never criticized economic growth and the industrial and social division of labor, nor any of the major subsequent environmental impacts.

The violence of the crisis of **capitalism**, especially since 2008, has led labor unions in two directions. On the one hand, confronted with the destruction of employment and a historically high increase in bankruptcies, the big unions appear less open than ever to the thematics of degrowth or of "shared frugality." In the short term, they have concentrated all their efforts on defending workers' employment and wages, and they have supported economic policies which are supposed to boost **growth**. On the other hand, however, new alliances are also emerging between some unions and degrowth activists. Not surprisingly, these connections involve small, even marginal, unions historically opposed to the reformist strategies of big unions, or dissident sections within major unions. Most of them are rooted in the revolutionary-syndicalist movement or are at least implicitly influenced by it. Examples are the Confédération Nationale du Travail (CNT), or the Union Syndicale Solidaires (SUD), in France; and the Confederación General del Trabajo (CGT), in Spain (65,000 members, the largest libertarian union in the world with 65,000 members).

A pro-degrowth stance is thus clear within the French CNT, which recently declared: "the defense of the environment implies the fight against **capitalism**; our labor class union is ecologist and in favor of degrowth" (Confédération Nationale du Travail 2011). For the Spanish CGT, the exploitation of both nature and labor imposes a similar strategy of class struggle that could draw from the idea of degrowth. At odds with the theory defended by reformist unions as well as capitalist ideologists that **growth** creates conditions for a more cohesive society, CGT denounces the "slave's way of life" (*"modo de vida esclavo"* – Taibo Arias 2008) imposed by mass production and consumption. The union points out the risk of a *forced* economic degrowth because of the overexploitation of natural resources, which is likely to take place in brutal conditions. The violence of the economic recession in Greece or Spain since 2008 may well prefigure such a social and economic collapse.

Of course these revolutionary unions, if they don't want to lose their modest influence also have to fight for employment in the economic sectors where it is threatened if they don't want to lose their (modest) influence. As a result, they may find themselves defending jobs even when these are ecologically and ethically questionable (car industry, nuclear plants, toxic factories). But these are precisely the difficulties the degrowth movement has to face when it moves away from academia or small groups of activists and engages in the daily reality of the millions of workers in industry, agriculture, and the public or private services sectors.

Wage earners in industry, services, or administration are neither the owners of capital nor the masters of their own work. Unlike farmers, who can develop agro-ecological practices on their own farms and initiate co-operative links with consumers, wage earners cannot act as producers in the direction of degrowth. There are few signs, however, as we can hope that limits are reached in the sacrifices asked of workers reaching their limits, and the current crisis creates a suitable context for the re-emergence of worker-run co-operatives, supported by unions after occupations and strikes to oppose redundancies or "fire-sales." Examples include the Vio-Me plant in Greece, the New Era Windows factory in Chicago, production of tea (Scop Ti) and ice cream (La Belle Aude) in France, and more than 300 factory workshops in Argentina. Once tools are increasingly in workers' hands, one may expect that ecological and health issues in the work place will raise to prominence, considering the growing concern for occupation diseases.

As far as we know, the Spanish CGT is the only union that provides a stimulating reflection on the links between work and degrowth – a result of its cooperation with the association Ecologistas en Acción. In an interesting document of the union, "work" is given a broad definition since it applies not only to the "use of nerves, muscles, brain," that legitimates the wage paid by private or public bosses (and which defines "labor force"), but also to domestic or collective work (food, health, educating children, taking care of old parents, developing neighborhood relationships, culture). This includes the work people do for themselves (food, health, culture) carried out for self-reproduction (see also **care** and **feminist economics**) (Confederación General del Trabajo y Ecologistas en Acción 2008: 18–19). This approach challenges the traditional opposition between "labor", "work" (both subject to necessity and opposed to freedom), and "action" (equated to "the realm of human freedom" [see Arendt 1958]), and thus differs clearly from contemporary theories known as "criticism of labor". Considering the reality of the exploitation of the labor force, some unionists want to free concrete work from the domination of **capitalism**, in other words, the abolition of the labor market.

Indeed, there is a growing class conflict in European countries which is trying to enlarge the area of human activities that can justify a wage. For example, an unemployed person should be considered a worker in the double sense that he/she doesn't get any property incomes (interests, profits) and that seeking a job, health care, and domestic tasks *are* work. Therefore all the unemployed should earn a salary and not a minority of them as it is now the case because of the limits and restrictions that apply to unemployment (and others) benefits – currently threatened by neo-liberal policies. That's why, even within big unions, there are growing demands for "professional social security" and for guaranteed decent wages for all workers, employed or not. Unlike the demand for "**basic income**," this proposal could be implemented through a reinforcement of existing institutions of social security already effective in most developed countries. Considering the increase of poverty produced by the economic crisis, such claims should be priorities, as they would put an end to the "employment blackmail" to which workers are subjected by massive unemployment, while questioning the sense and finality of human work.

Such a conception of work suggests that the end of "labor" is a pre-requisite for the degrowth project. As the economy of **growth** appears as "a vast accumulation of environmental nuisances," economic degrowth as viewed by radical unionists would involve a massive reduction of production (and consequently of environmental nuisances) and the destruction of employment; in other words, a destruction of labor exploited by capital. But work would still exist! No longer dominated by capital, human work could generate, with new tools – or an alternative use of some of the existing machines – a more co-operative and sustainable society. If work were under the control of workers, human work would be much more likely to be environmentally friendly, since under **capitalism**'s property rules and the imperative of **growth**, labor is *forced* to be environmentally harmful. Therefore, degrowth appears as a potential path to the end of the exploitation of both nature and human work by capital. A common goal for degrowth activists and radical, if not all, unionists?

References

Arendt, H. (1958/1998), *The human condition*, Chicago, IL: University of Chicago Press.

Arias, T. C. (2008) Intervención en las jornadas CGT "Una realidad de lucha y compromiso contra la crisis del capital," 26 de septiembre [Taibo Arias C. (2008), speech for the meeting of the Spanish CGT "A reality of struggle and commitment against the crisis of the capital," on September 26]. Available online at www.cgt.org.esgeb (accessed 17 August 2013).

Confederación General del Trabajo y Ecologistas en Acción (2008), *Ecologia y Anarcosindicalismo*, Manual Corso [General Confederation of Labor and Ecologists in Action- Spain (2008), *Ecology and Anarchosyndicalism*, Handbook Available online at www.cgt.org.es/sites/default/files/IMG/pdf/pdf_ecologismo_y_sindicalismo.pdf (accessed September 15 2013).

Confédération Nationale du Travail (2011), "Sortir du nucléaire? Le minimum syndical," communiqué du 7 mars National Confederation of Labor – France (2011), "Fazing out nuclear power? The least we can do," communiqué, on March 7.

46

URBAN GARDENING

Isabelle Anguelovski

ICTA (INSTITUTE OF ENVIRONMENTAL SCIENCE AND TECHNOLOGY),
AUTONOMOUS UNIVERSITY OF BARCELONA

Urban gardening is a practice through which people grow plants and crops in cities. It is a term often used interchangeably with urban agriculture, although the latter is generally practiced at a larger scale. What is known as "allotment gardens" were born in Germany in the nineteenth century to respond to food insecurity. During World War I, World War II, and the Great Depression, "liberty gardens" and "victory gardens" sprouted in the USA, Canada, Italy (under the name "Orticelli di Guerra"), and the UK, in which people grew produce and herbs to reduce pressures on food production and support war efforts. In the USA many were cultivated by European immigrants, especially Italians. Today, more than 800 million people participate in urban agriculture throughout the world, even though in many cases, especially in the Global North, the size of gardens is too small to provide produce every day for the gardeners and their families. Urban agriculture has reached much political visibility, the latest example of it being the media frenzy over Michelle Obama planting a garden with school children within the White House.

The numerous benefits of gardening have been largely recognized. First, urban agriculture supports greenhouse gas emission targets by promoting local, low-impact, and fresh food production to nearby customers. Gardening enhances the environmental quality of urban neighborhoods by mitigating storm water runoff, filtering air and rain water, mitigating urban heat island effects, serving as a sink for urban waste through decentralized composting, and helping to prevent soil erosion – even if in some cases gardening is practiced in heavily contaminated soil and requires much technical support. As gardens sprout in the city, they also provide greenery to neighborhoods that were formerly considered blighted, such as Haddington in West Philadelphia. In many instances, they thus help beautify places. However, neighborhood greening through urban gardening entails risks of gentrification and displacement, as newly attractive neighborhoods start being valued again by investors. In cities such as Delhi, New York, or Boston, urban gardens are indeed increasingly being managed by recently arrived, higher-income residents, while the proportion of lower-income gardeners and gardeners of color has decreased.

From a social standpoint, through gardening, relationships in the neighborhood are strengthened and renewed, as gardeners actively engaged in garden clean-up, production, and maintenance. They enhance the connection between people and their neighborhood and provide a greater sense of community. Growers often build a collective project without appropriating spaces for private uses and enclosing it, share responsibilities, and imagine a different use (than speculative use) for the land (see **commons**). Gardens facilitate networking, promote interactions between groups, and promote local pride and citizens' participation (Lawson 2005). From a health standpoint, they provide relaxation, healing, and trauma-recovery benefits, and also offer recreational and leisure opportunities for residents who might tend to remain isolated at home.

Last, and maybe most importantly, urban gardening addresses inequalities in food provision throughout the city by offering affordable sources of food for low-income residents and residents of color, who often tend to live in food deserts. For instance, in Los Angeles, the LA Regional Food Bank created a 14-acre farm, South Central Farms, in 1993, which brought fresh food to more than 350 poor Latino families until it was bulldozed by the City in 2006. In the Global South, urban gardening has always been woven into the urban landscape and been has increasingly supported by governments, NGOs, and farmer groups in places such as Harare, Nairobi, Rosario, Delhi, or Havana to support residents' income (Mougeot 2005).

The concept of metabolic rift, as advanced by Marx, is helpful in exploring the relationship between degrowth and urban gardening. Indeed, urban gardening contributes to addressing three dimensions of metabolic rift: the ecological rift, which is the rift in biophysical metabolic relationships (i.e. nutrient cycling), as humans are constantly in search of new spaces for ongoing accumulation, and the corresponding rescaling of production and search for technological fixes (i.e. fertilizers); the social rift, which is related to the commodification of land, labor, and food, best exemplified by the dispossession of rural populations from their land; and last, the individual rift, through which humans become alienated from nature and from the products of their labor (McClintock 2010).

Rescaling these nutrient cycles, reducing dependence on petroleum-based food production, and recycling organic waste through planting nitrogen fixing crops are at the center of the potential of urban gardening to mitigate the ecological rift. Urban gardening is a response to the social rift by cultivating under-exploited land, limiting the expansion of agri-businesses and processes and packaged food items in poor neighborhoods and beyond, and ensuring small-scale or subsistence production (while indirectly allowing ongoing accumulation at a more macro level) so that the market does not fully control the soil and the people. Here, urban gardening as alternative food movement can contribute to reclaiming resources formerly seen as commons from the enclosure of capitalist forces (see **commodification**) in ways that makes food available and affordable to everyone. Last, gardening in cities addresses the individual rift by reconnecting people with their metabolism and processes of food production and consumption.

Urban gardening and degrowth have a close relation. Often, activists have engaged in urban gardening, such as residents of Can Masdeu (Barcelona) or leaders of the Urbainculteurs (Québec), aiming to demonstrate the value of small-scale, non-commercial, low-impact farming where food is grown in ways that benefit local residents and engage them in food production. They are community initiatives embodying a transition towards a low-carbon economy and an alternative to a corporate agri-chemical intensive agriculture focused on returns. Urban gardening is often a non-capitalist practice. Through urban gardening, the distance between food production and consumption decreases. Urban gardening fosters face-to-face relationships between producers and consumers and might lead to what some call "civic agriculture," the reconnection between farm, food, and community (Lyson 2004). People are more aware and interested in the origin and quality of their food, and in ensuring that farmers have control over the means and process of production. Such interest is exemplified by the growing demand for farmers' markets and food co-operatives.

References

Lawson, A. (2005) *City Bountiful: A Century of Community Gardening in America.* Berkeley: University of California Press.
Lyson, T. A. (2004) *Civic Agriculture : Reconnecting Farm, Food, and Community, Civil Society.* Medford, Mass., Lebanon, NH: Tufts University Press; University Press of New England.
McClintock, N. (2010) "Why Farm the city? Theorizing Urban Agriculture through a Lens of Metabolic Rift." *Cambridge Journal of Regions, Economy and Society* 3(2): 191–207.
Mougeot, L. (ed.) (2005) *The Social, Political, and Environmental Dimensions of Urban Agriculture.* London: Earthscan.
Schmelzkopf, K. (1995) "Urban Community Gardens as Contested Space." *Geographical Review* 85(3):364–80.

47

WORK SHARING

Juliet B. Schor

DEPARTMENT OF SOCIOLOGY, BOSTON COLLEGE

In a shrinking capitalist economy, fewer people are necessary to produce declining levels of production. Working hours will almost certainly fall. The conventional case is where reductions in hours come in the form of unemployment. With intentional degrowth, work is to be shared by reducing the schedules of all workers, thereby avoiding unemployment for some. This is called work sharing.

Work sharing has been an important feature of economic policy in Europe since the 1980s but is less common in North America. Since the global financial panic of 2008, work hours have fallen in most wealthy countries. In some European countries, shorter work time policies were enacted as a response to the downturn. Germany, Italy, France, Austria, and the UK remain on a trajectory of declining hours. However, in the US and the Netherlands, economic recovery has reversed the shorter hours of the recession period. In Sweden and Spain, hours are considerably higher today than before the recession. Significant differences in average hours remain among nations. German employees work an average of 1,396 hours per year, British workers are at 1,660, and Americans are at 1,708, as measured by data from employers. Some mainstream economists argue that high labor costs are an obstacle to job growth; however, the current crisis is due to weak aggregate demand and the long term effects of the corruption of the financial sector rather than high wages. Indeed, real wages have declined in many countries since 2008.

The degrowth movement aspires to expand work sharing in the Global North beyond its current status as a temporary policy. If output is intentionally shrinking, hours must follow a parallel path of reductions, except in cases where the labor force and labor productivity are also declining. However, labor force shrinkage is unlikely even in the low fertility countries of Europe, because wealthy countries will need to accept climate refugees. (The majority of refugees are likely to be of working-age, given the current age structure of populations in Global South countries that will be most affected.) Similarly, growth in labor productivity is likely to continue. Innovations in digital technology can replace large amounts of human labor, particularly in the labor-intensive service sector. There is also a potential for significant productivity increases associated with eco-efficient production methods. A counter-argument is that the end of cheap energy will require higher inputs of labor (see **metabolism**). It is impossible to know the net effect of these opposing trends in productivity growth and energy costs, particularly because energy use and productivity are not independent from one another, but it is those variables that will determine how much work sharing is required to keep the labor market in balance.

How can working hours be reduced in a way that is consistent with the larger goals of the degrowth movement? Conventional work sharing entails the use of unemployment insurance to replace at least part of workers' lost wages. Replacing income is important in order to retain popular support for declines in yearly hours of work, especially for lower-paid workers. In degrowth scenarios, wages are typically assumed to remain constant and reductions in working time are financed through productivity growth. Reducing hours at a constant pay rate raises hourly wages and could lead to lower labor demand by employers.

Another approach is voluntary trading of income for time, through four-day workweeks, permanent part-time (with benefits and career ladders) and job sharing. These approaches were first introduced in the 1970s, although they remain relatively rare outside a few Western European countries. Trading income for time is more popular among highly educated professionals than manual workers. A primary obstacle to voluntary working time reduction is opposition from employers, who resist allowing short schedules for highly paid workers. A landmark law passed by the Dutch government in 2000 gives employees a statutory right to reduce their hours. Another option is to reduce the length of working lives by earlier or phased retirement, a promising approach but one that requires significant reform of pension systems.

Degrowth advocates also support work sharing because it yields additional benefits. Recent research on wealthy OECD countries shows that those with shorter hours of work have significantly lower carbon emissions and lower ecological footprints. Countries with shorter hours are producing less than their full production capacity, which means their pollution levels are lower. These nations also tend to grow more slowly over time and workers do less commuting. The second reason is that when households have more free time they are able to live more sustainable lifestyles, because low-impact activities are often more time-consuming. Mobility is a prime example: to get somewhere faster requires using more carbon.

A third benefit of work sharing is the value of free time itself. In the work-centric societies of the Global North, family, community, and political life suffer as people do not have sufficient leisure for social activities. Social relations are time-intensive; long working hours reduce investment in social connections and produce higher television viewing and exhaustion. Similarly, short working hours are essential for robust participation in democratic governance.

For degrowth, a key challenge is to transform underemployment and part-time work into a desirable way of living. Many degrowth advocates believe that the high levels of work effort of the full-employment era are no longer attainable; and besides, they are ecologically unsustainable. The alternative is to provide public goods, basic income, and access to inexpensive, but high-quality, goods and services so that working less is a freely chosen lifestyle. Innovative ways of meeting people's needs include public or collective provisioning of basic services such as housing, energy, and transportation. Internet-enabled peer-to-peer sharing schemes in which people rent, share, or give access to lodging, vehicles, consumer goods, and space, are growing (see **digital commons**). **Urban gardening**, barter schemes, time trading, and **community currencies** are also expanding. These more time-intensive ways of living are only possible when hours of work are not onerous. The degrowth movement envisions that the transition to shorter hours will also lead to new patterns of producing and consuming goods and services.

References

Coote, A. and Franklin, J. J. (eds.) (2013) *Time on Our Side: Why We All Need a Shorter Working Week*, London: New Economics Foundation.

Gorz, A. (1999) *Reclaiming Work: Beyond the Wage-Based Society*, Cambridge: Polity.

Knight, K. W., Rosa, E. A., and Schor, J. B. (2013) "Could Working Less Reduce Pressures on the Environment? A Cross-National Panel Analysis of OECD Countries, 1970–2007," *Global Environmental Change*, 23(4): 691–700.

Schor, J. B. (2011) *True Wealth: How and why Millions of Americans are Creating a Time-Rich, Ecologically-Light, Small-Scale, High-Satisfaction Economy*, New York: Penguin.

PART 4
Alliances

48

BUEN VIVIR

Eduardo Gudynas

LATIN AMERICAN CENTER OF SOCIAL ECOLOGY (CLAES)

The term 'Buen Vivir' (living well) originates in South America and signifies critiques of and alternatives to conventional ideas about development. It brings together a diverse set of questions and alternatives, ranging from the more superficial to deeper ones concerning the conceptual and practical bases for **development**.

The direct precursors of Buen Vivir are to be found in diverse concepts among some Andean indigenous groups. The first references with meanings similar to the present appeared in the 1990s, particularly in Peru, and became much more significant in Bolivia and Ecuador in the years after.

Three uses of the label Buen Vivir can be recognised:

- A generic use. This is employed in generic criticisms of different forms of conventional **development**. It has been used in questioning the practice of corporations (for instance, blowing the whistle on companies that pollute), or as a slogan to characterise alternative projects by progressive South American governments (for example, classifying as Buen Vivir the construction of pedestrian zones in the city of Quito or social support policies such as cash transfer programmes for the poor in Venezuela).
- A restricted use. This corresponds to more complex criticisms of contemporary **capitalism** that call for another, post-capitalist type of **development**. Most such criticisms are linked to the socialist tradition and the questioning posed is profound and involves a debate about different kinds of desirable **development**. Although this use does not necessarily question the goal of **economic growth** or the utilitarian use of Nature, it does convey specific views on the ownership of resources and the role to be played by the State in the allocation of such resources. The best-known expressions in this stream involve Buen Vivir as 'republican bio-socialism' in Ecuador, or as 'integral development' in Bolivia.

- Substantive use. This relates to a radical criticism of all forms of **development** at their conceptual foundations, and a consequent defence of alternatives that are both post-capitalist and post-socialist. These alternatives draw from indigenous knowledges and sensibilities, as well as critical Western strands of thought. Substantive use is a plural and intercultural set of ideas still under construction. This was the original formulation of Buen Vivir, whereas the two former formulations are more recent.

Buen Vivir corresponds most closely to the concept of degrowth in its substantive use, since other positions express positions that are more accurately described as 'development alternatives' – that is, instrumental arrangements that do not question fundamental ideas, such as the need for industrialisation, the myth of progress or the duality that separates society from Nature. In comparison, Buen Vivir, in its substantive sense, constitutes an 'alternative to **development**' (in the sense of Escobar 1992).

If Buen Vivir in its substantive sense is a plural field under construction, already there exist key consistent elements. Buen Vivir radically criticizes different types of conventional development, foundations both conceptual and practical, as well as its institutions and legitimising discourses. In particular, Buen Vivir rejects the idea of a predetermined historical linearity in which 'development stages' must be followed by all nations (imitating industrialised nations), but rather defends the multiplicity of historical processes. It does not accept the concept of progress and its derivatives (particularly **growth**) or the idea that welfare depends only upon material consumption.

In its substantive sense, Buen Vivir defends the diversity of knowledges. The dominance of Western ideas is replaced by a promotion of 'interculturality' under which Western ideas are not rejected but seen as one among many options. The separation of society and nature is not recognised and is replaced by a notion of expanded communities, which may also include different living beings or elements of the environment in territorial contexts. Buen Vivir is only possible within communities of extended or relative ontologies. This involves recognising intrinsic values in Nature, thus breaking with the prevailing Western anthropocentric position in which humans are the only subjects of value. Furthermore, Buen Vivir rejects the instrumentalisation of Nature by humankind.

This and other factors make Buen Vivir a non-essentialist perspective, relative to every historical, social and environmental context. Such a characteristic also accounts for the plurality underlying the term.

This plurality can be appreciated in its different variants. One of the best-known forms is the category *suma qamaña*, expressing the sensibility of some *aymara* communities in Bolivia. It is a notion of wellbeing, or a fulfilled life, which can only be achieved by deep relationships within a community. In turn, the sense of 'community' is extended as it integrates other living beings and elements of the environment located within a territorial framework (*ayllu*). A sense of fulfilment is only possible within the framework of these kinds of amplified rationalities and sensibilities.

The idea of *sumak kawsay*, from Ecuador, is also well known. This concept is similar to the previous one and highlights a welfare system that is not only material but that is also expressed within extended communities, both social and ecological. Unlike *suma qamaña*, *sumak kawsay* does not contain a concept like the Bolivian *ayllu*.

Several indigenous peoples have analogous concepts, such as the *ñande reko* of the Guaraní people, the *shiir waras* of the Ashuar in Ecuador or the *küme mongen* of the Mapuche in southern Chile.

Buen Vivir is also based on critical thought within the Western tradition. The two most important sources are **environmentalism**, which proposes the rights of Nature, and new feminism, which questions patriarchal centralities and claims an ethic of **care**.

Thus, Buen Vivir represents the confluence of knowledge of different origins, and it cannot be restricted to be an 'indigenous' idea. This is because there is no such thing as an indigenous knowledge in the singular, as this is a colonial category. Thus, Buen Vivir incorporates some concepts and sensibilities of some indigenous groups, as each one has a specific cultural backgroundthe *suma qamaña* posture of Buen Vivir among Aymara communities is not the same as *sumak kawsay* of the kichwas in Ecuador. These are positions pertaining to each social and environmental context, which, furthermore have been affected, hybridised or mixed in different ways with present-day or modern thought, even though they have no relationship with ideas like the 'good life' in the Aristotelian sense or in any of its Western derivatives.

Buen Vivir is not a return to the past; rather it confronts current situations with an eye to the future. This occurs in an intercultural context and even generates reciprocal challenges (for instance, for Western critical knowledge, the challenge of understanding the visions of extended communities regarding non-human aspects, and for some indigenous views, dealing with male chauvinism). An example of this involves the explorations of a transition from **environmental justice**, based upon third-generation human rights (quality of life or health), to ecological justice, specifically based on the rights of Nature (those independent from human appraisals).

Buen Vivir should be interpreted as a shared platform or field in which different positions converge in a criticism of **development** in particular and of Modernity in general. Buen Vivir proposes alternatives that also present complementary senses.

Buen Vivir is not presented as a unit or an academic discipline or a plan of action. It is a set of ideas and sensibilities deployed on another level, which could be said to be located in 'political philosophy', to use an available Western term, as occurs with ideas such as participation or equality.

Buen Vivir in its original radical sense influenced the drafting of the new Constitutions of Bolivia and, in particular, of Ecuador. In both these countries, however, there have been political decisions and new laws or resolutions that limit the components of the radical criticism of **development** inherent in Buen Vivir. This has been displaced by a new form of acceptable **development** (this is the case of 'integral development' in Bolivia) or, in a restricted sense, by a socialist option *sui generis* in Ecuador (Gudynas 2013).

As Buen Vivir in its substantive sense does not accept the conceptual bases of the different types of contemporary **development**, links with degrowth can be established. This is especially true with regard to Buen Vivir's criticism of growth or consumerism. In any case, Buen Vivir displaces the discussion of growth to that of social and environmental fulfilment. Thus, in a Latin American context some sector must be downsized and consumerism rejected, but the improvement in other sectors, such as education or health, may result in economic growth. From this perspective it could be said that degrowth is one of the possible consequences in certain contexts and not an objective in itself. Unlike degrowth, Buen Vivir, due to its intercultural perspective, follows more ambitious objectives placed in changing present-day cosmovisions of humans, society and Nature.

Bibliography

Escobar, A. (1992) 'Imagining a Post-Development Era? Critical Thought, Development and Social Movements', *SocialText* 31/32: 20–56.

Gudynas, E. (2011a) 'Buen Vivir: germinando alternativas al desarrollo', *América Latina en Movimiento, ALAI*, 462: 1–20.

Gudynas, E. (2011b). 'Buen Vivir: Today's Tomorrow', *Development* 54(4): 441–7.

Gudynas, E. (2013) 'Development Alternatives in Bolivia: the Impulse, the Resistance, and the Restoration', *NACLA Report on the Americas* 46(1): 22–6.

49

ECONOMY OF PERMANENCE

Chiara Corazza¹ and Solomon Victus²

¹ CA' FOSCARI UNIVERSITY
² TAMILNADU THEOLOGICAL SEMINARY OF SERAMPORE UNIVERSITY

'The Economy of Permanence' is an economic model proposed by J.C.Kumarappa (1892–1960) – an Indian Christian native of Madras. It was conceived for Indian villages and shaped from Gandhi's principles of economics. It aimed to establish democracy on a small basis, managed by people themselves, by providing primary needs, helping small village industries and subsistence agriculture. According to the economics of permanence, everyone had to provide for their own self-sufficiency with agricultural activity or by providing a useful service to the village by practicing a craft, such as spinning khadi, the typical Indian hand-made cloth, carpentry, iron smithy, pottery, water control and artisan works (Kumarappa, 1958a). Peasants and artisans would then exchange their own products through barter, without using money, and the village would become a self-sufficient entity. A village council – or panchayat – would have the task of regulating the administration of the village itself. In the economy of permanence women had fundamental importance in the education of young people and children to create future men and women capable of guaranteeing their own self-sufficiency (Kumarappa 1958a).

Kumarappa defined permanence' in the sense that 'inanimate life, the secret of nature's permanency, lies in the cycle of life by which the various factors function in close cooperation to maintain the continuity of life' (Kumarappa 1945: 1). He discerned that nature has the capacity to sustain a permanence of life and that humans should learn from her. Kumarappa argued that the Western economic system was intrinsically transient, based on large-scale production, export oriented markets, consumerism and individualism (Kumarappa 1958a). The Economy of Permanence does not conceive economics as a 'disembedded' discipline, but in coexistence with nature, its resources and future generations. It conceives an inseparability of economics, ethics and politics.

The Economy of Permanence is a less familiar term than "Gandhian economics" because the former refers to a specific alternative economic model while the latter is a mix of economic ideas related with Gandhi. Gandhi's economic ideas were founded mainly on two principles: Truth and Non-Violence. He also used other related concepts such as swaraj (self-rule), sarvodaya (welfare of all), swadeshi (self-reliance), home-made khadi. He made the chakra (the spinning wheel) a symbol of his economic programme (Kumarappa 1951).

The Economy of Permanence was conceived in the 1940s. During this period, India had long been involved in the struggle for Independence, and Kumarappa had worked closely with Gandhi, who was imprisoned for more than a year in 1942 during the Quit India Movement, since 1929. On several occasions, Kumarappa had opportunities to closely examine the economic situation of the Indian villages. He observed the elimination by British colonialism of the countless crafts and farming practices that had once animated rural life, and which transformed the Indian village economy towards the production of raw materials for England's industries. In this context, the economy of permanence was born out of desperation. Kumarappa was motivated by an aspiration to restore the ancient prosperity and sustainability of India on small-scale rural and self-sufficient bases ensuring a livelihood for everyone.

In 1945, Kumarappa published the book *Economy of Permanence*. Written in prison, the book articulated a model that its author had practised and experimented with in rural India since the second half of the 1930s and was not purely academic. Two organizations were created by Gandhi and Kumarappa to support Indian handicraft activities, at the time strangled by English industrial competition: the All India Spinners Association and the All India Village Industries Association.

The objectives of these associations were the promotion of Indian khadi, Indian traditional products, skills and technicalities and the teachings of ancient crafts, reviving them and helping the villagers to gain economic self-sufficiency. The overall goal was the eradication of a poverty that for Kumarappa was directly linked to the colonial British tax system.

After India's Independence, the Economy of Permanence presented itself as a suitable model for the newborn nation. However Kumarappa's views collided with the figure of Jawarlal Nerhu, the first popular Prime Minister of Independent India in 1947. Fabian Socialist, Westernised and fascinated by modernity, Nehru believed that Gandhi and Kumarappa's ideas were inapplicable. He followed an industrial policy in a developmental fashion and came into conflict with Kumarappa, who – like Gandhi – abhorred industrialism because it furnished cheaper products in large quantities in fierce competition with small artisans and hence caused their unemployment. An open dispute between Nehru and Kumarappa arose concerning the question of what should be the basis of the Indian economic development plan – cities or villages? Although Gandhi was with Kumarappa in spirit, he politically supported Nehru, although he tried to strike creative compromises between the two models. Once Gandhi died, Nehru, with his political power, took the upper hand and implemented an urban-centred industrialization process that sidelined Kumarappa's model.

Kumarappa withdrew from the national political scene but continued campaigning for the Economy of Permanence at a grassroots level. Today, many organizations are still active and new ones have formed, applying the principles of the Economy of Permanence, such as the Kumarappa Institute of Gram Swaraj founded in Jaipur in 1965 and the Kumarappa Institute of Rural Technology and Development, based at the Gandhi Niketan Ashram, active since 1956, in Tamil Nadu. The model's popularity is now growing among neo-Marxist Indians.

Degrowth thinkers and practitioners could be inspired by Gandhian economic thought. *The Economy of Permanence* shares many features with degrowth, such as an attention to the vulnerability of natural resources; a focus on creativity and the revolutionary potential of the grassroots; the idea of an alternative path to economism; the importance on spiritual values as opposed to material contentment alone; organic agriculture; the value of labour; the care of others; mutual aid and the revival of interpersonal relationships and permanence as a desirable alternative value opposed to conspicuous consumerism.

Kumarappa's economic model has indirectly been an important source for degrowth, even if up to now this has not been recognized and researched. In fact, Kumarappa influenced the forefathers of degrowth, such as Ernst Schumacher and Ivan Illich. Schumacher quotes Kumarappa in his book, *Small is Beautiful*, urging a study of the economics of permanence, for they imply a profound reorientation of science and technology. Illich acknowledged Kumarappa's influence and visited T. Kallupati, where Kumarappa spent his last days (Victus 2003). Illich was impressed with Kumarappa's holistic understanding, Schumacher with his appropriate technology concept. From an Indian perspective, degrowth is an expression of Gandhian economic thought in the West.

Finally, the Economy of Permanence is very close to degrowth in practice. The model is still practised today by many Indian villages that rely upon subsistence incomes in spite of the multi-frontal onslaught by neo-liberalism and Indian heavy industries or corporations. There have been many past and present Indian social movements and organizations influenced directly or indirectly by Kumarappa's and Gandhi's thinking about fervent **growth** and **development**: the Lakshimi Ashram, the Chipko Movement, the Narmada Bachao Andolan, Navdanya, the National Alliance of People's Movements, the Kumarappa Institute of Rural Technology and Development and the Kumarappa Institute of Gram Swaraj. These have been involved in promoting organic agriculture, small dams, decentralised development and supporting local industries and production. These are the natural allies in India of the degrowth movement in the West.

References

Kumarappa, J. C. (1945) *Economy of Permanence*, Varanasi: Sarva Seva Sangh Prakashan.

Kumarappa, J. C. (1951) *Gandhian Economic Thought*, Bombay: Vora & Co.

Kumarappa, J. C. (1958a) *Economy of Permanence: A Quest for a Social Order Based on Non-Violence*, Wardha (India): Sarva Seva Sangh.

Kumarappa, J. C (1958b) *Why the Village Movements?* Rajghat: Akil Bharat Sarva Seva Sangh (ABSSS).

Lindley, M. (2007) *J. C. Kumarappa: Mahatma Gandhi's Economist*, Mumbai: Popular Prakashan Pvt. Ltd.

Victus, S. (2003) *Religion and Eco-Economics of J.C. Kumarappa: Gandhism Redefined*, New Delhi: ISPCK.

50

FEMINIST ECONOMICS

Antonella Picchio

WELL_B_LAB*, SPIN OFF, UNIVERSITY OF MODENA AND REGGIO EMILIA

Feminist economics introduce a shift of perspective in the way we see the economy. This new perspective is set by seeing women as autonomous subjects not definable on the basis of the male norm that has transformed sexual difference into a social inferiority. The feminist standpoint, free of a reductive and distortive male bias (Elson 1998), allows for a deeper and broader insight into the economy. It is deeper, because women's experiential knowledge leads us closer to the complexity of real life, and broader, because it extends economic analysis to domestic, non-market activities.

The power to change perspective is rooted in the international feminist movement of the late 1960s and early 1970s. At that time, as now, the feminist political wave was concentrated on women's resistance against the use of their bodies as a means of production and reproduction on the part of the State and the Church and of men's control of them (Dalla Costa and James 1972).

Feminist economic thought is a rapidly expanding field of studies, a heterogeneous and pragmatic effort open to different approaches, paradigms and empirical methods. The main areas of research and debate are:

- the sex disaggregation of economic data, to highlight overlooked persistent forms of gender inequalities and their impact on labour markets, development processes, trade and public policy;
- the extension of micro and macro economic dimensions to non-market activities;
- the position of social dimensions in economic analysis and policy;
- the feminist critique of current mainstream and heterodox theories, for their methodological blindness to the social reproduction of human beings.

A very important academic institution of the community is IAFFE (International Association for Feminist Economics), which publishes the journal *Feminist Economics*.

According to my feminist analysis, economic systems are characterized by specific relationships between the production of means and the social reproduction of people. Production and reproduction relationships are grounded on the division of productive and reproductive labour, the distribution of income and resources and sex and class power relationships (Picchio 1992).

The capitalist system is based on a specific structure of historical processes: production of commodities, market exchange, distribution of income and, last but not least, social reproduction of the population. These processes are all connected in a circular flow, which is not automatically sustainable and it adapts through recurrent crises.

The capitalist system is characterized by the wage-labour market, i.e. by the buying and selling of the capability to work (labour force), which is treated as a commodity (see **commodification**). Classical political economists (Smith, Ricardo and Marx) defined wages as the normal costs of the conventional necessaries that enabled the 'labouring population' to work and reproduce their 'race' (the term they used). Actually, in a capitalist context, the lives of workers become means of production that are to be kept, for the sake of profit, within the limits of efficiency and social control. This process of transforming lives into capital is a moral and political battlefield that makes the link between economics and ethics indissoluble and sex and class conflict endemic in capitalism.

Capitalism is a dangerous and inherently destructive system: on the whole, it is unsustainable precisely because of the conflict between profit and the well-being of the labouring population and the exploitation of the environment in order to hide real costs of production and discharge social responsibilities.

Economic theories are not neutral or innocent with regard to the functioning of the system of provisioning. The main economic paradigms differ when it comes to the definition of profit, capital, wages and distribution of incomes. In particular, the way the social reproduction of the labouring population is connected to other structural processes entails major paradigmatic differences. Given that in classical political economy, profit is defined as a residuum between production and whatever goes to the labouring population under any title (wages, public services and transfers), and that the process of distribution of the surplus is explained on the basis of class power relationships, the process of reproduction of the labouring population falls at the centre of the analysis of value and distribution and at the core of a structural conflict.

In the present context of growing insecurity, social inequality, fears of new wars and ongoing destruction of the environment, the sentiments of the degrowth critique and, even more so, the varied experiences of local convivial living, are appealing and, what is more, are capable of producing more humane living conditions at the local level. Yet, from a feminist perspective they have some limitations. Macro feminist economics and the degrowth perspective differ in the way they order and see structural processes, and in the attention they give to the distribution between profit and subsistence of the (labouring) population. The degrowth perspective dwells extensively on production and consumption, giving subsistence economy a mythical role, but it does not pay enough attention to the sex and class body-politics of social reproduction in the capitalist context we live in.

At the micro level, the provisioning of goods and services for direct use may take into account the need to live a healthy, sociable, just life, but at the macro level the degrowth narrative does not challenge the structure of **capitalism**. The current crisis shows that there is a small group of financial profiteers endowed with the power to rule public expenditure, i.e. to decide on the suffering of the bodies and minds of the population. Any sensible person should be outraged by such developments, but a mere moral reproach aimed at the ways we produce and consume is equally unsatisfactory. The real challenge is to set out and defuse the structural forces at the root of such destructive and alienating dynamics.

In order to understand the material and moral features of the capitalist system, we need theories that grasp its structure and its dynamics. The classical surplus approach offers powerful tools to this end. Not only does this approach show surplus to be the leading motive of production, in conflict with a sustainable well-being of the labouring population, but it shows also that the distribution between wages (social wages included) and profit (plus rent) is the result of a political, institutional confrontation based on unequal class and sex power relationships (Picchio 1992). Once the politics of distribution are made clear, and real living conditions emerge as crucial and at the heart of the social conflict, the so-called 'objective constraints' that condemn so many people to poverty and social exclusion, and women to more and more unpaid labour, will loose their grip. The use of social reproduction as capital and as a reason to control women's bodies and agency could also explain the long history of violence exercised against women since the beginning of **capitalism** (Federici 2004).

The more recent analytical tools of the capability approach developed by Amartya Sen and Martha Nussbaum can enrich the classical surplus approach. They expand the concept of standards of living: no more a basket of commodities, but a multidimensional set of individual functionings that defines effective well-being within a space of multiple capabilities. The freedom to compose our lives according to our values as autonomous individuals, embodied agaand embedded in a social context, becomes a fundamental dimension of a good life.

Drawing from the toolbox of the surplus and of the capability approaches, the feminist perspective on women's experience – on what it *really* means to be embodied and embedded in a social context – proposes a 'reproductive, extended macro economic approach' (Picchio 2003) as a basis for a transformative **Care** Economy.

The degrowth perspective is not broad enough to include the critique of the macro-dynamics of the present capitalist system and not deep enough to reveal the complexity of real lives and the use of women's activities to make it sustainable. It thus shares the general blindness which dumps any caring reproductive responsibility onto the domestic space, and this means, among other things, that human vulnerability, including the vulnerability of adult males, remains a woman's issue.

References

Dalla Costa, M. and James, S. (1972) *The power of women and the subversion of the community*, Bristol: Falling Wall Press.

Elson, D. (1998) 'The economic, the political and the domestic: businesses, states and households in the organization of production', *New Political Economy*, 3 (2), 189–208.

Federici, S. (2004) *Caliban and the witch: women, the body and primitive accumulation*, New York: Autonomedia.

Picchio, A. (1992) *Social reproduction: the political economy of the labour market*, Cambridge: Cambridge University Press.

Picchio, A. (2003) 'An extended macroeconomic approach', In *Unpaid work and the economy, a gender perspective on standards of living*, London: Routledge.

51

UBUNTU

Mogobe B. Ramose

DEPARTMENT OF PHILOSOPHY, UNIVERSITY OF SOUTH AFRICA

Ubuntu is a philosophy of the Bantu speaking peoples in Africa. Underpinning the philosophy is the belief that motion is the principle of being. Accordingly, through motion, all beings exist in an incessant complex flow of interactions and change (Ramose 1999: 50–9). In Ubuntu, to be human one must practice giving, receiving, and passing on the goods of life to others (Griaule 1965: 137). This worldview takes the ethical position that to be a human being is to **care** for oneself and others. *A person is a person through other persons*, is the motto of Ubuntu. A human is being and becoming in relation to and interdependence with others.

Here, the concept of others also includes all other entities that are not human beings and, therefore, the concept relates directly to a care and a concern for the environment. The Ubuntu philosophy's ethical position takes as its point of departure the principle that one must promote life and avoid killing (Bujo 1998: 77). The Sesotho proverb *feta kgomo o tshware motho* is a statement of this principle. It means that if and when one ought to choose between preservation, especially of human life, and the possession of excess wealth, one must opt for the preservation of life. The philosophy of Ubuntu (*botho* or *hunhu*) is anchored on the ethical principle of the promotion of life through mutual concern, care and sharing between and among human beings as well as with the wider environment of which the human being is a part. Ubuntu philosophy understands life in its wholeness (Bohm 1980).

According to Ubuntu philosophy, a community is a triad comprised of the living, the living-dead (ancestors), and the yet-to-be born. The community of the living answers to the living-dead by remembering them constantly through various rituals, which pertain to the different stages of individual and family life. It is believed that maintaining the relationship with the living-dead in this way promotes well-being and harmony and thus the living avoid affliction imposed by the displeased living-dead. It is also believed that one of the benefits of the harmony between the living and the living-dead is that the latter will provide whatever is necessary so that the former fulfil their obligation to the third rung of the community, namely, making the yet-to-be-born real by bearing children. Bearing children is incomplete without the means to nurture and rear them; the necessaries for the preservation of life must be available. This is the node and vital point at which the concept of life extends to the environment and future generations, reaffirming the philosophy of wholeness. Here arises the responsibility to promote life by actually practising the ethics of concern and care for the environment. From the point of view of the Ubuntu philosophical understanding of life as wholeness it may be suggested that the environment forms the fourth dimension of the community.

In practice, the protagonists of Ubuntu philosophy continue to care for the environment through various fertility rituals, the observance of taboos and respect for totems.

Global warming threatens life in its wholeness, a threat paralleled only by the silenced, but still real, threat of nuclear holocaust. The stubbornly inexorable march towards collective suicide through the destruction of life as hitherto known parallels the unbridled pursuit of money, and in particular, profit. This challenges the Ubuntu concept of community and the attendant ethical principle of *feta kgomo o tshware motho*. The community of the yet-to-be-born has the same right to life as the living have.

Ubuntu offers the philosophical basis for an alternative **imaginary** to **growth** and **development**, and thus it can be a source of inspiration for degrowthers. If degrowth challenges the idea of **development** in the Global North, imaginaries such as those of Ubuntu challenge it in Africa and elsewhere. The point is not whether the North has to degrow for the South to grow, but whether we can leave space for alternative native imaginaries to be part of shaping the future. Ubuntu's emphasis on connection, and of being in relation to others, resonates strongly with the notions of **commons** and commoning. Ubuntu also expresses a strong principle of community solidarity materialized into a redistribution of wealth. Its spirit of 'extroverted communities' resonates with degrowthers' call for localized economies with open borders and flows. Group work and cooperation are privileged over self-promotion, in line with the cooperativist spirit of degrowth, though there is also recognition of individuals' difference and uniqueness. The abstractness of modern urban societies has undermined a community socialization that is central to Ubuntu, but this can be regained through an ethic of collective responsibility and commitment to a collective prosperity.

Despite the suppression of the Ubuntu's voice in South Africa, for more than three centuries Ubuntu philosophy has not died. Its continued practise is an important challenge to the unfolding environmental problems, not least global warming. The time for change is now, and the practise of the philosophy of Ubuntu is one of the appropriate ethical responses to the necessity to halt and reverse global environmental change.

References

Bohm, D. (1980) *Wholeness and the implicate order*, London: Routledge and Kegan Paul.
Bujo, B. (1998) *The ethical dimension of community*, Namulondo Nganda Cecilia (trans.) Nairobi: Paulines Publications Africa.
Griaule, M. (1965) *Conversations with Ogotommeli*, Oxford: Oxford University Press.
Maathai, W. (2009) *The challenge for Africa*, London: William Heinemann.
Ramose, M. B. (1999) *African philosophy through Ubuntu*, Harare: Mond Books Publishers.

FROM AUSTERITY TO DÉPENSE

Giacomo D'Alisa, Giorgos Kallis, and Federico Demaria

– [A] big duel, Uncle . . . Great things are in the offing, and I don't want to stay at home . . .

– You're mad, my boy, to go with those people! They're all in the mafia, all troublemakers. A Falconeri should be with us, for the King.

– For the King, Uncle, yes, of course. But which King? . . . If we want things to stay as they are, things will have to change.

Giuseppe Tomasi di Lampedusa, "The Leopard"

[A]ll that city . . . You just couldn't see an end to it . . . It wasn't what I saw that stopped me, Max. It was what I didn't see. . . . In all that sprawling city, there was everything except an end . . . Take a piano. The keys begin, the keys end. You know there are 88 of them . . . They are not infinite, you are infinite. On those 88 keys the music that you can make is infinite. . . . But you get me up on that gangway and roll out a keyboard with millions of keys, and . . . there's no end to them, that keyboard is infinite. But if that keyboard is infinite there's no music you can play.

From the movie "The Legend of 1900"

[A] human sacrifice, the construction of a church or the gift of a jewel are no less interesting than the sale of wheat . . .

It is not necessity, but its contrary . . . "luxury" that presents living matter and mankind with their fundamental problems . . .

Georges Bataille, "The Accursed Share"

The core question in the aftermath of the economic crisis in Europe and the U.S has been framed as one of austerity vs. spending. Should governments implement austerity or deficit spending measures in order to re-launch growth? While the EU went mostly for the first option, the U.S. opted largely for the second. In conventional economic terms, one could argue that austerity is not working: most European countries are still in recession, while the U.S. is slowly growing again. But in degrowth terms, neither austerity nor deficit spending are the solution. They are the problem. Both, indeed, aim to re-launch growth; degrowthers oppose them precisely because they are ideologically rooted in the growth imaginary. Even those who want spending and growth only for the short-term to exit the crisis, and hope to move beyond growth afterwards, do not realize that this "after" will never come, since it is precisely through the spectre of recession and crisis that growth is legitimated eternally.

To depict the substantial differences between the degrowth society we envision and the contemporary Westernized society in which we live in, it seems useful to briefly deconstruct the austerity and spending imaginaries using two examples from the news.

Cut 1. November 11, 2013: David Cameron's speech about austerity in the Lord Mayor's banquet. The UK Prime Minister called for a "fundamental culture change." He condemned idleness and invoked the traditional British value of hard work. "Put simply," he said, "no country can succeed in the long term if capable people are paid to stay idle and out of work." People are trapped into unemployment by high benefits, Cameron noted: "for generations, people who could work have been failed by the system and stuck on benefits". Benefits will be lowered, he promised, and *no one will see any reward in staying idle* or working less: "We are ensuring that for every extra hour you work and every extra job you do, you should always be better off." In Cameron's talk, the State is the problem, not the solution; it has to be shrunk, become leaner and limit itself to setting and enforcing rules, letting markets and the private sector produce wealth. His talk was a celebration of private enterprise: "the UK economy should be based on enterprise . . . we need to support, reward and celebrate enterprise . . . make sure it is boosted everywhere, promoted in schools, taught in colleges, celebrated in communities."

Cut 2. November 16, 2013: Paul Krugman comments on Lawrence Summers' talk at the IMF, where the latter raised the spectre of a "secular stagnation" for the U.S. economy, that is a long-term zero growth state. For Krugman this is the result of a liquidity trap, which makes state spending vital. Ideally such spending should be productive; but even unproductive spending is better than nothing, Krugman argues. The important is to get circulation going. Hide money or gold in caves and have enterprises dig it up, as Keynes proposed, Krugman says. Fake a threat from non-existent space aliens and spend for military protection (Krugman's "own favourite"). Or get U.S. enterprises "to fit out all their employees as cyborgs, with Google Glass and smart wristwatches everywhere." Even if this does not pay off, "the resulting investment boom would have given us several years of much higher employment, with no real waste, *since the resources employed would have otherwise been idle.*"

The two discourses appear on the surface to be worlds apart. Cameron calls for an unprecedented cultural change, but in fact re-invokes Locke's instructions to the emerging bourgeoisie, what Max Weber later called "the protestant ethic": work hard, and deny self-indulgence and pleasure. This way capital will accumulate and enterprises produce wealth, Cameron suggests. In the current conjuncture there is no doubt that Cameron's project is classist, redistributing upwards. The working classes are asked to tighten their belt and accept the loss of services provided to them, free or subsidized, by the common wealth, so that the rich do not have to shoulder higher taxes to sustain the common wealth in the absence of growth. The Keynesian project instead seems to put the employment of the working classes first; its advocacy of public spending seems, at least in principle, not to be regressive (even if it is not destined to what one would normally call public services).

However, we maintain, what is common between the two discourses is more instructive than what separates them. Both Cameron and Krugman are concerned with "investment." The former thinks that investment will be unleashed by raising the confidence of the markets that State expenditures are under control. The latter wants the State to kick-start investment by pouring money in the economy. They differ on the "how," but what both want is to see capital circulating and expanding again. The second feature they share is their abhorrence of "idleness." For Cameron, the problem is the idleness of workers and the resources wasted by the State to support it. For Krugman the problem is the idleness of capital and the waste of productive resources that could otherwise be invested. For Cameron, the problem is the worker who doesn't work; for Krugman, the capital that doesn't flow.

On the contrary, we degrowthers are not afraid of idleness. Paul Lafargue's provocative "The right to be lazy" is our inspiration. A society that has developed so many resources surely can extend the right to idleness from the few rich to everyone, Lafargue argued in 1883, and André Gorz elaborated 100 years after. We degrowthers also are not afraid of the idleness of capital; we desire it. Degrowth involves slowing capital down. The essence of **capitalism** is the continuous reinvestment of surplus into new production. Wealth in industrialist societies is what can be invested again.

The spending proposed by Krugman and Summers appears wasteful and unproductive in the short-term, but is productive in the long-term: it is a utilitarian spending whose goal is to value capital, so that it does not stand idle, re-launching its circulation and **growth**. Worse, implicit in their proposal is the assumption that public policies must not engage with the meaning of life and the creation of a political collective. On the contrary, for us, the current socio-ecological crisis urges to overcome **capitalism**'s senseless **growth** through the means of a social **dépense**. **Dépense** refers to a genuinely collective expenditure — the spending in a collective feast, the decision to subsidise a class of spirituals to talk about philosophy, or to leave a forest idle – an expenditure that in strictly economic sense is unproductive. Practices of **dépense** "burn" capital out and take it out of the sphere of circulation, slowing it down. Such collective "waste" is not for personal utility or for the utility of capital. It aspires to be **political**. It offers a process through which a collective could make sense of and define the "good life," rescuing individuals from their illusionary and meaningless privatized lives.

Dépense generates horror, not only among the supporters of austerity, but also among Keynesians, Marxists, and radicals of all sorts, including some environmentalists. To return to our examples, witness the reaction to the set-up for Cameron's talk. Progressives reacted because the Prime Minister was calling for austerity while standing in a sumptuous hall surrounded by furniture crafted in gold. Instead, we are not particularly concerned with such lavish expenditure, by a public institution such as the City of London Corporation that was founded in the Middle Ages. The gold of the Mayor's Hall is an unproductive expenditure with the anti-utilitarian essence of a by-gone era that preceded **capitalism**. For Keynesians, what was appalling in this picture is the display of idle wealth; not for us. The contradiction is not between Cameron's call for austerity in the midst of golden furniture; the real contradiction is between his call for an austere state, in the midst of a place that symbolizes an era during which sovereigns were not shy of **dépense**.

The Mayor's Hall is a form of public **dépense**, which we do not want to reproduce, but that we not reproach *as such*. We are aware that the gold in London's Guildhall is the outcome of the exploitation of workers, colonies, and ecosystems by the British Empire. We are against such dispossessions and depletions. But our point here is about the destiny of surplus, not its origin. Social surplus *might* be, and has often been the outcome of exploitation, but it doesn't *have to*: commonwealth can be generated without exploitation. The progressives who took issue with Cameron's talk condemned the contradiction between the display of wealth and his call for austerity. We see nothing contradictory between this wealth being a product of exploitation, and Cameron's call for austerity, i.e. more exploitation of workers.

Many environmentalists will find it hard to accept a non-utilitarian waste of resources, because their **imaginary** is so strongly wedded to the idea of natural scarcity. But scarcity is social. Since the stone-age we have had more than what we need for a basic standard of living. The original affluent societies of Sahlins did not experience scarcity not because they had a lot, but because they did not know what scarcity means and thought they always had enough. They consumed what they gathered, and they never accumulated. Scarcity calls for economizing and accumulating; this is why the common sense in industrial society is that scarcity is the major problem of humanity. This is why scarcity is the *sine qua non* of **capitalism**. Our message to frugal ecologists is that it is better to waste resources in gold decorations in a public building or drink them in a big feast, than put them in good use, accelerating even more the extraction of new resources and the degradation of the environment. It is the only way to escape **Jevons' Paradox**. Accumulation drives **growth**, not waste. Even in a society of frugal subjects with a downscaled metabolism, there will still be a surplus that would have to be dispensed, if **growth** is not to be reactivated.

For those who are concerned that there are not enough resources to secure basic needs, let alone waste them uselessly, let us note the incredible amount of resources currently dispensed in bubbles and zero-sum positional games, whose aim is nothing else than the circulation of capital (in fact what Krugman calls for). Economists realize now that bubbles are not an aberration; they are vital for **capitalism** and **growth**. Think of the immense amount of resources spent on professional sports, cinema and commercial modern art, financial services, or all sorts of positional consumption (the latest cars, houses, or gadgets whose only fleeting value is that they are the latest). A football game was as pleasant as 50 years ago, when sports were practiced by amateurs, and a movie or a painting no better today than then, despite the huge amounts of capital that circulate to finance and market sports and arts. "Ferraris for all" is the elusive dream of **growth**, but when everyone has a Ferrari, the Ferrari will be the Fiat of its generation. Economists have called for limits on such zero-sum competition for positional consumption, limits that would liberate resources for real **growth**. We instead want to liberate these resources to secure basic needs and to collectively feast with the rest to avow **the political** of a new era. We in degrowth have made considerable advances in thinking about the State and autonomous institutions that will cater for the satisfaction of basic needs. Now we need to think about the institutions that will be responsible for the socialization of unproductive **dépense** and the ways in which circulating surplus will be limited and expended.

At the same time that capitalist discourses blame the idleness of the "factors of production" at the societal level, they also foster the privatization of wasteful consumption: the individual can get drunk, spend all his or her savings at the casino, organize private parties with champagne and caviar for his or her entourage, deplete accumulated resources in luxurious hobbies or conspicuous shopping, or lease beautiful bodies of women and men for orgiastic VIP parties. All this personalized **dépense** is allowed in the name of the liberty of each individual to elusively search in his or her personal sphere for the meaning of life. The unquestionable premise of a modern society is the right of each person to accumulate resources beyond basic needs and use them for realizing what he or she thinks is a "good life." As a consequence, the system has to constantly grow to allow each and every one the opportunity to pursue this right, as it pretends to do in the abstract.

This central feature of modernity has affected many strains of Marxism too, which pushed the dream of collective emancipation to the extreme by means of a life of material abundance for everyone. Actually existing socialist regimes found that basic needs could well be satisfied for everyone. But in doing so, they repressed private **dépense** and disavowed socialized **dépense** (counting out military parades and ceremonies in honour of Stakhanovite bureaucrats). The hypothesis put forward here is that it was the stifling of both private and social **dépense** that led to the failure and eventually collapse of these regimes.

In the degrowth society that we imagine, **dépense** will be brought back to the public sphere, but sobriety will characterize the individual. This call for personal sobriety is not in the name of financial deficits, ecological limits or moral grounds; ours is not the Protestant call of the supporters of austerity. Our claim for sobriety is based on the premise that finding the meaning of life individually is an anthropological illusion. Consider for example those rich individuals who after having it all, get depressed and don't know what to do with their lives. Finding meaning alone is an illusion that leads to ecologically harmful and socially unjust outcomes since it cannot be sustained for everyone. The sober subject of degrowth that we envisage, does not aspire to the private accumulation of things because he or she wants to be free from the necessity to find the meaning of life individually. People should take themselves less seriously, so to say, and enjoy living free from the unbearable weight of limitless choice. Like the pianist in "the Legend of 1900" the sober subject knows well not to desire a piano with limitless keys. Like the pianist, he or she will always prefer a limited vessel, to the limitless city. The sober subject finds meaning in relations, not in itself. Liberated from the project of finding individually the meaning of life, he or she can be devoted to a daily life centered around **care** and reproduction and participate to the societal **dépense** democratically determined. Anthropologically, this subject of degrowth already exists. It is the subject of the **nowtopians** and **eco-communities**. It is to be found among the **back-to-the-landers** who work the land, or the city dwellers cultivating **urban gardens**, or occupying the squares. The open question is how it can spread and replicate; but this is a political question, not an individual question.

The pair personal sobriety-social **dépense** is to substitute the pair social austerity-individual excess. Our dialectical **imaginary** is **"political"** in the deep sense of the term. Compare it to the supposedly "political" economy of Krugman, who like the character in the Leopard, wants to change everything (even invent aliens!), just for things to stay the same. It is indeed the paradox of the contemporary political economy that it must not be political, i.e. it must not participate to build the (new) meaning of life, the latter being an affair let to individuals and their private networks. Instead, we maintain that once basic needs have been secured, it is in deciding collectively "what to dépense" that a sense of the "good life" can be constructed and the political of a new era be liberated. The realm of meaning starts where the realm of necessity ends. A degrowth society would have to build new institutions to choose in a collective way how to dedicate its resources to basic needs on the one hand, and different forms of **dépense** on the other. The political does not end with the satisfaction of basic necessities; it starts there. The choice between collective feasts, Olympic games, idle ecosystems, military expenditures, or voyages to space will still be there. The weight on democracy and on deliberative institutions will be more intense than now that the dogma of **growth** and continuous reinvestment has evaded the difficult questions of what we want to do once we have enough. The political economy will be interested in the sacred again. And the economy of austerity, for the most and private enjoyment for few will give its place to an economy of common feast for all sober individuals.

Vive la décroissance conviviale! Pour la sobriété individuelle et la dépense sociale!